PRESERVING
CHARLESTON'S PAST,
SHAPING ITS FUTURE

Susan Frost as a fiercely determined reformer, circa 1920. From Charleston *Post and Courier* Collection.

PRESERVING CHARLESTON'S PAST, SHAPING ITS FUTURE

The Life and Times of Susan Pringle Frost

SIDNEY R. BLAND

UNIVERSITY OF SOUTH CAROLINA PRESS

© 1999 Sidney R. Bland

Published in Columbia, South Carolina, by the
University of South Carolina Press

Manufactured in the United States of America

03 02 01 00 99   5 4 3 2 1

Library of Congress Cataloging-in-Publication Data

Bland, Sidney R.
    Preserving Charleston's past, shaping its future: the life and times of Susan Pringle
Frost / Sidney R. Bland. — [2nd ed.]
        p.   cm.
    Includes bibliographical references (p.) and index.

    ISBN 1-57003-290-4 (pbk.)
    1. Frost, Susan Pringle.   2. Charleston (S.C.)—Biography.   3. Historic
preservation—South Carolina—Charleston.   4. Social reformers—South
Carolina—Charleston—Biography.   I. Title.
    F279.C453 F763   1999
    975.7'915—dc21   98-40218

For my mother, Helen Wilson Bland,
and for Linda, Laura, and Wil

$\mathcal{C}$ONTENTS

ILLUSTRATIONS

OREWORD

When I was young, I often heard my mother speak in glowing terms of Miss Susan Frost. I never understood why until I read this fascinating and valuable book. The experience has been an *eclaircissement*—the clearing up of something hitherto obscure in my own life. I now understand far better my Charleston past, which has obviously been the background for all of my writing on South Carolina history.

Susan Frost began her career in 1901 as private secretary to Bradford Gilbert, the New York architect who had the central role in planning the West Indian Exposition of 1901–1902. The most enduring physical legacy was Hampton Park, but in the mind of the people there was also a change in attitude to a forward-looking optimistic view, particularly with reference to the place of women in the local society. Led by Susan Frost, the women of Charleston began to make an impact not only on the cityscape and the arts, but also on the social and political affairs of the state.

In order to make the exposition a successful affair, the women formed a network, and from that network they moved to influence the growth of the city, the political life of the community, most notably in the suffrage movement and ultimately the preservation movement.

Susan Frost's roots went back to the beginning of South Carolina, but the wealth of the family had been lost in the Civil War. Her father tried to reestablish the family fortunes by once again planting rice on the North Santee, but he failed in that effort and had to be satisfied with the role of public health officer in Charleston, which took him into the most decayed parts of the ancient city. What the Frost family held on to were two magnificent buildings—4 Logan Street (the Humphrey Somers House) and 27 King Street (the Miles Brewton House). Susan Frost represents what those once privileged could do amid adversity. Through her father's career she learned of the blight that was around her, but it was her vision and her will that drove her along the path to become the "Patron Saint of Preservation." She started her real estate business in 1909. In November 1918, she became the first woman to rent an office on Broad Street, and in July 1919 she began the buying and selling of houses.

The city council in the fall of 1909 began to cooperate with the West End Development Company, which intended to extend the southwestern perimeter of the city by reclaiming the marshes of the Ashley River. In 1909 the sea wall from White Point Gardens to Tradd Street was begun, and when it was completed two years later Murray Boulevard was laid out behind it. The low marshy land was filled and lots were sold. Miss Frost took "two unpretentious frame houses on a little triangle of land near the marshes at the west end of Tradd St. and thus began her preservation efforts."

My mother, a native of Knoxville, Tennessee, and my father, a native of Charleston, were married in December 1913 in Knoxville and arrived in Charleston on January 1, 1914, to establish their first home. It was my mother who urged my father to buy a very ramshackle frame house at 190 Tradd Street, but it was Susan Frost who showed my mother how she could improve the purchase by an addition of an iron fence across the front and wooden columns to support a new piazza. Whenever a house was torn down or a dwelling remodeled, Miss Frost was there to purchase unwanted ironwork and woodwork which she stored behind her home on King Street. At this time Charleston lost many interior rooms to the museums of St. Louis, Minneapolis, and Delaware. Miss Frost attempted to stop this export of Charleston artifacts by salvaging what she could.

I was born in 1922 after my parents moved into 190 Tradd, and thus I grew up amid the pile drivers on the marshy lots and the unpaved streets. Pluff mud and rats were part of the natural scene. Perhaps that was implied when one said one grew up "below the drain." One turned an ugly necessity into a mark of distinction. But now I can clearly see that there were good minds at work trying to make the city a better place in which to live. Why would my mother have taken us to live in such an area, which was periodically submerged by passing hurricanes and spring and fall high tides? She certainly had absorbed some of Miss Frost's vision.

These women had character, strong wills, and a sense of humor. Susan Frost could even poke fun at herself. She had grown quite fat by middle age and once commented that when people saw her coming down the street, she "must have looked like a house on legs."

But out of the tumbled-down houses, the decay and the dirt, there could arise a whole culture of art and literature. In order to find persons to purchase the remodeled structures, Miss Frost looked for artists and found them. She led them to the east end of Tradd Street as well as to Rainbow Row on East Bay where at one point she owned six houses, although the carrying charges forced her to sell them one by one. Miss Frost in a sense created the setting for the Charleston Renaissance of the 1920s. Elizabeth O'Neill Verner and Alfred Hutty captured the "before"; Miss Alice Huger Smith, the romance; and Mrs. Ravenel, the place and the people. Somehow I must have internalized what was going on, although I did not understand the whole picture until I read this book in manuscript.

It was Dubose Heyward (1885–1940) who in his novel *Porgy* (1925) described Catfish Row, the kind of dwellings that her father must have inspected many times in his work as health officer. DuBose Heyward himself grew up on the west end of Tradd Street in the period prior to World War I, when his father was the manager of the Chisholm Rice Mill. He would have been suffused by scenes such as Susan Frost altered. The intertwining of the old and the new, the good and the bad, the nostalgia, and the vision were threads of every story that came out of the Charleston Renaissance.

Above all, what I would like to emphasize was that these ladies created homes. For me looking back in time, it was a home. Children had vacant buildings at the rear of almost every lot to explore, walls to keep one's feet from the ground as groups played "follow the leader" looking down into gardens, or up to the rooftops always stepping gently so as to avoid any cut from the crushed glass that had been placed on top of walls to discourage intruders. Wisteria vines in the gnarled, old oaks were the greatest challenge for the youthful climber; the omnipresent umbrella trees provided the safest ascents for the smaller children.

The designation uppermost in the minds of the Susan Frost set was "dwelling house." In 1917 Alice R. Huger Smith and her father D. E. Huger Smith published *The Dwelling Houses of Charleston, South Carolina*. That was a central work of those years. Sidney Bland captures quite clearly what it had meant to Susan Frost to have grown up in Charleston in this quotation: "She saw it partly through a golden haze of memory and association, not only for its buildings, and streets, and vistas, but also for those men and women she had known, or of whom she had been told, who dwelt here, and created, through a period of many generations, the town wherein she herself was privileged to dwell. . . . She never lost this personal feeling for the spirit of Charleston."

Having experienced this feeling so intensely, she wanted to preserve the experience for future generations. Thus began the preservation movement. She was therefore present at exactly the right moment—to stop the rot, to hold back the bulldozer. If she and her sisters were to preserve the ancestral home, they had to organize. Susan Frost described her work on Tradd Street as "pyramiding," saving one house at a time. It also led to the paving of Tradd Street in 1919. But that work had to be topped off. The preservation of the Joseph Manigault home was the test case.

The author has not ignored the contributions of African Americans to the cultural enrichment of Charleston, nor did Susan Frost. She used the skills of the African-American craftsmen, particularly those of Thomas M. Pinckney who became "Sue's right-hand man."

> He was among the most prized artisans of his day. Educated in Charleston's public schools and Clark University [in Massachusetts] night school, he became a stair builder (his father was a cabinet maker), and then apprenticed with a contracting company before starting his own firm. He focused on restoration of old buildings and was particularly adept in handcarved woodwork, especially mantelpiece sunbursts. Many talented tradesmen were in his employ, and Pinckney taught his skills to numerous other African Americans.

In 1994 South Carolina recognized the contributions of this group by electing Philip Simmons, the master African-American blacksmith, to the South Carolina Hall of Fame. Susan Frost helped to create jobs for members of the African-American community.

Restoration on the grand scale also required outside capital. Through family associations Susan Frost had ties to the DuPont family of Delaware. "Rebe" Frost, Susan's sister, was personal secretary to Irene DuPont in November 1918 when Susan and her sisters had to raise funds to buy out the other heirs to the Miles Brewton House. DuPont loans "guaranteed the three Frost sisters were sole proprietors of the Miles Brewton House."

Few had access to such a source of funds. Susan Frost thus began to think of revolving funds and citywide organizations. To rescue the Joseph Manigault House, the Society for the Preservation of Old Dwellings was called into being and has evolved into the Preservation Society of Charleston. Her concept of revolving funds was a vehicle used by the Historic Charleston Foundation to save the houses of Ansonborough.

"Susan Frost was ahead of her time in envisioning saving communities, not as museum settings such as Williamsburg, but as places where people lived and worked throughout the year." She wrote to the *News and Courier* in 1937 to distinguish between reconstructing and restoring, explaining that "we do not have to reconstruct as at Williamsburg, only to restore what we already have in such profusion from one end of the city to the other." Her work has gone forward year after year. Sidney Bland comments at the end of his book that we do not need a marker to explain what she did: "After all, like the renowned English architect, Sir Christopher Wren, her monuments are all about her."

George C. Rogers, Jr.

PREFACE

Longtime Carolina lowcountry journalist Thomas R. Waring, Jr., described Susan Pringle Frost as "a sort of Tugboat Annie personality, short, buxom, fast-talking in the Charleston patois and accustomed to pushing causes" (letter, Thomas R. Waring, Jr., to author, September 16, 1980). In her four score and seven years, Frost championed a host of major issues, most notably women's rights, a more active and accountable local government, historic preservation (the cause most dear), and, quite often, better treatment of African Americans. She could be, and was frequently, equally passionate on other questions ranging from animal rights and prevention of cruelty to animals to ending capital punishment and testing atomic weapons. Although her gender, her deviance from convention and her array of eccentricities, including gardening in middy blouse and bloomers and chauffeuring her dogs through Charleston's narrow streets with abandon, brought routine dismissal by some (including her more provincial local kin), Frost's courage, perseverance, and impeccable lineage ensured that she would be heard and that, over time, many battles would be won.

Not only was Susan Frost important and quirky, but also much interest accrues to her as a transitional figure. She was both a child of the Old South and a New South woman, and her causes extend beyond class and locality. In bridging chronological, regional and social chasms, her life serves as a prism through which to view directions in voluntarism, meliorism, women's rights, professionalism, and the attitudes of cities toward their material and cultural heritage. She both followed in the footsteps of nineteenth-century reformers who sought to eradicate major social evils like slavery and "demon rum" and served as a model for women in a new age to move beyond regional traditionalism and effect, even direct, community betterment.

Therein lies part of the puzzle of Susan Pringle Frost, however. In reviewing her career, one might ask, Whom were her reforms most designed to benefit? Was she more interested in achieving social justice or maintaining social control? Put another way, did her work for change look more forward or more backward? Should she be remembered as a pathbreaking Southern feminist who foreshadowed today's independent female professionals and gender advocates? Or was she, in the final analysis, a "lady bountiful" in the conservative tradition of good works, more patrician than progressive? As a preservationist, should Susan Pringle Frost be remembered as a ruthless real estate operator, driven primarily by the profit motive as she displaced blacks and resurrected the rundown city of her birth? Or was she a visionary whose approach to rehabilitating slums proved a viable formula for maintaining architectural treasures and opening the door to tourist dollars?

Answering such questions is challenging, for Susan Pringle Frost was a complex and often inconsistent crusader—wherein lies part of her charm. She stood astride two generations, one still hurting from war and focused on "the lost cause," and the other concentrating on economic revitalization and coping with the forces of modernism. Susan Frost's life is, therefore, uniquely suited to facilitating an understanding of the larger changes in the twentieth-century urban United States.

My initial forays into the world of reform history in the United States came years ago in seminars with Robert Harris Walker at George Washington University. Both Walker and Keith Melder of the Political History Division of the Smithsonian Institution made me aware of the potential and the excitement of being a scholar in the rapidly expanding field of women's history. Melder shepherded me through a dissertation on the suffrage militancy of Alice Paul and the National Woman's Party, where I first learned about Susan Pringle Frost. Everyone who labors in Southern women's history owes much to Anne Firor Scott, and I am indebted to her for the depth and range of her scholarship on New South women and for her encouragement and support of this project at various stages. Dr. A. Elizabeth Taylor, a pioneer researcher on the woman suffrage movement in the South, kindly wrote letters supporting several of my grant proposals. Dr. Charles Hosmer, "dean" of preservation historians, shared critical findings about Charleston preservationists and others of like ilk nationally, while critiquing key chapters and alerting me to the pitfalls of "doing" historic preservation. I am saddened that he never saw the final product he so influenced.

Many Charlestonians provided vital information during several research trips. Journalist Thomas R. Waring, Jr., was a key source on local history. Frances Ravenel Smythe Edmunds, director of the Historic Charleston Foundation for nearly forty years and a resident in one of the buildings Susan Frost restored on Bedon's Alley, shared her depth of knowledge about the preservation movement. Of Susan Frost's coworkers in the preservation vineyards in the 1920s, only Alston Deas was alive to recall the challenges and frustrations of the early days and his own crucial role as Frost's successor as Preservation Society president. Mrs. Edward Manigault, a cousin who cared for Susan Frost in her dying years, furnished vital family history. Information on the family was also forthcoming from two other cousins, Margaretta Childs and Eleanor Hart, whose mother, Nell Pringle, was an unsung heroine of the Charleston preservation movement as well as a painful victim of the overextended realtor Susan Frost. Peter Manigault, whose recent extensive rehabilitation of the Miles Brewton House (MBH) arrested years of decline, provided access to the MBH photograph collection. Richard Côté's extensive knowledge of the Pringle family saved me from several errors; he also generously shared portions of his own research that impacted on my study. Dr. George C. Rogers, Jr., long the state of

South Carolina's preeminent historian and a native of Charleston, graciously consented to write a foreword that shares personal reflections on the impact of Susan Frost's vision on his own family. His death in the fall of 1997 left a huge void in the countless lives that he touched through his teaching, scholarship, and gentlemanly charm and wit. Other Charlestonians, including Elise Pinckney, Elizabeth Verner Hamilton, and Dorothy Legge, recipient in 1993 of the first annual Susan Pringle Frost award for exceptional achievements in the cause of historic preservation, added valuable perspective. Thanks are also due David Hamilton, grandson of Elizabeth O'Neill Verner, and the Tradd Street Press for ensuring that the Verner etching of Charleston's oldest thoroughfare could grace the cover of this paperback edition.

The Preservation Society of Charleston (PSOC) and its current executive director, Cynthia Jenkins, have both encouraged and facilitated research on their organization's history and its founder. The former executive director, John Meffert, was of invaluable assistance as I completed this biography to coincide with the PSOC's celebration of its first seventy-five years of fighting to preserve the city's old architecture and its historic neighborhoods. The latter have recently been celebrated anew by Jonathan H. Poston of the Historic Charleston Foundation in what will likely be a standard reference work on the city's built environment, *The Buildings of Charleston: A Guide to the City's Architecture* (Columbia: University of South Carolina Press, 1997).

Over several years a coterie of directors, archivists, and staffers at the South Carolina Historical Society have patiently and courteously responded to my needs and requests, including Gene Waddell, David Moltke-Hansen, Stephen Hoffius, and especially Harlan Greene. I also want to acknowledge the cooperation and support I received from the staffs at the Library of Congress, the Bancroft Library, the Rockefeller Archives Center, the Society for the Preservation of New England Antiquities, the Eleutherian Mills Historical Library, the Perkins Library at Duke University, the University of South Carolina, the Archives of American Art, Winthrop University Archives, and the Charleston City Department of Archives and History and County and City Libraries.

Many of my colleagues at James Madison University have provided encouragement and assistance at crucial stages. Two exceptionally supportive department heads, Raymond C. Dingledine, Jr., and Michael Galgano, provided released time from teaching responsibilities, wrote grant support letters, gave constructive criticism, and effectively utilized a balance of stick and carrot measures. I benefited substantially from a thorough review of the manuscript in its latter stages by Jean Cash, with whom I team teach a course titled "Southern Women in Literature and History." Laboring together through many of the same stages of writing, rewriting, seeking publishers and juggling teaching and research roles, Cameron Nickels and I have taken turns exchanging ideas and buoying each other at regular lunch meetings. Paula See has provided valuable secretarial help on many occasions, and I am not sure I can ever adequately thank Raymond "Skip" Hyser for helping me enter the computer age and patiently answering my many distress calls. James Madison University, through its Office of Sponsored Research and its Programs of Grants for Faculty Assistance, has generously endorsed my scholarly endeavors, and the American Philosophical Society, through its Penrose Fund, also offered backing. The JMU Center for the MultiMedia, and particularly Erik Mundel, were of invaluable assistance in readying the hardback for publication. I am gratified by the enthusiasm and commitment of the University of South Carolina Press to ensuring that the Susan Frost biography will receive a wider readership. In his capacities as former executive director of the South Carolina Historical Society and, currently, acquisitions editor of the University of South Carolina Press, Alex Moore has both supported my research and made readying this edition a pleasure.

Finally, there is the love and support of family. My mother, Helen Bland, inspired me with her courage, independence, and active mind, and I shall always be in her debt for allowing me to read books in the summer during lulls in hauling woods dirt to her flower beds. Her recent death at age 95 in the fall of 1997 has left a large personal void. Both parents took turns signing report cards during my school years, and though as a textile worker my father was far less educated than my elementary school teaching mother, Robert Bland both championed my endeavors and sacrificed to ensure that I would function in a world different from his. My brother Lamar, also a college professor, has been steadfast and a comfort in both good times and bad. I shall always treasure savoring the sights and smells of Charleston with my daughter, Laura, and son, Wil, during extended research trips, and their "How is 'Miss Sue'?" inquiries over a longer period than I care to remember demonstrated they never lost faith. The unconditional love, understanding, advice, and encouragement of my wife, Linda, have sustained me throughout.

PRESERVING CHARLESTON'S PAST, SHAPING ITS FUTURE

$\mathscr{I}$NTRODUCTION

By all odds Susan Pringle Frost (1873–1960) should never have become what she became—a pioneer career woman, feminist, and civic activist who spearheaded the historic preservation movement in Charleston, South Carolina. To be sure, the image that prescribed narrowly defined roles for Southern women never fit the actual reality of the lives they led, either in Charleston or anywhere else in the South. The "woman's sphere" that became highly elasticized with men off fighting Civil War battles did not return to its original confining dimensions in the postwar era. Countless casualties of war also produced a generation of women in dire need of employment, with one result being that by the 1890s more "well-bred" women were at work in the South than anywhere else in the world.[1] Those who remained in the domestic sphere found the whole structure of their lives changed by the myriad of factory-made products in the Victorian era. With their burdens somewhat lightened, many middle- and upper-middle-class women began to group themselves in ever-increasing numbers of associations devoted to achieving personal, religious, and civic betterment. Numerous Southern women thus developed a high degree of individuality and independence in the years of change after 1865 as the myth of the Southern lady was juxtaposed against a new image—the image of the "new woman" in the New South.[2]

The image of the lady had deep roots, however,[3] and the "new woman" represented but a small minority of all women in the South. The virtues ingrained in the cult of the lady—purity, piety, submissiveness, and domesticity— still commanded widespread allegiance after the Civil War, with the pressures of a life on the pedestal being strongest among the elite. The force of the cultural image of the lady was so powerful that those Southern women seeking political emancipation and social change had to assume "various protective colorations" to safeguard their pursuits, often apprenticing in such outwardly safe associations as church societies and the Women's Christian Temperance Union before venturing into club work and suffrage activity. For some, the ideal was so stifling as to preclude even the thought of participation in such groups. A member of Charleston's aristocracy who grew up in the Reconstruction period recalled the dilemma of his mother: "My mother would have regarded with horror the idea of belonging to women's clubs, or of attending political meetings. She regarded war and politics as a man's game, in which, it is true, women were incidentally, and often tragically, interested; but about which they knew, and should know, nothing. On such subjects I have never heard her express an opinion, not even against the Yankees, although the war had cost her favorite brother. My mother always seemed girl-like, and never "grew up" to be a mature person."[4]

Born in one of Charleston's grandest homes in 1873, Susan Pringle Frost was nurtured in the same clearly delineated woman's sphere. It was a world she could vividly recall three-quarters of a century later: "We came into this world at a period when it was still considered that young girls should not go out into public life; that their avocations should be confined to within the family circle and within the home." Options were therefore quite few: "we could do embroidery, receive and pay social calls, entertain in the home but never in public places," Frost remembered. The routine custom of spending the day with friends or cousins was a never-ending one for Susan Frost and her two sisters, Mary and Rebecca ("Rebe"). Many days were carbon copies of preceding ones, with departure immediately after breakfast and return home only after a late supper. The routine seemed to have been broken only on Fridays, when a friend and her mother spent the day at the family home on King Street. Two years of boarding school as a teenager only brought a return, in 1891, to the same circumscribed world; to fill the hours she "took a Bible course by correspondence from Miss Smiley in New York, did some sewing, made some shirtwaists for my younger sister who was then at boarding school."[5] Susan Frost clearly was annoyed with some of the constraints. Most exasperating, she remembered, was that women were not even allowed to go to the post office and buy postage stamps, and their letters would remain for days in men's coatpockets, entirely forgotten and unmailed.[6]

Susan Frost's mother, Rebecca Brewton Pringle, more than fulfilled the injunctions of the cult of true womanhood. One of thirteen children herself, she made home and hearth her own raison d'être and dutifully bore three daughters and three sons. Susan Frost's father, Francis LeJau Frost, likened his wife to a prized possession who was raising their "bright, happy little children" in a wholesome Christian atmosphere, instilling in them virtues of the highest order: "She is an infinite blessing and treasure to me and our dear little ones. She is a woman of very rare excellence of character and with age develops in all Christian and womanly virtues and goodnesses, and day by day commands more and more my highest respect and esteem, and my purest and most elevated affections. I prize her infinitely as my wife, but above this even, do I prize her in the most sacred character on earth of mother of my children. She is so full of good sense and of sound judgment and holy affections, that I feel that her character is the sure guarantee that her children, through her example and training, will possess the same high qualities and traits."[7] Coming into Charleston to bear each of her children, Rebecca Brewton Pringle quickly returned to her husband on the family rice plantations he tended after the Civil War. But life on a plantation after the Civil War hardly fit the romantic ideal attached to such an existence. "She works very hard and takes but little rest for herself," Frank Frost wrote of his spouse in 1871. "Last night she got very little sleep, but is in her usual state of activity and health this morning."[8]

Susan Pringle Frost's father, Francis LeJau Frost, like many a loyal aristocratic son of the Old South, was a man whose life was regulated by performance of duty to family, church, community, and country. A promising medical career[9] was short-circuited with the outbreak of the War between the States, but he served with distinction as personal and staff surgeon to General A. P. Hill and, after Hill's death, to General James Longstreet. Wounds at the Battle of the Wilderness in 1864 almost cost Frost his life. Widespread devastation and a dramatic change in labor conditions compelled the Charleston physician to try and salvage both Frost and Pringle Santee River rice plantations after the war. The effort was back-breaking and doomed to failure.[10] Frank Frost continued to practice medicine as a moral and community obligation, making late-night plantation calls to slaves along the Santee,[11] occasionally attending the sick during summer retreats to Saluda, North Carolina, and serving, late in life, as Charleston city health officer, but he spent the bulk of his years, not in the medical career he had envisioned, but in the fertilizer business, opening an office in downtown Charleston as Reconstruction ended. Later civic responsibilities included service as city registrar and member of the city council. Generations of Frosts had long been part of the backbone of St. Michael's Episcopal Church, and as a bishop-blessed lay reader, Dr. Frost sometimes conducted services at the Charleston Home for the Indigent, the Roper Hospital chapel, the family plantation church, and, occasionally, the Church of the Transfiguration in Saluda.[12]

Prominence in government, church, medicine, business, and the social affairs of Charleston and the state of South Carolina was deeply rooted in the families of Francis LeJau Frost and Rebecca Brewton Pringle, and Susan Pringle Frost and her sisters and brothers were accustomed to hearing of the brilliance and accomplishment of the ancestry. It also surrounded them at every turn in the King Street home of their grandparents, the Miles Brewton House (then known as the Pringle House), where their formative years were spent.

The Frost lineage went back to the Reverend Thomas Frost, widely respected rector of St. Philip's Episcopal Church. Dr. Frank Frost was named for a famed Anglican missionary ancestor, the Reverend Francis LeJau (born a French Huguenot), whose education and baptism of slaves and Indians (as well as his abolishment of customary baptism fees) brought renown.[13] The Pringles had Scottish roots. Robert Pringle (1702–1776), the ancestor of the Pringle family in Charleston, became a successful colonial merchant in the business district of Tradd Street; the later Pringles developed and maintained expansive lowcountry plantations such as Runimede, Richfield, Pleasant Meadows, and Beneventum.[14] Susan Frost was also a direct descendant of Miles Brewton, a major colonial merchant prince and public official, and via the Mottes, Alstons, Pringles, and Frosts the Georgian mansion of Brewton on lower King Street ultimately passed to the three Frost daughters. The history of the Miles Brewton House and the ancestry of Susan Pringle Frost are in no small way a history of Charleston itself.[15]

Some of the courage, perseverance, commercial acumen and independence of spirit that Susan Frost exhibited in her business career and historic preservation activities is rooted in the lives of several strong women of the Pringle/Frost family tree. The fearlessness and patriotism of Rebecca Motte, sister of Miles Brewton, in coping with the British occupation of the Brewton House and her plantation home on the Congaree generated one of the most enduring legends of the Revolutionary era in the Carolina lowcountry. Susan's sister, Rebecca Motte Frost, was named after this famed heroine.[16] An earlier ancestor exhibited considerable determination and business skill in managing six rice plantations after the death of her husband.[17] Susan Frost long admired her cousin, famed lowcountry rice planter Elizabeth Waties Allston Pringle. A long-awaited visit to Chicora Wood in 1908, when she was contemplating venturing into real estate, provided Frost with much-needed inspiration as another courageous family role model.[18]

Family has always been a prime factor in determining Southern identity.[19] After the Civil War, family was a particularly vital core of Southern life, serving as a source of warmth and strength in a time of significant readjustment as well as continuing to provide a powerful basis of self-identity for the old aristocracy. Because the South remained a kin-dominated society after 1865, with family networks a principal influence in determining sexual, domestic, marital, and work roles, major changes in the social status of women were still some years away.[20]

Large numbers of kin have always resided in close proximity to each other throughout the South. After Appomattox, kin often, of necessity, lived with each other. "We spent our childhood in the old home with our parents and grandparents and our Aunt Susan Pringle," wrote Susan Frost of her own kin network at the Miles Brewton House. "There were five adults and five children comprising the household in those early days. Needless to say, we had a happy childhood amid such surroundings."[21] The Pringles retained several family servants in the years after emancipation. Use of existing rooms in the Miles Brewton House changed as grandparents aged and children became teenagers.[22] Post–Civil War social life in the South was home-centered. For the Frost children, the visits of cousins, aunts, and uncles were special occasions, eagerly anticipated and requiring special preparation. Susan Frost's sister, Mary, recorded the joy and excitement of such times in her *Chronicles and Reminiscences:* "When a niece or nephew came from New Haven, California, France, then indeed was fullness of soul. The great room must be made ready, the great bed with the old blankets and counterpane and lamp. Mary must light the fire in the morning and bring a kettle of water for the tub. Bella (Aunt Bell) must do her best cooking. Cousin James must be at the station. Robert must be at the door to open in welcome. The thrill of meeting Cousin James, of arriving at the old home, of running up the steps; of Robert at the door; of Aunt Sue waiting in the hall upstairs—the

embrace, half tear, half laughter! The rush of memory; the remainder in coun-
tenance or voice or laugh!"[23]

Despite the loss of thousands of male lives during the Civil War and the
measure of independence that accrued to women during this time, the South
continued to be highly patriarchal long after the guns had ceased firing. Family, church, the law, and the community all reinforced this long-entrenched traditional order. The father was head of the family and the ultimate final authority
on matters affecting his children—their education, their spirituality, their
friendships, indeed their overall existence and well-being. Fathers were frequently stern (probably more so in image than in reality) and usually meted out
larger doses of assertiveness training to their sons than their daughters. Daughters, in contrast, frequently experienced their fathers as more loving and were
less likely to be pushed toward independence of thought and deed. More of the
everyday rearing of females (and males) fell to mothers than to fathers, and
numerous stereotypes developed to accompany the historically sharp divisions
between males and females and family responsibilities.[24]

Francis LeJau Frost was a patriarch who was keenly involved in the rearing
of his children after the Civil War, and he did not always conform to stereotypes
in his role. The Frost offspring received moral and religious values from both
parents, who held to the belief that they were solely responsible for the religious
teaching of their children,[25] but Frank Frost was vitally involved in the process.
One of Susan Frost's earliest recollections of her father was his Sunday morning instruction in church catechism and "all the old time church hymns." As
nurturer and teacher, Dr. Frost instilled other "high principles" and "maxims."
Among the earliest teachings his daughter Susan retained was the injunction
never to help herself to the best of anything, for to do so implied she was leaving the worst for others.[26] Francis LeJau Frost's "strong Christian faith" was
passed on to his son Francis LeJau Frost, Jr., who served as Anglican priest on
Staten Island for thirty-five years. Though confirmed at St. Michael's Episcopal
Church at age eleven, Susan Frost's religious training continued with Bible
classes offered by a private teacher.

Francis LeJau Frost also provided the best in formal educational instruction
for his family. Like most of the contemporaries of their social class, the Frost offspring were educated in the private schools of lower Charleston. However, the
training that Susan, Mary, and "Rebe" Frost received at the Legare Street school
of the Misses Victoria and Malvina Murden and their nieces who succeeded
them, the Misses Mary E. and Jane du Bose Sass, differed substantially from that
of their brothers. Like her cousin Elizabeth Allston Pringle a generation before
her, Susan Pringle Frost was sent to private school for "finishing touches" (and
some educational discipline). All such young ladies received less instruction in
math, history, and the sciences than they did in the fine arts of conversational
French, music, painting, sewing, and moral training and scripture reading.
Expectations were clearly defined. Ornamental training and skills in the social

graces would ready women like Susan Frost for the marriage market and, in turn, success as a social matron with a large family.[27]

Although they had the best of tutors and private schools, Susan Frost and her sisters and brothers were allowed to explore the world around them and learn from it as well. On countless occasions, despite the expectations and pressures on him as provider for a large family, Francis LeJau Frost was escort and companion for an afternoon of adventure. Cousins and friends often accompanied them. One of Susan Frost's favorite "jaunts" was "to hire a strawberry patch" in the sparsely inhabited area north of the city. Once the season was over and the best of the crop was shipped to northern markets, Frank Frost took his children "up the road" and paid the owner of the patch a total of 25 cents, entitling the entire entourage to pick from the remaining culls. More adventuresome and no less a popular childhood outing was bouncing on the rafts of lumber being floated down the Ashley River to the local mills. The daring found plunging into the water from the closely moored bundles of logs was a more satisfying experience than swimming in the protected pools of the often ill-kept and overcrowded bathhouses jutting out from the peninsula.[28] For Susan Frost memories of the pleasure of jumping from raft to raft on the Ashley were always accompanied by the "vivid and terrifying" recollection of a sister caught between two rafts, feet dangling in the air, head under water, a story with a happy ending because of her father's heroic rescue. "Of course," the well-known Charlestonian wrote years later, "we thought our father the most wonderful person in the world and that he could do anything."[29]

Like many a child of the old aristocracy of the lowcountry of South Carolina, Susan Pringle Frost stored up countless memories from years of summering in the western North Carolina mountains. Distinguished Charlestonians of means, with names such as Baring, King and Memminger, developed places like Flat Rock ("Little Charleston of the Mountains") to escape the summer coastal heat and demonstrate their prosperity. By the mid–nineteenth century, mountain towns like Hendersonville and Morganton annually received an economic and cultural boost from a summer wave of migrants from the tidewater.[30]

Frank Frost ultimately purchased both a cottage and an orchard in Saluda, and Susan Frost spent her first summer there at age twelve. Opening of the Spartanburg and Asheville and the Western North Carolina Railroads in the 1880s dramatically lessened what had been a ten- to fourteen-day journey from the seacoast for pre–Civil War rice planters, but the lowcountry teenager found travel in Saluda itself antiquated until well into the twentieth century as the town passed through such phases of locomotion as "the old shanks mare," the "ox and wagon period," "the mule team period," and "the horse drawn age."[31] In Saluda, as in Charleston, Frank Frost provided numerous avenues of adventure and exploration for his children. Susan Frost treasured "the unselfish devotion of our father and his thought of always giving us the advantage of every interesting experience within the range of his opportunity," remembering fondly the regular twenty-mile hikes he led through the western Carolina mountains.[32]

Though stigmatized throughout much of Southern history and frequently stereotyped as such in fiction and film, maiden aunts were often cherished members of family circles and played influential and indispensable roles in shaping the lives of the children around them.[33] Susan Pringle played such a role in the large kin circle at the Miles Brewton House. It was from her Aunt Susan that Susan Pringle Frost gained a deep and abiding sense of her family's past and its role in shaping the destinies of Charleston and the lowcountry of South Carolina. In carving out her separate identity as a spinster in a large household and developing a significant measure of financial independence amid the general poverty after the Civil War, Susan Pringle taught her niece Susan important lessons in survival and in stretching the perimeters of the narrowly defined sphere of proper behavior for Southern ladies.

Susan Pringle occupied a place of prominence in Mary Frost's history of the Miles Brewton House; she was "the last of a long and notable generation," Susan Frost observed on her aunt's death in 1917.[34] Born in 1829 and an obvious spinster by the time of secession, Susan Pringle became a fixture in the marriage fashioned by Francis LeJau and Rebecca Pringle Frost. Several Frost offspring either slept with their aunt or in an adjoining room. In such childhood play as "rolling hoop, skipping rope, bouncing on the joggling board . . . rehearsing scenes from our history lesson," and the games of "Prisoner's Base" and "King George and his army," Susan Pringle was a daily monitor who, in the words of Mary Frost, "was very forebearing with ourselves and our playmates."[35]

Susan Pringle's great passion was flowers, and with the assistance of a gardener who remained after emancipation she transformed the expansive backyard of the King Street Georgian mansion into a temple of natural beauty, full of orange trees and an endless variety of flowers. Susan Frost and her sisters performed regular religious and patriotic duty by helping their Aunt Susan convert spirea, ivy, magnolia, and other flowers and ribbon grass into "crosses, wreaths, anchors and stars" for the altar of St. Michael's and the graves of Confederate dead at Easter and Memorial Day. Susan Pringle regularly won prizes for her pansies at the Meeting Street Agricultural Hall flower shows. Most of all, however, flowers were, for Susan Pringle, a business. Throughout the spring months, her best specimens were sold to visitors at the Charleston Hotel. She sometimes garnered as much as $10 a day from sales, and on more than one occasion her profits ensured that tax obligations on the family home place would be met. On the one hand Pringle's enterprise bespeaks old aristocracy coping with fortunes considerably depleted after the Civil War. In a more important sense, Susan Pringle, through her hard work and ingenuity, emerged with an independence and sense of self-worth accorded to a minority of women, and fewer maiden aunts still, in nineteenth-century Southern society. Susan Pringle Frost's lifelong love of gardening was inherited from her Aunt Susan, and after World War I

Frost established her own florist business in her effort to ensure adequate funds for her real estate and home mortgages.[36]

It was also from her aunt that Susan Frost developed an understanding and appreciation of the material artifacts and historical and architectural importance of the stately mansion in which she was born and spent most of her life. As teenagers, the Frost girls often sat in on portions of the regular twelve noon to two o'clock visits of ladies to the Pringle home and heard, "in gentle voice," tales of ancient youth and family distinction. They learned that the beautifully detailed woodwork around them resulted from a London-born carver hired by Miles Brewton, that the Georgian-style townhouse and the original Waterford crystal chandelier in the upstairs drawing room had survived occupancy by two foreign armies, a major earthquake, and numerous storms and fires, and that the heavy iron bar with spikes (a "Chevaux-de-frise") atop the wrought iron fence in the front of the Pringle house had possibly been added after Denmark Vesey's slave insurrection in the early 1820s. They soon knew which master painter was responsible for which family portrait. Remembering her aunt as "a gifted raconteur," Susan Frost never tired of her story of the untimely demise of Theodosia Burr Alston, beloved daughter of Aaron Burr and a relative of the Frost sisters as a result of her marriage to their grandmother's brother, Joseph Alston, one-time governor of South Carolina.[37] The three Frost sisters nursed their aunt in her final days, and they ultimately assumed ownership of the valuable but rundown King Street property in 1919, despite meager resources, because of the deep concern shown by their ancestry, particularly their Aunt Susan Pringle, for the Miles Brewton House and its history. One Frost cousin concluded: "The three felt it was a trust, an act of loyalty and love to their parents and their forebears to live in the house, keep it as best they could, and use it to interpret to who ever would come the dignity, bearing and courage of their and other Charleston families."[38]

The post-Reconstruction South in which Susan Frost was raised was politically controlled by conservatives once more. One of Charleston's own, Wade Hampton, was idol of the state. "If they had been royalty in England, they could not have been treated with more deference," Frost's uncle remarked on attending a reception for two of the former Confederate general's sons.[39] With Hampton, governor from 1876–1880, then U.S. senator, 1880–1891, came white Democratic control of state and local governments, now redeemed from the evils of Republican carpetbaggery. Paternalistic on the racial issue, Wade Hampton largely kept his political promises and allowed African Americans to participate in the political process in the 1870s and 1880s. In Charleston, however, the story, for the most part, was different. "Through the operation of the separate ballot-box law, the colored vote amounted to nothing and Democratic officials were hardly opposed for election," wrote Theodore Jervey of his politically redeemed "Ellentown."[40] The Charleston City Council quickly became an all-Democrat body after 1876, and after 1883 no African American was elected to that group until 1967.[41] Former Confederate captain and operator of a successful shipping and commission business, William Ashmead Courtenay, served as a popular two-term Democratic mayor of Charleston in the 1880s and did the bidding of the powerful Broad Street financial and legal community.[42] For old-line lower peninsula Charleston families like the Frosts and Pringles, these were times for political rejoicing. Like most young Southern ladies being carefully groomed for a future already defined for her, Susan Frost was not to become burdened with the weighty matters of government.

Charleston politics in the 1870s and 1880s were highly volatile. Riots and deaths surrounded the election of Wade Hampton in 1876, and the racially tinged murder of influential *News and Courier* editor Francis Warrington Dawson in 1889 brought forth an outpouring of grief in the city unlike any seen since the funeral of John C. Calhoun.[43] One prominent businessman who lived near Broad Street recalled that African-American political demonstrations often took place at night on the steps of City Hall, with orators exhorting those assembled on appropriate candidates to support.[44] Although her support of Irish Catholic Mayor John Grace and her regular interaction with the local political establishment in the twentieth century made Susan Frost a highly visible figure, as a teenager in the 1880s she was for the most part politically sheltered, unable to remember anything substantive about the man many regarded as Charleston's finest mayor, William Courtenay.[45]

One political event, however, Susan Frost never forgot, and neither did many other Charlestonians, for it was one of the old city's most memorable demonstrations. Grover Cleveland had always been popular among the ruling elite there,[46] and his reelection as president in 1892 triggered a great celebration, highlighted by a vast procession, with wagonloads of fireworks, "bands of music" and some five hundred marchers bearing torches in the shape of guns, each with a large wick and containers on the end "holding about a pint of kerosene oil." In the parade of Susan Frost's memory, the tremendous fire risk and the danger of being trampled by frightened cavalry horses remained sublimated by the overall excitement of the occasion and the affirmation she received as being a lady "with spunk enough" to march in such an event, all of which, she later acknowledged, had only been possible because of her father's support.[47]

Susan Pringle Frost grew up in a Charleston that physically was racially integrated. African Americans outnumbered whites by more than four thousand in 1870, and they remained a majority well into the twentieth century.[48] Numerous African Americans settled on the city's lower east side after the Civil War in areas once inhabited by some of Charleston's most prosperous colonial merchants, and blacks and whites lived in close proximity throughout all the wards of the lower peninsula. Said one observer: "The magnificent and the mean jostle each other very closely in all quarters of the city; tumble-down rookeries are side by side with superb houses."[49]

Though physically integrated, Charleston witnessed enforced institutional segregation of the races and a quickening of the pace of discrimination by the late 1870s. The process greatly accelerated after the state codified segregation laws in 1895.[50] "The Jim Crow law made friends into enemies overnight," recalled Mamie Garvin Fields, a prominent mid-twentieth-century African-American activist who grew up on the peninsula in the 1890s. Reporting for a job as a cross-stitcher at the front door of a south of Broad Street home, Fields suffered the indignity of being ordered to use the back entrance customarily reserved for servants. Mamie Fields never remembered Charleston's famous landmark, the Battery, ever being segregated "because of a real law," but by the 1880s the spot often populated by blacks and tans in the Wade Hampton era, had become, a "forbidden place."[51]

Lone exceptions to that "unwritten" law by the end of the nineteenth century were New Year's Day, the day the Emancipation Proclamation took effect in 1863, and the fourth of July, left uncelebrated by many white Charlestonians for a generation after the Civil War because it was considered a Yankee holiday. On those occasions the Battery came alive with African-American bands and militia. "So glad to get down to where they were allowed only once (or twice) a year," Mamie Fields wrote, "the mothers and grandmothers cooked up a storm, and they would bring everything for a barbecue and a picnic." For Mamie Garvin Fields those July celebrations on the Battery had special meaning because "many of our parents were actually celebrating their own freedom."[52]

Forced to spend much of the summer in Charleston before her father bought property in the western Carolina mountains in 1884, Susan Pringle Frost remembered the fourth of July as "a great day among the Negroes," with "great numbers" streaming past their King Street home bound for the benches, shade trees and ocean breezes of the Battery. Continuing to try and survive in as grand a manner as possible amidst the uncertain economic times of the late nineteenth century, the Pringle household opened the carriage gates on the holiday, and their servants sold such lowcountry favorites as benne cakes and "monkey meat" (sweetened coconut cakes), as well as watermelon and lemonade.[53] Susan Frost was reared in a household replete with "faithful old time Negro maumas," and she documented yet another generation of family faithfully maintaining the stately Miles Brewton House (and thereby actively perpetuating the history of the Old South) by including photographs and brief biographies of the servants and their children and grandchildren in her history of the structure.[54] Ironically, while living near African Americans on the narrow land mass of the lower peninsula for several decades, Susan Frost, through her twentieth-century restoration of many of the city's old houses and her highly visible role in the historic preservation movement, would in no small way be responsible for creating a largely all-white Charleston south of Broad Street by World War II.

Susan Pringle Frost left the familiar world of lower Charleston in 1889 and for two years attended Saint Mary's in Raleigh, North Carolina, a prominent Episcopal women's boarding school that as an antebellum academy had provided education for offspring of some of the best known planters in Virginia, the Carolinas, and Georgia.[55] Frank Frost was a close friend of Dr. Albert Smedes, the son of the school's founder, and was thus assured his daughters would receive final educational training that would reaffirm the values of the elitist patriarchal family to which they belonged. The all-female world of institutions such as Saint Mary's, while existing to fashion future Southern ladies and wives, promoted close sisterhoods, bonding that allowed antebellum young women to develop relationships independent of family.[56] Susan Frost wrote of her experience: "I formed warm friendships at St. Mary's which have been a source of happiness ever since." Frost also established close ties with some of the "fine set of teachers" at Saint Mary's, corresponded with them over the years and entertained some at the Frost Saluda mountain cottage.[57]

For most of the young women who attended Saint Mary's, even at the end of the nineteenth century, schooling was followed by a return to home and parents. Cut adrift from the community that nurtured them, not knowing if they would see friends again with, perhaps, no steady male relationships nor wishing any, many found the return distressing. Susan Pringle Frost left Saint Mary's in June 1891 as a partial graduate, having pursued no strict degree requirements but rather a sequence of desired courses plus a fine arts component. She came back to Charleston with little option but to enter the dizzying round of galas and parties reserved for young ladies of the old aristocracy until she made her debut at the only ball that really mattered, that staged by the St. Cecilia Society. "If one is not eligible to the St. Cecilia one simply is not a debutante," wrote one of the city's renowned newspapermen about the elite club with early-eighteenth-century origins.[58]

Immediately after Saint Mary's, there was also the excitement of helping her parents bring order to the only home exclusively theirs, the Logan Street residence built by Frank Frost's father in about 1859 and bought from his mother's estate in 1891. For the most part, however, Susan Frost's next several years were spent in spasms of sewing, visiting cousins and friends, traveling, performing ladylike functions on religious and patriotic occasions, and, of course, summering in Saluda and socializing during the season on the peninsula. Her life may never have changed but for one of those monumental natural disasters for which Charleston is famous. The 120-mile-an-hour winds of the hurricane of August 27, 1893, destroyed much around it, including the Battery promenade and the new bridge across the Ashley River, and it triggered the downfall of the Ashley Phosphate Company belonging to Francis LeJau Frost.[59] Like many of the surviving planter class who entered the business, Frank Frost had seen the manufacture and sale of commercial fertilizers as an avenue to hold on to an old order rather than promote a new.[60] And like the over twenty manufacturing companies with plants in South Carolina by the mid-1880s, the Ashley Company profited substantially in the short run, with Southern cotton farmers furnishing much of the demand as they struggled to revitalize their own lands.[61] Frank Frost joined many of the old aristocracy who annually escaped the repressive summer heat to mountain cottages by purchasing his own retreat, and he outfitted his south of Broad Street home in the style of those around him. He sent his youngest daughter Rebecca to boarding school, not in nearby Raleigh, but in New York State.

Long-term luxury was not to be, however. A variety of factors, including labor problems, state regulations, and production costs, plagued the phosphate industry from the beginning. Conditions worsened significantly in the early 1890s. Governor Benjamin Tillman, in his disdain for the conservative aristocrats in "the greedy old city of Charleston," doubled the state royalty on phosphates, licensed other companies to enter river mining and generally exerted tougher regulations. Competition outside the state, especially from Florida and Tennessee, virtually ended the South Carolina monopoly. The hurricane of 1893 provided the final knockout blow. South Carolina's production of phosphate dwindled to less than 7 percent of the national total by 1910,[62] and the lowcountry economy remained in crucial need of revitalization and stability as the nineteenth century ended.

The winds of economic fortune and misfortune that affected the South Carolina coast in the late nineteenth century left the prestigious old Frost family in a topsy-turvy state. For Frank Frost it had been a tragic roller coaster ride; his rebound after the failure of the family rice fields was, in a decade or so, followed by much greater financial disaster. He was left a somewhat broken man, mortified because he was no longer the family provider. Susan Frost called it "a heartbreaking experience in our father's life."[63] Little did she know that it would also be the event that would allow her to escape the imprisoning folds of an image that had long held Southern women in its grasp.

Susan Pringle Frost never forgot that early morning of November 5, 1895, when her father drove up to Captain Charles Pinckney's residence to take the final steps "in assigning all he had in favor of his creditors."[64] Like Margaret Mitchell's Scarlett and countless nonfictional Southern females who overcame the deprivations of war, Susan Frost would rise above family misfortune to see a better day. She would ultimately be a giant force, through her rehabilitation of significant sections of the southeastern peninsula and her championing of historic preservation, in ensuring that her beloved Charleston also witnessed a new dawn. In later years "Miss Sue" was fond of striking a Scarlett O'Hara–like pose, looking a person squarely in the eye and proclaiming, "I am a fighter, for my father was a fighter."[65] At the heralding of a new century, this middle daughter of distinguished but failed old aristocracy would need all the resolve she could muster.

CHAPTER 1

"*W*HILE THE PEBBLE HAS BEEN DROPPED INTO VERY STILL WATERS, THE CIRCLES WILL WIDEN RAPIDLY"

Ida M. Lining, *The Exposition*

Susan Pringle Frost's new day did not come quickly. Following family bankruptcy, she struggled to learn typing and stenographic skills, but after five years and at twenty-seven years of age she had managed only an unsalaried position in a law office on Broad Street. The city of Charleston fared little better in its own battle with economic adversity. For both Susan Frost and Charleston, the South Carolina Interstate and West Indian Exposition of 1901–1902 promised to better their fortunes. For Susan Frost the exposition would be a critical juncture on the road toward self-identity and life as a professional. It would also acquaint her with women's larger accomplishments and networks of women seeking to better their own lives.

Industrial fairs, or expositions, were prevalent in the New South; New Orleans, Atlanta, and Nashville all had celebrations in the last quarter of the nineteenth century. With major harbor improvements recently completed and interest in overseas trade stimulated by the Spanish-American War, lowcountry exposition leaders pinned their hopes for economic revitalization on development of trade relations with the West Indies and Central and South America and the national and international exposure such an event would yield. Sparing no expense, organizers hired a prominent New York architect and Yale honor graduate, Bradford Lee Gilbert, to plan the exposition grounds. Gilbert's specialty was heavy construction work such as churches and public buildings, and he helped design the Metropolitan Opera House. His fame ultimately rested on his design of railroad terminals, however, and the erection of structures for various railroad interests at the Columbian Exposition in Chicago. Similar duties for the Cotton States Exposition in Atlanta in 1895 earned him gold medals and brought him to the attention of South Carolina Exposition planners. Charlestonians welcomed Bradford Gilbert with open arms and predicted that his purchase of a "handsome and commodious" South Battery residence in January 1901 would result in the city's ultimately becoming his permanent residence.[1]

Exactly how and when Susan Frost met Bradford Gilbert is not clear. What is certain, however, is that the fourteen months she served as Gilbert's stenographer/secretary left an indelible imprint on her life. She quickly developed a "tremendous admiration" for the architect in chief, and she experienced him, as did other Charlestonians, as "not in any sense a club man, but devoted to his family, home and church work."[2] Susan Frost's professional responsibilities with the Charleston Exposition included acting as liaison between Bradford Gilbert and the work staff on the fairgrounds. Among those with whom she had "pleasant contact" was Louis Godebrod, a young sculptor who had studied under Augustus St. Gaudens in Paris and whose pieces for the Charleston Exposition were highly regarded. On occasions when he returned to his New York office, Gilbert expected progress reports. Frost frequently had the architect's Charleston driver ready horses and carriage and drive her to the exposition site, where she relayed instructions to a wide variety of workers. She later confessed she knew nothing about a cantilever "or any other" construction in 1901–1902 and was astounded that workmen on the Cotton Palace and other buildings would "defer to me as if I knew and understood it all."[3]

As personal secretary to the chief architect of the exposition, Susan Frost sometimes performed family household duties, including Christmas shopping for his daughter. On occasion Miss Frost accompanied Bradford Gilbert to his New York office and Brooklyn home. To her amazement she found that "this man of unusual personality" had values similar to those she had been taught, and she was particularly surprised to find a picture of Christ's Last Supper on the dining room wall of his home. Long after she had emerged as a prominent realtor and leader in the Charleston historic preservation movement, Susan Frost acknowledged that her thoughts often returned to the thoughtful, caring architect and the "interesting, unusual and delightful" experiences of their months together. Those recollections also reminded her of women's sheltered lives at the turn of the twentieth century. Frost was regularly escorted home after late-night work, on Gilbert's orders, by a Western Union messenger. "The company would send a small boy and he and I would ride home on Logan street on our bicycles," she recalled; "I do not know what the small boy would or could have done if anyone had molested us, but it was the custom of the times for girls not to be alone on the streets after dark."[4]

The South Carolina Interstate and West Indian Exposition furnished Frost a crash course in architecture and design. It doubtless also quickened her awareness and appreciation of Charleston's own rich architectural heritage. Praise from exposition designers such as sculptor Louis Godebrod, who labeled Gilbert's secretary an "efficient stenographer,"[5] and her good personal and professional relationship with the chief architect himself brought important self-confidence to the heretofore sheltered daughter of Charleston's old aristocracy. The experience defined her own emergence as a professional. Frost remembered the exposition as crucial in her development: "the start of my long and interesting business career; it made a lasting impression on me."[6]

For many sheltered Southern ladies such as Susan Pringle Frost, industrial expositions were consciousness-raising experiences that opened doors to larger worlds. Increasingly after the Civil War, such events became showcases for the accomplishments, preoccupations, and goals of women. The Philadelphia Centennial of 1876, the New Orleans Exposition of 1884, the Chicago World's Columbian Exposition of 1893, the Atlanta Cotton States and International Exposition of 1895, and similar fairs in Nashville and Buffalo soon thereafter provided avenues for women to celebrate their history and achievements and to share the evidence of their education and training with other women. Women honed their organizational and managerial skills in planning and governing separate women's buildings at such fairs, generating, in turn, women's networks and female solidarity that generated important benefits for American feminism in the late nineteenth and early twentieth centuries.[7]

Some women's lives were forever changed by participation in these separate female spheres. Sallie Southall Cotton of North Carolina spent nearly three decades in "busy domesticity" with her seven children until her appointment by the governor as one of the state's "lady managers" at the Chicago World's Fair in 1893. Cotton returned sympathetic to women's social, professional, and political advancement, and she spent the next three and a half decades of her life as a force in the North Carolina women's club movement, crusading for reform.[8]

The women of Charleston distinguished themselves as fund-raisers and organizers at the South Carolina Interstate and West Indian Exposition of 1901–1902, and the Woman's Building became the "gem" of the exposition's "ivory city." Great zeal and ultimate success in raising the necessary $25,000 to operate their antebellum mansion produced envy in male counterparts and high praise from the *News and Courier*, which somewhat grudgingly noted near fair's end that "they have managed their business and financial affairs with rare success."[9] President Theodore Roosevelt dined in the restaurant in the Woman's Building. Thousands viewed with some degree of surprise the elaborate display of inventions of women, and visitors applauded the efforts of Charleston's women to comply with the overall goals of the exposition by promoting home-grown tea and launching an ambitious campaign to resurrect the once highly visible silk industry.[10] Federal Judge William Brawley saluted their accomplishments at the special "Woman's Day." At fair's end, the city fathers offered similar sentiments in gratefully accepting the $2,000 bank balance of a free-from-debt Woman's Department to cover a portion of the severe "pressing embarrassments" from a financially troubled Exposition: "How they accomplished so much within the time limit and with the narrow means at their command was little short of miraculous. . . . Never since the foundation of the town was there so much attempted and so much accomplished; and in all that was done the same strong business sense was displayed. . . . It is certain that no such record was ever made by the women of any other community in this or any other country."[11] Susan Pringle Frost, like all Charlestonians, took pride in the achievements of the Woman's Department. Despite her own busy schedule as Bradford Gilbert's private secretary, she served on the Silk Culture Committee and promoted its goals.

Although the South Carolina Interstate and West Indian Exposition of 1901–1902 failed to provide the long-term stimulus for an ailing lowcountry economy, it enhanced Susan Frost's secretarial skills and became the critical springboard for improving her own fortunes. In 1902 she won a competitive examination for a position as United States District Court stenographer,[12] and for the next sixteen years she traveled with a trio of federal judges through three states. The position offered Frost a measure of financial stability and independence as she struggled to develop long-term career interests. The district court system also acquainted Miss Frost with some of the horrors that the industrial system and a more complex social order had produced and heightened her awareness of both social inequities and inequalities toward women. At the same time, because all three federal judges had deep roots in the lowcountry, with one of them a prominent publicist of state and local history, Frost broadened her understanding and depth of feeling for her own elitist culture and heritage. In the role of court secretary, Susan Pringle Frost earned a niche in history; she was, maintained Charleston newspaperman Thomas R. Waring, Jr., "a pioneer among her sex in such employment."[13]

Frost shared impeccable antecedents and secure family position in the lowcountry of South Carolina with the three federal district court judges whom she served, Charles H. Simonton, William H. Brawley, and Henry Augustus Middleton Smith, and she was a blood relative of at least one of them.[14] Frost found her job draining and exhausting. "Court work is absorbing," she confessed to suffragist Elsie Hill in 1915.[15] Several days of every month were spent taking testimony. Regular court terms took her to Aiken and Columbia, South Carolina, for ten days at a time, but often called her elsewhere, and there were frequent early morning and late evening train rides. Frost was delighted that a one-day session in November 1908 would bring her to Georgetown, where she could visit her cousin Elizabeth Waties Allston Pringle at Chicora Wood plantation. "I must leave here Tues. at 6:10, and the Reference begins at 10:30, and I would be able to leave Geo. for your home that aft.," wrote Frost of her busy schedule. "I shall of course not stay longer than the night, returning the next evg. to Chas. . . . no end of duties here."[16]

The Charleston *Yearbook* of 1904, in a memorial tribute to Charles Simonton, suggested something of the pace of Frost's life during those first two years as court stenographer: "He [Simonton] took no vacation. . . . His industry was untiring, his labors unceasing."[17] Work was no less hectic for Susan Frost under Simonton's successors, however. "Have only time for a note, as up to my eyes in work," she told cousin "Bessie" Pringle shortly after the Chicora Wood visit; "brought back about a thousand pages of testimony fr. the Col. Term to write up, order fr. lawyers . . . am working until one and two at nights, and two sets of lawyers pushing me for cases, so must not stop for more."[18] Court schedules and the volume of work heavily impacted on the time Susan Frost could give to causes she later became involved with, especially woman suffrage, and to her real estate career in its infancy. In 1915 she complained to National Woman's

Party coleader Lucy Burns: "I find it always so difficult to sandwich in important suffrage work [in] between my various terms of Court when I have to be out of town."[19]

The majority of Frost's court years was spent in serving with the most distinguished of the trio of jurists, Henry Augustus Middleton Smith. Appointed judge for the Eastern District of South Carolina in 1911 by President William Howard Taft, Smith inherited large tracts of land from both his parents, including Middleton Place Gardens where he made his home, and he successfully managed one of the largest planting enterprises in the lowcountry. He was a respected amateur botanist, poet, lawyer, and civic leader, but his most significant and enduring contribution was as historian/scholar. Judge Smith did extensive research into the records of abandoned towns and settlements of lower South Carolina and traced early proprietary grants and titles through the Civil War. His studies of baronies, plantations, and river communities were judged "path-breaking both in methodology and historical perception," and Smith fostered historical studies of the locality and state through his own writings and support of historical institutions. He was a founder of the South Carolina Historical Commission, forerunner of the Department of Archives and History, helped establish the *South Carolina Historical (and Genealogical) Magazine* and for twenty years was vice president of the South Carolina Historical Society.[20] Henry Augustus Middleton Smith's rich historical and genealogical scholarship dovetailed with Susan Frost's intense interest in the rich but decayed Charleston architectural landscape by the second decade of the twentieth century. He doubtless voiced approval of her early crusade to save the quaint antiquated structures on Tradd Street and the lower east side.

In the last three decades of her life, Susan Pringle Frost was highly visible for her outspokenness on social and political issues. That pattern began during her years as court stenographer as she gained familiarity with Progressive Era problems and with how her own city and municipalities all over the country were responding, or not responding, to them. Well before she completed her sixteen years as court stenographer, Susan Frost became convinced that women were needed to help solve society's ills, many of which she learned about in the courtroom of Judge H. A. M. Smith. Smith was widely recognized as a compassionate arbiter, a judge who agonized over many of the sentences he handed out.[21] The social issues over which Judge Smith pondered ultimately quickened the social conscience of his court stenographer.

Frost developed keen humanitarian concerns for the poor and less fortunate while serving under Judges Simonton, Brawley, and Smith, and she believed city government had "a moral and Christian charge" to aid the underprivileged, especially the young and the elderly. "There should be no essence or tinge of politics in the selection of officers where the life and happiness of those less fortunate than some of us are involved and often sometimes even at stake," Frost once admonished Mayor T. T. Hyde on hearing the rumor that well-liked, capable officials at the Charleston Home were likely to be replaced after the next election.[22] Miss Frost often expressed compassion for children; child abuse cases left her exhausted and emotionally drained at day's end.[23] Growing social concerns resulted in Susan Frost and her sisters' becoming regular visitors to many of the city's charitable agencies.[24] Frost strongly opposed capital punishment[25] and advocated humanitarian and Christian remedies instead. Prostitutes, Frost argued, should be escorted to church, not sentenced by the courts.[26]

In addition to its stagnant economy, Charleston faced a myriad of municipal problems as it entered the twentieth century, the most acute of which were in the area of public health. Frost learned about many of those problems, not in the chambers of Judges Simonton, Brawley, and Smith, but in her Logan Street home from the lips of her father. Never to return to business after the disaster that befell the Ashley Phosphate Company, Francis LeJau Frost spent his last years as a public servant, serving as city registrar, as member of the city council, and as city health officer prior to his death in 1912. In the latter role, Frank Frost faced enormous challenges.

Although smallpox was virtually eradicated from Charleston between 1903 and 1908, cases of diphtheria, typhoid, and scarlet fever showed significant increases. As late as 1919, the city's rat population was estimated to equal the human population of 70,000.[27] In the early years of the century, citizens still cluttered the streets with trash. Twelve thousand privy vaults remained throughout Charleston in 1905, many on the lower peninsula below Broad Street.[28] Water problems were equally acute. Frost's annual report to the city in 1905 revealed a plethora of cow lots and butcher pens on the peninsula, breeding and transmitting diseases. Attempts to regulate licenses in the dairy industry during the typhoid scare of 1906 ran into the usual outcry that individuals such as widows would be adversely affected.[29]

As city health officer, Susan Frost's father vigorously promoted reforms. A series of recommendations in 1905 included regular inspection of city baths along the waterfront, "obliteration" of privy vaults by private owners "as quickly as possible," filling of low lots to prevent mosquito breeding, a municipal abattoir (slaughterhouse) to replace private butcher pens, and the appointment of competent meat and milk inspectors and the hiring of a bacteriologist to test milk. John Patrick Grace later achieved great fame as the mayor who removed cows from the Charleston peninsula, but Frank Frost, concluding that "personal friendships must give place to the public good," dramatically lessened the cow population (then numbering 434) by allowing them only if needed for infants, invalids, or "delicate digestions," with no more than "one or two" per property owner.[30]

Armed with more and more data, gained from both her father and district court judges, about such pressing civic issues as education, crime, child welfare, health, and city beautification, Frost became an increasingly vocal advocate of reform in Charleston. Rights and opportunities for women in the city would also gradually emerge among her list of important concerns as well. "I never hesitate to ask for what I wish," Frost once bluntly wrote to a cousin.[31] With the highly visible "Miss S.P. Frost, Stenographer, U.S. Court" at the top of her stationery, Frost regularly typed letters to Charleston mayors in the early twentieth century, beseeching them to be more active. One missive detailed several assaults and burglaries in her own neighborhood, including that of her sister "Rebe," and argued for more police protection and better street lighting in Charleston's narrow alleyways. Another chided sluggishness in street-paving activity, suggesting politics was to blame for keeping rundown neighborhoods from being reclaimed. Frost saw greed, partisanship, and the spoils system in the administration of the Charleston Home for the elderly and advocated an equal number of women on that and other publicly administered agencies to end corruption and better municipal government.

In suggesting a social housekeeping role for some of Charleston's women, Susan Frost championed the work of Georgie Fowler, a YWCA "Traveler's Aid" at the Charleston train station, to make her case. Fowler performed a variety of police-type duties at the rail yard, including intercepting cadets absent without leave from area military schools. Like her counterparts throughout the United States in the Progressive Era, however, one of Fowler's key duties was to prevent young girls from being lured into prostitution. Revealing a growing social awareness of modern municipal government, as well as a nascent feminism, Susan Frost observed that "in all important cities now it has been found advisable and needful to have women on the police force," and she implored then Mayor Tristram T. Hyde to make Georgie Fowler a salaried city police officer. Hyde found the idea "deserving of consideration" and promised to implement it in the next year.[32]

Old family connections, her father's long business and public service career in Charleston, and her own employment with one of the lowcountry's most distinguished jurists allowed Susan Pringle Frost both to criticize local governmental officials and, ultimately, to become aligned with them. Her most controversial alliance was the one she forged with John Patrick Grace, probably the most unconventional, flamboyant politician in Charleston's history.

Grace was once described as "an urban politician in a rural state, a Roman Catholic in the most Protestant area of the nation, a liberal Democrat in an aristocratically conservative city, a nationalist in the most rabidly sectionalist area of the country."[33] As a second-generation Irishman who championed the cause of the common man, John P. Grace won, lost, won, and then lost again the mayoralty of Charleston in the wildest, most hotly disputed, violence-marked elections in the city's history. His opposition to American entrance into World War I, a war that brought an increase in jobs for the Charleston Navy Yard and spurred the growth of north Charleston, led critics to brand him pro-German, and the city's aristocrats regularly railed against his liberalism and bossism politics. Numerous Grace positions sparked great controversy, including ridding the peninsula of cows, building the Cooper River Bridge, and establishing municipal ownership of the city docks. None doubted his love of his native "City by the Sea," however, and his death in 1940 brought accolades from even his staunchest adversaries.[34]

Over the years Susan Frost often earned family disdain for her unconventionality, and relatives long remained embarrassed over her ties to the Irish mayor and her glowing letter of tribute on his death. Frost admitted to twice voting for Grace, who won four-year terms in 1911 and again in 1919, and she once spoke on his behalf at a large mass meeting. One relative maintained that the endorsements could be traced to Miss Frost's lifetime penchant for politically always "taking the side of the underdog."[35]

There were other reasons, however, for Frost's fascination with John Grace. The Irish mayor enacted into law the public health concerns of her father, and Grace's waterfront reform and his program of paving Charleston's streets coincided with her own emerging real estate and preservation interests by the second decade of the twentieth century. "In the Society for the Preservation of Old Dwellings, we always felt we could count on his support and interest," "Miss Sue" wrote years after Grace's controversial terms of office.[36] Ultimately, Frost also saw in Grace's career circumstances that closely paralleled her own. John Grace fought courageous uphill battles over issues he strongly believed in, and he sometimes offended the sensibilities of those whose perceptions of order on the Charleston peninsula were tenaciously fixed. "He was working against the interests of his own friends, and yet he never faltered," Frost said of Grace's vision for a better Charleston; "he felt it was for the good of the city and he made no exceptions; he was without fear or favor when he required cows to be removed from the city."[37]

Frost became actively involved in women's club work and woman suffrage in the second decade of the twentieth century; she found Grace to be especially progressive on women's issues. A staunch woman suffrage supporter, the mayor broke precedent by appointing females to the Alms House Board and the Board of Park Commissioners, and he added another woman to the Playground Commission and created a women's bureau of the Police Department. In his annual review of 1921, Grace expressed gratitude for the support of Susan Frost, among others, who "added the weight of their influence and intelligence" for city purchase of the rundown waterfront docks from the Charleston Terminal Company. He also appointed the then-active female realtor and preservationist to membership on both the Bath House and Juvenile Welfare Commissions. Frost's final tribute to Grace was a glowing one: "I have seen mayors come and go. I have heard of men like Mayor Courtenay and the good they did for the city, but within my personal experience, I have not known a mayor, who did such constructive work for the city, who had the welfare of the city so deeply at heart, or who worked so faithfully for its best interests. . . . the tremendous improvements he made in the city of a constructive nature will live after him for generations."[38]

Although Susan Frost's years as court stenographer and her father's public service kept her attuned to political and social concerns in and around Charleston, she only gradually became preoccupied with women's issues. While startling in light of her eventual career as an outspoken and independent woman, like many a Southern female surrounded by years of tradition regarding appropriate gender roles, Frost had early reservations about such issues as the franchise. Having the distinct impression that the state of Virginia was poised to enact a suffrage measure in early 1912, Frost wrote to her California cousin Nina Pringle: "I don't see how you will ever have the courage to vote; I should never know how; it terrifies me to think of it, and I hope the laws will not be passed in S.C. for some time, I don't care for the responsibility."[39]

Nearing age 40 by 1910, Frost was more concerned about personal matters and the increased workload under Judge Smith than about the future of women. Her father was in declining health, as was her Aunt Susan Pringle, and Susan Frost and her sisters were juggling nursing duties between their Logan Street home and the Pringle House on King Street. A long-term suitor still sent an occasional overture, but marriage seemed further and further away. The court stenographer reluctantly acknowledged that spinsterhood would likely be her fate, admitting, "I hope I shall be an interesting old maid." With middle-age plumpness clearly manifesting itself and fearful she would be alone in her old age, Frost tried hard to keep her cousin Nina Pringle committed to a "pact" to share their later days.[40] While labeling her professional duties "dreadfully strenuous," Frost nevertheless found them stimulating and rewarding, and she seemed content with her lot. In late 1911 she wrote: "Nina, you speak the truth when you say I have a most interesting time of it; and no one realizes or appreciates that fact more than I; I frequently feel that I have too much happiness for one person, and it kind of frightens me, and then I pull myself together and argue that in all the yrs. I have always gotten thro,' and that if further changes come I hope I may rise to the occasion always, but I feel that I have more than my share, a most delightful position, interesting work, fine pay, perfectly charming home, and sisters and friends, and in fact, it seems to me, everything that mortal could wish."[41]

Though generally satisfied with her professional responsibilities in the early years, Frost soon found that men and women were not necessarily treated equally in the workplace, and it was while employed with Judge Henry Augustus Middleton Smith that her interest in women's issues quickened. Discovering in early 1912 that male court secretaries performing the same duties as she were paid more, Frost resolved to attend the upcoming Appeals Court proceedings in Richmond to "find out all there is to learn about salaries."[42] Judge Smith ultimately pledged to seek a salary increase for his female staffer. Her role as court stenographer in succeeding years, as well as her first few years in a real estate business quietly begun in 1909, revealed to Susan Frost that women suffered other inequities. Frequently taking testimony in citizenship proceedings, Frost ultimately exploded over the discrimination against women inherent in the naturalization process, thus revealing that earlier anxieties about woman suffrage had dissipated. She angrily wrote to a South Carolina suffragist: "we are not asking the Nat. Government to give us any special privileges, but simply to take away the barrier of sex, that because by the accident of birth I am born a woman, though I am the possessor of 15 houses in this town, and my people have lived here for generations, moulding the destinies of the Country, yet that after 60 yrs. of the earnest labours of the women of the Country because of that accident of birth, I am not fit to vote, but a foreigner of the most ignorant class can come here and in 7 years attain the full measure of a citizen . . . it makes my blood boil."[43]

Challenging convention as a female court stenographer and verging toward a still move controversial career as a woman realtor at the end of the first decade of the twentieth century, Frost increasingly began to exhibit the competitiveness and daring that made her a legend in Charleston. "You know I always did enjoy being out in the broad stream, and in the midst of the battle," Frost told her California cousin; "I hate to be stuck off in a corner, I like to be *doing things.*"[44] Each year stockholders of a Cuban fruit grove company in which she had shares elected one of their own to inspect the property, and in 1913 Frost volunteered for the task, receiving twelve votes. Nina Pringle received an account of the incident: " Of course I was the only woman applying, in fact I think I am the only woman stockholder, and I had not the least expectation of getting even one vote, I only applied for fun; four men got much fewer than I did; one got only 2, and one got 1 vote, so I felt very much pleased. May be I will get it next time."[45]

By World War I, Susan Pringle Frost had clearly become identified in the Charleston community as both a business professional and an advocate for women's advancement. As her local visibility increased, so did her willingness to speak her mind. In August 1916, asked to contribute the initial article of the "Women's Section" for a beginning Charleston daily newspaper, Frost heralded with considerable pride the ever-widening civic and economic accomplishments of and opportunities for American women. Citing as evidence the twenty policewomen in Chicago, a female assistant governor in Colorado, New York City's female commissioner of corrections, the more than twelve seats women held at the recent Democratic Party convention that year, as well as examples of women in positions of trust in agriculture, commerce, and assorted occupations ranging from wholesale dealers to quarry operators and stockherders, the District Court stenographer concluded: "The signs of the time," are ever more and more hopeful for the advancement of her [woman's] position in the world, the handwriting on the wall is more legible every day. . . . Surely we are coming into our own in this marvelous day and generation."[46] Frost became a member of the National Federation of Business and Professional Women's Clubs of Charleston during World War I and joined the Division of Business Women to march in a crowd of five thousand for the 1916 Flag Day parade.[47] That same year the lowcountry recognized Susan Frost the professional in placing her "among the first" in a "most popular woman" contest conducted by the *News and Courier.*[48]

Frost's expanding role in the professional sphere both brought her in contact with other successful women and acquainted her with obstacles facing those who sought to break from convention. Like many other Southern women in the Progressive Era, Susan Frost was also steered toward activism in the public sphere and toward women's issues as a result of membership in women's clubs.

Southern women may have been a generation behind their Northern counterparts in forming women's clubs, but at the end of the nineteenth century female associations were much in evidence. By 1890 the city of New Orleans had at least six women's clubs.[49] Other Southern urban centers also witnessed middle-class women moving in familiar patterns of organization, gradually gravitating from "safe" literary and church groups, including the Women's Christian Temperance Union (WCTU), to women's clubs and federations of women's clubs that began to tackle pressing social issues and, eventually, their own inequality. By 1910 the women's movement in the South was "moving out in the open," with the regional press "publicly rubbing their eyes in astonishment at some of the accomplishments of the women's groups."[50]

Southern industrial expositions played an important role in fostering the growth of women's organizations and networks of women interested in educational, social, and political reform. More than thirty-four congresses of women were held during the three months of the Atlanta Cotton States and International Exposition in 1895, and the Atlanta Women's Club was launched during its fair.[51] The *News and Courier* reported that "innumerable women's societies and associations" had been induced to hold sessions in Charleston during the South Carolina Interstate and West Indian Exposition. In addition, the National American Woman Suffrage Association dispatched several luminaries, including new president Carrie Chapman Catt, to the lowcountry.[52] Although a few new suffrage recruits resulted from all the exposure, an optimistic Ida Lining of the staff of *The Exposition* was not discouraged; "while the pebble has been dropped into very still waters," she wrote, "the circles will widen rapidly."[53]

In reality, the circles of women's club activity were widening dramatically in Charleston at the turn of the twentieth century, and they would ultimately embrace Susan Pringle Frost in their sweep. The key years in Charleston's women's club history were 1899–1900, and the critical early leadership came from Louisa, Christie, and Mary Poppenheim, sixth-generation Charlestonians and all graduates of Vassar College. President of the Century (literary) Club, Louisa Poppenheim was elected state recording secretary at the organizational meeting of the South Carolina Federation of Women's Clubs in 1899 and began a climb to regional and national prominence in the movement. She returned from the state meeting to organize the "City Union" (later the Charleston City Federation of Women's Clubs), an amalgam of women's groups that were particularly concerned about child welfare, education, and civic betterment. The federation's future was guaranteed with the addition shortly thereafter of the Civic Club, founded by Christie Poppenheim in 1900, and the Council of Jewish Women, a large and influential group from whose ranks four of the initial eight members of the City Federation's Hall of Fame were drawn. Beginning in 1899, and for fourteen years thereafter, Louisa and Mary Poppenheim published *The Keystone,* which became the official organ of Federations of Women's Clubs in Mississippi, North Carolina, Florida, Virginia, and South Carolina, as well as the United Daughters of the Confederacy divisions in several states and the South Carolina Audubon Society.[54]

Charleston's women's clubs compiled an impressive array of social reforms in the Progressive period and, with additional leadership to complement the Poppenheim sisters, made great strides in advancing the cause of women in a bastion of traditionalism. The Civic Club numbered among its signal accomplishments the organization of an African-American kindergarten and a Colored Civic League, the opening of the first municipal playground in South Carolina, legislation requiring covered garbage cans in the city, the Charleston Free Library, and reforms leading to the establishment of a Domestic Relations Court. The club was also involved in a host of other sanitation and beautification activities.[55] A celebrated several-year campaign spearheaded by Louisa Poppenheim on behalf the Federation of Women's Clubs resulted in the hiring of police matrons at the Charleston city and county jails. In addition, under federation auspices a Parent-Teacher Association was organized and domestic science departments were inaugurated in the local schools.[56] Steady pressure on the city council resulted in more female appointments to boards and commissions, especially those focusing on child welfare.[57] The three Pollitzer sisters rivaled the Poppenheims in championing social reform and women's rights in Charleston and beyond. Carrie Pollitzer, a pioneer kindergarten teacher and administrator, led the successful fight to have women admitted to the College of Charleston in 1918, and sisters Mabel and Anita were active suffragists, with Anita later heading the National Woman's Party.[58]

Although 40 percent of the Civic Club charter membership consisted of Frosts and Poppenheims,[59] Susan Pringle Frost was not part of her family's contingent. Exposition responsibilities and then learning the ropes of the circuit court world, with its demanding travel schedule, precluded her involvement with the women's club movement during its takeoff period. Love of Charleston and an increased social awareness placed her in sympathy with the civic betterment activities furthered by local women's groups, however, and travel, reading, and correspondence attuned her to wider reform. "Do keep me posted as to your gay city life, I am so interested, and also as to the Civic Club meetings," Frost urged her California cousin in early 1912.[60] Before World War I ended, Susan Frost had added involvement with women's clubs to an already crowded schedule of professional and volunteer activities.

Frost's years of taking court testimony in cases involving children as well as the national focus on child labor and the general welfare of the nation's young prompted her to gravitate toward the Civic Club's active Child Welfare Committee. The Civic Club largely underwrote the Charleston visit of the noted judge of the Denver Juvenile Court, Ben Lindsey, in November 1920. It also undertook to raise $7,000 to establish an emergency home under the direction of the city's Juvenile Welfare Commission, and the club eagerly anticipated local implementation of the landmark Sheppard-Towner Act of 1921, which extended federal aid for the welfare and health of maternity and child care.[61] Susan Frost quickly emerged "in the forefront of advocating care for the city's children,"[62] and she was appointed to the Juvenile Welfare Commission by Mayor John Grace in 1923. For many years the court stenographer/realtor provided financial support and encouragement to the well-known Jenkins Orphanage for lowcountry African-American children.[63]

Frost succeeded Mabel Pollitzer as chair of the Civic Club City Betterment Committee in early 1919 and quickly charted her own aggressive agenda for an already active committee. Her projections included trying to improve unsanitary housing conditions; urging owners of property to place city water in all houses, whether occupied by white or African-American tenants; bettering conditions in the Charleston train station waiting room; and pressuring, perhaps through investigation, for cleaner streets in the city.[64] For the next quarter century, as her commitment to restoring the city's old homes and unique architecture deepened, Frost would utilize the Civic Club as a forum to advance the cause of historic preservation. At one of her early meetings after joining the Civic Club, she made a motion to have the group "unanimously endorse" a proposed plan which, had it been implemented, would have brought a Spoleto-type festival to Charleston much earlier than the 1970s.[65] Frost served on the Charleston Arts Commission from 1925 to 1930.

Historic preservation became Frost's consuming passion after World War I, and the war years marked the peak of her involvement in the women's movement. Her interest in seeing more women on local governmental and social agencies dovetailed with those of Charleston's women's clubs, and she supported the campaigns of the Federation of Women's Clubs to secure more female appointments. In the spring and summer of 1918, Frost was a member of the negotiating team of the federation that hammered out an agreement with the College of Charleston to admit women, and Frost worked with Carrie Pollitzer and other club members to raise the $1,500 required to guarantee that the first female could enroll in the fall.[66] The preeminent women's issue for Susan Frost during World War I, however, was not female appointments or women's education, but the right of women to cast a ballot.

Frost entered still waters as a female professional in the South in the early twentieth century, and her commitment to social reform and women's rights only gradually matured. The circles of her interest widened dramatically during the second decade of the twentieth century, however, as court duties, a developing real estate career, civic activism in both family and local women's groups, and an ongoing dialogue with her cousin in the progressive state of California sensitized her to social problems as well as to the lack of equality for women in the United States. From a position of anxiousness and uncertainty on the suffrage question as late as 1912, the lowcountry court stenographer had, by the spring of 1914, advanced to become president of the Equal Suffrage League of Charleston. Her involvement in the movement throughout its duration would be intense and highly controversial, for Frost cast her lot with the militants who advocated a federal suffrage amendment and who picketed the White House to achieve it. Although her ties to the National Woman's Party led to the split of one of the most active suffrage groups in the Southern states, they were vital to the shaping of her feminist thought and to her further emergence as a new woman in the New South.

Susan Frost (left) and sister Mary as children, 1876. From Charleston *Post and Courier* Collection.

Frost sisters, Rebecca, Susan and Mary, as debutantes, circa 1890. From Charleston *Post and Courier* Collection.

Frost Family at their mountain "cottage," 1900. From Charleston *Post and Courier* Collection.

Susan Frost (bottom right) hosting a suffrage delegation on Logan Street, 1915. From National Women's Party, Washington, D.C.

54 Tradd Street, circa 1900, as it appeared when Susan Frost purchased it. From Gibbes Museum of Art/Carolina Art Association, Charleston, S.C.

54 Tradd Street after restoration, circa 1917. From Gibbes Museum of Art/Carolina Art Association, Charleston, S.C.

Rainbow Row section of East Bay Street in the early twentieth century. From Gibbes Museum of Art/Carolina Art Association, Charleston, S.C.

Rainbow Row section of Charleston today. Photograph by J. Michael Krouskop, Charleston, S.C.

St. Michael's Alley prior to Frost's improvements, 1910. From collections of the
South Carolina Historical Society, Charleston, S.C.

Miles Brewton House and property, 27 King Street, which the Frost sisters
inherited, circa 1910. From Gibbes Museum of Art/Carolina Art Association,
Charleston, S.C.

Susan Pringle Frost

REAL ESTATE
Charleston, S. C.

SPECIALIZING IN SALE AND
RESTORATION OF OLD
CHARLESTON AND COLONIAL HOMES

April 28,1938

My dear Mr. Rockefeller;

      I have heard of course of your restoration at Williamsburg, and of the manifold things, cultural and benevolent, that you do, and wondered if you would care to make a donation of a thousand dollars towa the completion of the restoration of our ancestral home, in Charleston, S. C. My sisters and I own it, but we have to maintain it by our work, boarders, a taking visitors thro. it on admission fee of one dollar each. We have done much restoration with the money we have earned, and with a donation made by friends, but there are still a good many details which we have not been able to complete; the end is considered to be of benefit to our city and Nation, this home; we preserve it in the old atmosphere; we were born and raised in it, hence have a deep affection for it.I know you receive many such letters, but I believe the matter of the restoration of the worthwhile old homes is an interest that you care a good deal about;I wish if you are ever in Charleston that you would stop in and see us and the home.

      Very truly ,

Susan Pringle Frost

John D. Rockefeller, Esq.,

     Much lovely prose and poetry have been written about our home; I enclose a poem written by Mr. Van Zile of the Players Club in New Yor, who with his wife and daughter stayed with us one winter.

Rockefeller Family Archives
Record Group 2
Cultural Interests
Box 156

Susan Pringle Frost's business stationery and letter to John D. Rockefeller, Jr., 1938. From Rockefeller Archives Center, Sleepy Hollow, N.Y.

An elderly Susan Frost, with Alderman Alfred O. Halsey, views restored city market lights, circa 1948. From Charleston *Post and Courier* Collection.

Susan Frost at work in the Miles Brewton House drawing room, mid-1940s. From Charleston *Post and Courier* Collection.

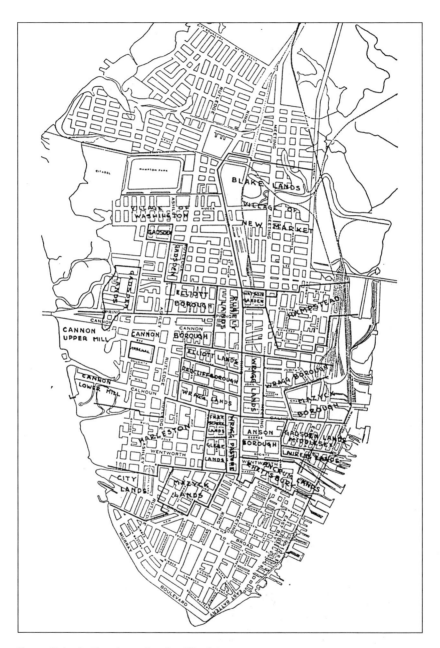

Susan Pringle Frost's peninsular Charleston

CHAPTER 2

"BY THE GRACE OF GOD I WILL LEAP OVER THE WALL"

Susan Pringle Frost, November 2, 1915

The suffrage waters were still quite tranquil in South Carolina as late as the beginning of the second decade of the twentieth century, with circles of interest only beginning to widen by the time Susan Pringle Frost joined the movement. Large, promising ripples had appeared in the stream in the 1890s when the work of Virginia Young and the South Carolina Equal Rights Association (SCERA) generated optimism among national suffragists, but these hopes were soon dashed against the rocky shores of traditional Southern conservatism. Young complained that South Carolina women had been too long "housebound" and "sunbonnetted" and decried "the pity of this pedestal business" as she fruitlessly sought converts to the cause.[1] Despite new hope generated by the visits of prominent suffragists Carrie Chapman Catt and Henry Blackwell to the South Carolina Interstate and West Indian Exposition, the woman suffrage movement in South Carolina, like that of the nation, was headed into a period of dormancy.[2] Susan Frost would ultimately be one of the key figures in revitalizing the movement in the state.

Although most suffragists in the South operated in a basically hostile environment, new conceptions of the proper role for women were emerging, even in Dixie. The cause of woman suffrage had achieved national respectability by the early twentieth century, and southern women who had private interests in women's rights but were afraid to voice them sometimes found, in the membership of a female church circle or at the meeting of a literary society, that there were others with like sentiments. Similar safe havens such as the WCTU and women's clubs provided the necessary protective coloration that allowed believers to gain strength and leadership skills to be developed. Such associations were "the incubators of the 'new woman'" in the New South.[3] From these groups came the activists who brought social and civic reform to the South in the Progressive Era and who in turn began to see themselves as victims and as the oppressed.

The New Era Club was one such group of New South women. In the fall of 1912 a group of thirty women, describing themselves as "progressive" and "abreast with the times," came together in Spartanburg, South Carolina, "to stimulate interest in civic affairs and to advance the industrial, legal and educational rights of women and children." Though ostensibly a civic study group, the New Era was, from its inception, concerned as much with women's advancement as with municipal issues. The group demonstrated its true colors in January 1914 when it decided to make woman suffrage its chief concern, thus signaling the end of suffrage's dormancy in South Carolina.[4]

Other New South women were drawn into social activism simply by experiencing at first hand the power and charisma of nationally known reformers. Belle Kearney knew nothing about the WCTU until she heard Frances Willard speak at a Mississippi convention; within two years she was a temperance lecturer and national organizer, and she moved on to become president of the Mississippi Woman Suffrage Association and still later was the first Southern woman elected to a state senate.[5] Virginia Young likened Carrie Chapman Catt to the magnetic temperance leader Willard on hearing Catt speak at the Charleston Exposition and renewed her own suffrage vows.[6]

Lila Meade Valentine had such an impact on South Carolina in 1914–1915, and Susan Frost was one of those responding to her call to action. A founder and president of the Equal Suffrage League of Virginia, Valentine became intent on awakening the social consciousness of the South following her visits to an England that had been aroused by Gladstone liberalism and the sensational suffrage campaigns of the Pankhurst family. The Virginia suffragist believed that public speaking was a key to advancing her cause, and hard work in developing platform skills soon earned her national attention as an orator. Valentine's 1915 address to the South Carolina House was so convincing, it was said, that "if a vote had been taken that night the [suffrage] resolution would have been adopted."[7] Lila Meade Valentine gave a public address in Spartanburg shortly after the birth of the New Era Club, and her trip to the state capital in March 1914 resulted in the creation of the Columbia Equal Suffrage League. Minutes of the Charleston City Federation of Women's Clubs reveal that the Virginia suffragist was equally effective in the state's tidewater: "Mrs. B. B. Valentine of Richmond, the guest of Miss Poppenheim, delivered a notable address on Woman Suffrage in South Carolina Hall. The immediate result was the organization of Charleston's Equal Suffrage League [CESL]."[8] Susan Pringle Frost was its first president, and within weeks she had aligned it with the suffrage clubs of Spartanburg and Columbia to create the South Carolina Equal Suffrage League (SCESL).

By the time new suffrage clubs and the state Equal Suffrage League developed in South Carolina, the national movement had emerged from the doldrums too. New life was injected into the U.S. woman suffrage movement in the early twentieth century by those such as Lila Meade Valentine who had witnessed first hand how the militancy of Emmeline and Christabel Pankhurst had dramatically revitalized the suffrage cause in England. Outdoor street meetings, deputations to Parliament and beautifully staged parades brought banner headlines and a wave of new discussion. However, these activities were soon followed by heckling designed to embarrass English political party leaders and to provoke police. Stone-throwing, window-breaking, and arson brought arrests, hunger strikes and forced feeding as the British movement became more extreme by 1908. The U.S. press devoted extensive coverage to the so-called British "suffragettes," particularly during several well-planned U.S. fund-raising tours.[9]

The increased sensationalism in the British suffrage movement brought increased debate among suffragists worldwide as to the wisdom of such measures. Busy with the International Woman Suffrage Alliance, Carrie Chapman Catt was "deeply stirred" by the upsurge of interest in the cause generated by the British militants, but she remained unconvinced that such tactics would work in the United States.[10] Others believed just the opposite. Harriot Stanton Blatch, daughter of Elizabeth Cady Stanton and participant in several British social movements, generated interest among the working class in New York through the color and pageantry of parades and outdoor meetings. Beginning in early 1913, Alice Paul, a New Jersey Quaker, and Lucy Burns, a Brooklyn Catholic, both imprisoned and force-fed while working with the Pankhursts, applied direct-action tactics toward a federal suffrage amendment in the United States while still members of the National American Woman Suffrage Association (NAWSA) and with the blessing of its president Anna Howard Shaw.[11] Although convinced that the British government's "departures from good faith" had been responsible for the eruption of militancy in that country, Lila Meade Valentine nevertheless went to great lengths to assure Charleston's ladies that she did not sympathize with the methods being used.[12]

Susan Frost wasted little time in energizing the forty-three women who had joined her in responding to Lila Meade Valentine's suffrage address. In the process, she demonstrated that, despite limited organizational experience, she had powers of persuasion and significant leadership potential. Frost also advanced sound strategies for the CESL in its battle to overcome rigidly fixed attitudes toward women and family. In crusading fashion, the court stenographer called those assembled "laborers together, pioneers in a great and a big cause" of which woman suffrage was but a single phase: "the ballot is only the voice without which we cannot go far in our endeavors, but the movement is much more than the ballot or the voice; its scope reaches far beyond and above that aim." Aware that those within the sound of her voice perhaps needed their confidence bolstered, Frost assured her audience that national suffrage advocates were neither advocating neglect of home and family nor trying to be like men. All suffrage supporters, she argued, should be possessed with "intense earnestness, strong conviction, great courage, high enthusiasm, tolerance, tact and judgment and lastly, but including all, . . . the highest type of womanliness." Frost advocated that the CESL be "strong, orderly, and intelligent" in pursuit of its goal, and she had the News and Courier assure its readers that the new organization, though "militant in its positiveness in going after the ballot," would not be "militant like the English suffragettes."[13] The CESL was soon organized into wards, each presided over by a captain, and Frost made regular visits to each of the units.

Once she accepted the presidency of the Charleston Equal Suffrage

League, Frost embarked on a crash course to learn more about the movement's past history and to keep apace as the cause picked up momentum in the war era. Her cousin Nina Pringle was a key resource. "I have quoted yr. let. about studying to vote on the new amendments, so often in my talks on suf., please send me some more details as to the working of the e.s. in Cal.; I made great use of the last," Frost typed in February 1915.[14] Frost regularly digested the NAWSA *Woman's Journal* and, after it began publication, *The Suffragist*, the organ of the Congressional Union (later the National Woman's Party). She watched with keen interest the four eastern suffrage referendum campaigns (Massachusetts, New York, New Jersey, and Pennsylvania) in the fall of 1915. A lengthy letter to the *News and Courier* following the New Jersey defeat cleverly refuted the antisuffragist claim that women were losing rather than gaining in state referenda, observing that the very size of the New Jersey vote offered proof of her position. Writing of women's march throughout the centuries toward an ever-widening role, the CESL president optimistically predicted: "The logic of the world's evolution [will] lead us to equal suffrage. We await the result of that evolution with confident expectation."[15]

Frost found the early months in the woman suffrage movement "fascinating" and "tremendously absorbing" with "no end to the possibilities of development." It "keeps my brain constantly on the alert to determine what is best to do next with the limited time left to me for court work," she exuberantly told her cousin.[16] "No end of Suffrage matters to see about, trying to secure good speakers for the winter, etc, and trying to get off for the first annual convention of the State League," Frost typed hurriedly in another update.[17] Insecurities still surfaced occasionally as she discovered that the presidency of the suffrage league required public speaking. In one confession she noted: "Have never done anything of the kind bef.; I conduct the meetings of the E. S. League of course, and have had a good many nice things said to me about my work in that direction . . . but have never actually delivered an ad. and fear I shall make a blunder. . . . I am afraid I am becoming too much of a pub. character."[18]

As her appearances increased locally, however, and with an occasional address elsewhere in South Carolina, Frost gained confidence in her oratorical abilities. Favorable press reports helped remove her lingering doubts. Billing her address as the first on woman suffrage in the city, a Florence newspaper observed: "Those who know Miss Frost's charming personality and brilliant mental gifts will be assured of a thoughtful and earnest treatment of the subject."[19] "The speaker presented the subject very ably and with good effect," the local press noted after the court stenographer appeared before the Charleston Jewish Educational Alliance.[20]

Charleston's earliest suffrage league meetings were held at Frost's home on Logan Street, which could comfortably accommodate the twenty-five to thirty regulars. But by the fall of 1915 the CESL had swelled to four hundred members,[21] and the organization had moved its meeting place to the YWCA building. Many on the roster were members in name only, however, and a small circle of activists carried the workload. Carrie and Mabel Pollitzer, both prominently involved in Charleston's women's clubs, were key insiders. Carrie Pollitzer was the membership chair and later corresponding secretary of the CESL, whereas her sister Mabel was in charge of publicity, a role she later handled for the National Woman's Party in the state.[22]

At the initial convention of the South Carolina Equal Suffrage League, Susan Frost had aligned the Charleston branch with the National American Woman Suffrage Association,[23] which was then still floundering under the ineffective leadership of Anna Howard Shaw, once Susan B. Anthony's most trusted lieutenant. Frost was impressed with Dr. Shaw when she visited Charleston in May 1915, describing her as "magnificent," and ensured a large audience to hear her.[24] A month later Elsie Hill, a largely unknown suffragist came to Charleston for a week of campaigning. Her presence dramatically affected Susan Pringle Frost and changed the course of the Charlestonian's suffrage career.

Elsie Hill was the daughter of a Connecticut congressman, a Vassar College graduate, and a member of the executive committee of the Congressional Union (CU), formed in 1913 after Alice Paul became disgruntled over NAWSA's static methods. As a result of its dramatic parade in Washington the day before Woodrow Wilson's inauguration, subsequent deputations to the president and its widely publicized 1914 congressional election campaigning against Democrats throughout the western states where women had the vote, the CU gained much visibility in a short period. Failing to reconcile strategic and tactical differences with NAWSA, the Alice Paul–led Congressional Union went its own way in early 1914.[25]

Frost had quite accidentally begun a correspondence with Elsie Hill at about the time the CU split from NAWSA. A Colorado suffragist had asked Frost to correspond directly with Hill, who needed evidence to refute claims made by South Carolina congressmen that women in their state did not desire the ballot. Elsie Hill was impressed with a letter Frost had written to Senator Benjamin Tillman, and the Connecticut suffragist began to regularly update the lowcountry court stenographer about CU events in Washington. On receiving Frost's discouraging letter of May 19, 1915, indicating little success in trying to organize "factory and store girls," Elsie Hill offered to pay her own way to campaign in Charleston. Without informing the CESL, Frost extended an invitation.[26]

Suffrage history was made in Charleston, and perhaps the South as well, during CU organizer Elsie Hill's week-long stay in the heat of the Charleston summer of 1915. Hill spoke twice a day, at noon and in the evening, not in the comfort of a convention auditorium, but outdoors in Charleston's commercial and legal district. "The first street work that has been done in this part of the world for equal suffrage," Frost proclaimed ecstatically.[27] At Carrie Pollitzer's insistence, two suffrage booths were erected on prominent corners and distributed literature throughout the week. Crowds grew larger, with most of the audience male, including "representative" businessmen, some from "the humbler classes" and, often in the late afternoons, personnel from the navy yard. A few men signed league pledge cards. Some praised Miss Hill's "moderate tones" and ladylike demeanor. Most simply listened politely. The experience left Frost stunned: "It was truly a remarkable sight. I never saw such attention accorded any speaker anywhere."[28] The week of suffrage campaigning was climaxed by the presentation of a petition to Representative Richard Whaley, First District congressman and member of the important House Judiciary Committee, on the steps outside Frost's Logan Street home, an event featured on the front page of the July 3, 1915, edition of *The Suffragist,* mouthpiece of the Congressional Union. Whaley pledged to have the petition printed in the *Congressional Record.*[29]

Frost was thoroughly captivated by Elsie Hill, deeply impressed by "the force of her personality," her "splendid command of the language," her "deep spirituality" and "intense conviction." "You have put new life into us all," Frost wrote in thanks for the visit.[30] Charleston's ESL president was not the only one pleased, and a steady correspondence soon ensued between Frost and CU leaders Alice Paul and Lucy Burns. Burns believed that the publicity from the Charleston open-air meetings and petition ceremony was valuable, and Alice Paul promptly urged Frost to have photographs taken of all suffrage deputations in South Carolina because as she said, "they tell the story so much better than long descriptive articles."[31] Burns, now editor of *The Suffragist* and head of the press department that became a vital nucleus of the Congressional Union, mailed Frost hundreds of copies of pamphlets, annual reports, membership cards, *Suffragist* subscription blanks, and a generous supply of the July 3, 1915, edition that showed her "entertaining" Congressman Whaley.[32]

Frost's flirtation with those endorsing English suffragette-type tactics brought instant controversy. The president of the South Carolina Equal Suffrage League, Mrs. M. T. Coleman of Abbeville, charged the Charleston branch president with acting in contravention of the states' rights policy of the state organization. Frost professed to be unfamiliar with such a stance. The Charleston league had never taken an official position on the most desirable route to achieve the end goal, Frost pointed out, and she let the state president know that several of the "most intelligent and earnest workers," including herself, favored the federal amendment route. While seeking to smooth ruffled feathers, Frost made it clear that she would be governed only by her convictions. She also left no doubt as to her national allegiance: "the Cong. Union has done more than any other body to bring the movement to where it now is, so that we can look forward to victory, I believe, in the not far distant future. They have given a back-bone and stamina to the movement that I feel is most marked."[33] In the *News and Courier* the CESL president answered local criticism that outdoor street corner suffrage meetings had "lowered our cause." Instead she argued: "we have elevated it to the highest heights. . . . We have shown a depth and breadth and dignity to the movement that I think few men have as yet realized it possessed."[34]

Her suffrage preferences no longer a secret, Frost formed a committee of the CESL to arrange a fall convention of the Congressional Union in Charleston for purposes of forming a South Carolina branch of the CU. Throughout the summer of 1915 Frost and CU officials haggled over the details. At times they nearly came to blows. Frost begged for money from a national organization that had little money to give. The annual summer exodus from the oppressive heat dictated that the convention be held later than CU officials felt it would have political impact. The large and "enthusiastic" contingent of Jews in the CESL dictated being sensitive to their religious observances.[35] Unable to make final convention arrangements, Lucy Burns soon became totally exasperated. Elsie Hill restored calm, with the CU coleader promising: "I will be kind to Susan P. Frost, but she drives me mad; every day she sends me a letter changing her plans so there is a constant criss-crossing of letters based on different suppositions. . . . her weak point is her tendency to postpone."[36] Alice Paul pledged to be in Charleston at whatever fall date was settled on; she concluded one letter to Susan Frost "with deepest appreciation of what you are accomplishing."[37]

Once the fall convention arrangements had been settled, Frost and the Congressional Union forged a close relationship. Concerned that the lowcountry suffragist might lose her enthusiasm over the summer months, the CU was delighted when Frost decided to attend its September Women Voters' Convention at the Panama-Pacific Exposition in San Francisco. "She ought to come home boiling with ardor over federal work," Lucy Burns wrote Elsie Hill.[38] Burns asked Frost to send her picture to the CU Washington office because of the obvious publicity benefits: "she belongs to one of the first families of Charleston."[39] In California Frost was one of the speakers at a reception in the home of Congressman and Mrs. William Kent (Mrs. Kent was a member of the CU Executive Committee), and before Frost returned to Charleston she had consented to join the Congressional Union's advisory council and have her name listed on organization stationery. The West Coast trip left Frost with still more questions to answer back home. She stubbornly maintained that news stories proclaiming support for a federal suffrage amendment were "her own convictions and did not represent an official CESL stance."[40]

Although Burns was never content to allow Frost's suffrage activity to go unmonitored, Burns developed a certain admiration for Frost and her dogged determination to succeed in overcoming life's obstacles. Burns particularly liked Frost's self-proclaimed motto, "By the help of God I will leap over the wall," a biblical reference that gave Frost courage and inspiration in hours of financial and personal distress.[41] Applauding the addition of Susan Frost to the CU Advisory Council and hoping to draw on Frost's social status to make other suffrage inroads in the nearby South, Burns projected an additional role for the court stenographer as a suffrage organizer. Burns directed Elsie Hill: "If Mrs. W. H. Cobb is willing to organize a deputation in Goldsboro, could you ask Miss Frost to go up there and start it going?; . . . the name of Miss Frost carries great weight in North Carolina."[42]

Frost's extended summer vacation and a return to court responsibilities and real estate ventures precluded both her serving as the Congressional Union leader desired and her being in the nation's capital when California suffrage petitions were presented to President Wilson. While Frost busily prepared for the November 1915 CU organizing convention in Charleston, she observed with great interest the political battles taking place both locally and nationally. Frost regarded President Wilson's pronouncements about woman suffrage on the eve of the eastern referenda as little more than efforts to keep the heat off the Democratic Party in the next national election. CU pressure directed against South Carolina Senator Benjamin Tillman prompted the lowcountry suffrage leader to write: "he is a hard nut to crack, but I feel that our movement has gained such strength now that we don't need the support of men of his type; they are fast getting to be back numbers."[43] The explosive and violent Charleston mayoral election of 1915 between John P. Grace and Tristram Hyde left Frost angry and more convinced than ever that woman suffrage was vital to cleaning up politics. Frost gave her California cousin a blow-by-blow account: "The rumours are wild, and it is hard to learn the truth; one story is that the ballot boxes have all been thrown out of the window, and the Wash. Light Infantry has been called out .... Could anything be *half* as bad not to say worse under Women's Votes; this is the result under the wonderful man suffrage that they wld. have us be contented with. ... the men were having the time of their lives infesting the polls and brewing trouble of all sorts. .... It makes my blood boil to see such a state of affairs as that and then have men say that women should not vote."[44]

Relations between Charleston suffragists and the more extreme national suffragists were formalized on November 17–18, 1915. Following a reception at her Logan Street home, Susan Frost presented Congressional Union President Alice Paul to an audience at Hibernian Hall, the city's largest meeting place. Miss Paul then outlined the federal amendment campaign. The next afternoon, a South Carolina branch of the Congressional Union was established. Pleased with what had transpired in the lowcountry, the CU weekly, *The Suffragist,* declared: "In no place has there been manifested a keener interest in the federal amendment than in Charleston, and high hopes are entertained for the development of a strong sentiment throughout that State which will cause the South Carolina congressmen to support the national amendment when it comes before them in the next Congress."[45] An enthusiastic Alice Paul signed her thank you note to her host Susan Frost, "with much appreciation for your delightful hospitality and your splendid efforts in the forming of the Union in South Carolina."[46]

Frost had developed considerable admiration for Alice Paul before she came to the peninsula, and the New Jersey Quaker's brief sojourn simply deepened her convictions. Frost also became party to the widely circulated stories about Paul's zeal and self-sacrifice for the cause of women's freedom, informing the SCESL president: "I am told by those who are close to her that she can go for days without rest or food if the work is needing her time and attention." Frost thus joined the ranks of those who regarded Alice Paul as a martyr willing to give her life for a noble calling. She reflected with awe: "Such earnestness of purpose is so lacking in me, that I can but deeply admire and revere it in others."[47]

As Christmas 1915 neared, Frost assessed her whirlwind suffrage involvement over the past several months. She concluded that she was overextended, telling her cousin "the responsibility of leadership . . . is too much with my regular work."[48] While outlining activities and speakers for the CESL for the new year, Frost looked forward most to a few days of relaxing at "the Ranch," her Isle of Palms cottage, and projected a future celebration for her and Nina Pringle: "One of the days there we will have a big din., with favours, suf. favours; and one of the days we will row over to Goat Island behind the Isle of Palms, where a queer couple lives, and where we have often been to have oyster roasts. I have always loved the island, and have for many yrs. had it in mind that some day I wld. buy it; I have always wanted to own a whole island."[49]

The new suffrage year began no less busy than the last, however, with monthly CESL study classes and two major addresses in Charleston by national women's rights advocates, the most important being that of Helen Ring Robinson, Colorado's first female state senator. Robinson left the lowcountry planning to write a story about Susan Frost's emerging real estate/preservation career.[50] Frost was now in demand as a suffrage speaker as well. In one of several addresses in early 1916, the Equal Suffrage League president thoroughly reviewed the progress of the women's movement before the Charleston People's Forum and predicted that women would have the right to vote in five years.[51] Weekends were often as hectic for Frost as weekdays. One particularly busy Sunday schedule included the usual watering of plants at the Miles Brewton House, early and midday church services at St. Michael's Episcopal, dinner and supper meal obligations, an afternoon of showing a house she was "fixing over" and typing court testimony for mailing, and, in the evening, a "special sermon on the woman question," one of several sermons that the rector at St. John's Church was preaching on "industrial questions."[52] Despite her pleas for a rotating presidency, the Charleston Equal Suffrage League reelected Frost president at its annual meeting in the spring of 1916, citing her "untiring" efforts which were a "source of pride" to the membership.[53]

Throughout the year 1916, the Charleston Equal Suffrage League maintained a cordial, though somewhat uneasy, relationship with the state suffrage organization and aided in the lobbying of state legislators during sessions of the General Assembly. Cognizant of the flirtations of one of its league presidents with the more extreme national suffragists, the SCESL had reaffirmed loyalty to the National American Woman Suffrage Association at its fall 1915 convention and subsequently omitted "Congressional Chairman" from its letterhead stationery because some had mistakenly connected that to the Congressional Union.[54] The state convention was held in Charleston in 1916, and Frost was elected treasurer.[55] By the end of 1916, however, additional responsibilities surrounding the impending death of her aunt, Susan Pringle, and the future of the Miles Brewton House, as well as her own overloaded agenda, left Frost no alternative but to curtail her suffrage involvement. Only one outside speaker came to Charleston during the SCESL calendar year 1916–1917. The CESL's wards continued to function, however, and with no one willing to step forward as president Susan Frost reluctantly accepted another term in March 1917, thanking members for being patient with "my shortcomings."[56]

Despite some tension within the SCESL, sentiment for woman suffrage was increasingly evident throughout the state by the time the United States entered World War I. Twenty-five suffrage clubs were reported in existence by late 1917, and several groups, including the WCTU, the Federation of Women's Clubs, and the Federation of Labor, had given their endorsement to the movement.[57] South Carolina suffragists had a strong supporter in the legislature in the person of Neils Christensen, a Beaufort newspaperman, and under the leadership of legislative chairman Ellen Cathcart of Columbia the SCESL mounted an aggressive lobby campaign for the 1917 session of the General Assembly.[58] Carrie Chapman Catt's "Winning Plan" had the National American Woman Suffrage Association reenergized and the national movement on a sound footing, with a huge financial bequest to NAWSA by Mrs. Frank Leslie, wealthy publisher of *Leslie's Weekly,* guaranteeing funds for the final push for suffrage.[59]

For its part, the Congressional Union (known as the National Woman's Party after March 2, 1917)[60] continued the political strategy it borrowed from the English militants—that of holding the party in power responsible for women's failure to vote—and in early 1917 zeroed in on the Southern states, long a Democratic Party stronghold. Recognizing that under President Woodrow Wilson Southerners held prominent positions in the House and Senate and that they predominated on the rules and judiciary committees, the CU aimed at creating branches in every state in Dixie and dispatched many of its best organizers to the region.[61]

The advance party to Charleston found nothing but frustration, however. With Frost performing court duty in Aiken and other CESL officers unavailable, Congressional Union national organizers arrived, unmet, in the dead of night. Lenten observances forced a change of meeting plans, leaving the two suffrage organizers muttering about "the church-mad South." Like much of the nation in early April 1917, Charleston was preoccupied with the United States entrance into World War I. "I thought Charlotte was bad enough, but this place is preposterous," a depressed Doris Stevens, one of the two organizers, wrote to Alice Paul. Labeling Charleston "as pacific as a tomb," Stevens concluded, "I'm sorrier than ever that the South didn't secede successfully. I almost hate it as suffrage territory."[62]

Stevens mellowed, however, when Frost returned within the week to organize a suffrage tea and assumed her usual take-charge role. Banners were soon flying at convention headquarters, the Charleston Hotel, and with special per-

mission from Mayor Hyde another round of suffrage street meetings was initiated as volunteers worked feverishly to arouse interest. The South Carolina
branch of the National Woman's Party was formed on April 11, 1917. Speaking
at the organizational luncheon, an optimistic Susan Frost pointed to the injus-
tice that permitted aliens and illiterates to vote and exercise governance over
educated women as she predicted: "It is because of the Woman's Party that I
believe we will pass our amendment through the Sixty-Fifth Congress and that
I think this may be my last suffrage speech."[63]

The National Women's Party chartered its Southern chapters amidst enormous controversy. Struggling to maintain visibility in the face of a revitalized
National American Woman Suffrage Association under Carrie Chapman Catt
and not totally satisfied with the results of their political campaigning, Alice Paul
again imitated the English suffragettes as she sent pickets to stand, silently with
banners, day after day, at the gates of the White House beginning in January 10,
1917. Special days recognizing states and professions varied the routine, and
when Wilson was inaugurated a second time a moving picket line four miles
long encircled the president's home. The National Woman's Party refused to
abandon its crusade for women's political freedom at the outbreak of World War
I. Indeed, the words and phrases on its colorful banners became increasingly
sharper, especially dramatizing the inconsistency of fighting a war to make the
world safe for democracy when the latter did not exist at home. Arrests followed, the first in June 1917, and the pattern of imprisonment, hunger strikes,
and forced feeding that sensationalized the British movement was repeated here
in the United States.[64] Such militancy prompted sharp criticism from newspapers across South Carolina.[65] Despite this hostility, the South Carolina branch of
the NWP supported the militancy in Washington, with the state president joining the White House demonstrators.[66]

Although Frost's involvement in suffrage throughout 1917 was sporadic, she
was still deeply committed in principle, and the Charleston court stenographer/
realtor regularly monitored National Woman's Party happenings. Observing that
war service was earning women the franchise in other parts of the world, Frost
and the Charleston Equal Suffrage League tied the issues of war, women, and
democracy together in a one-day membership campaign in the summer of
1917. Charlestonians were urged to sign a suffrage card at one of several stands
in the downtown area, thereby pledging they supported "full and lasting
democracy regardless of sex, first within the borders of our own Country before
we presume to extend it to others in foreign lands."[67] Frost's own views on the
NWP's controversial militancy were made quite clear as suffragists began to be
arrested and jailed in Washington. The Suffragist shared a portion of her resound-
ing endorsement: "What a magnificent stand the picketers are taking! When the
smoke of opposition and prejudice and ignorance rolls away, and the nation
comes to regard the matter in its true light, and with the splendid vision that
has been granted the Woman's Party, the work that the picketers have done will
be regarded as one of the truly great and majestic and far-reaching episodes in

the onward march of equal suffrage."[68] NWP Vice President Lucy Burns acknowledged the letter of support and begged Frost to join in demonstrating against the "unlawful arrest" of NWP members.[69]

Determined that the nation as a whole should know of the repressive measures that a government fighting a war to make the world safe for democracy was imposing on women asking only for political liberty, the National Woman's Party took its case to the people in the fall of 1917. For two months some of its biggest names crisscrossed the country. In a "suffrage car" driven by a female companion, executive committee member and labor advocate Maud Younger traveled throughout South Carolina. Despite the recent death of her aunt, Frost assisted with Charleston logistics and was in attendance at Hibernian Hall where "hundreds of men and women" heard Younger's indictment of the Wilson administration.[70]

Frost soon added her own indictment—a letter of protest to the president of the United States. Assuring the chief executive of the place she and her family had played in the annals of Charleston and that she was "no renegade," the outspoken court stenographer nevertheless maintained that it was no longer possible to submit quietly when women were giving unstintingly of their time and talents in furthering the war effort and yet were being arrested for asking for liberty and were being imprisoned under conditions "so revolting that a civilized nation shrinks from crediting their existence." Although Frost saluted all the demonstrators, she saved her greatest praise for their leader, Alice Paul, then frail from seven months of imprisonment and a hunger strike. She is "the Kerensky of this country," Frost wrote President Wilson; she is "sacrificing herself on the altar of liberty."[71]

Frost's social standing in Charleston and her ties to Elsie Hill and Alice Paul produced a small but loyal faction within the Charleston Equal Suffrage League that supported the more aggressive suffrage strategies of the National Woman's Party. "Most of the talk here because of Sue was on Alice Paul's side," former Charleston Museum Director Laura Bragg recalled.[72] Newspaperman T. R. Waring, Jr., suspected that his aunt lent her name because "someone more militant invited her to sign up."[73] Both Estelle McBee and her sister, Dr. Mary Vardrine McBee, a Smith College graduate and the founder of the renowned Charleston private girls school, Ashley Hall, were National Woman's Party supporters.[74] Mabel Pollitzer and her younger sister Anita were also NWP loyalists.[75] Anita Pollitzer joined the NWP following completion of the art school at Columbia University in 1916 and quickly became a force within the national organization—so much so that in her later years Laura Bragg recalled, erroneously, that it was Anita Pollitzer who first interested Susan Frost in the militants.[76]

The inevitable showdown over which national suffrage group the Charleston Equal Suffrage League would be permanently allied with occurred in December 1917. Despite the advance notice advertising a proposed amendment to its constitution, only 64 of the 650 members attended the pivotal CESL meeting, evidence that tended to support the claims of both Mabel Pollitzer and

Laura Bragg that the woman suffrage movement in Charleston was not always sustained over the years.[77] A "lively and at times heated" debate ensued, however. Pleading her case for alliance with Alice Paul and the NWP, CESL President Frost argued that the vote was purely over methods to achieve an end goal that all desired and had been striving toward for nearly four years, and that no hard feelings should result. A final tally revealed a near-even split in preference, with thirty members favoring change and thirty-four opposed, considerably short of the two-thirds vote needed. No other Southern state suffrage association came as close to affiliation with the NWP as did that in Charleston. Now that the die had been cast, Susan Frost and Carrie Pollitzer promptly severed their ties with the CESL; fifty-one other women ultimately joined them in casting their lot with Alice Paul's militants.[78] "Personally I am delighted we failed to carry it," stated Anita Pollitzer; "we would have taken over many unwilling and unsympathetic with all the bigness; this way we have only live, fresh material."[79]

Frost's farewell address to the suffrage organization she had chaired and to which she had devoted much time and energy expressed both gratitude for years of support and justification for the convictions that prompted her course of action. Frost was, in some measure, parting company with good friends for whom she felt affection, and she expressed "very great regret" in doing so. But serving as president of a suffrage league with whose policies she did not always agree had sometimes been frustrating, Frost confessed. "Old time methods" had been fine for the movement in its early days, but a "young and strong and virile" branch of suffragists had generated badly needed new energy and political pressure at the very doors of Congress, and she desired to be "free and unhampered" in expressing her support. Frost again exalted the vision of Alice Paul, likening her to a "meteor, a leader among women who is born once in a century, born to accomplish one great purpose." It was Paul's followers, Frost concluded, who were the "real workers" in the suffrage vineyards; it was they who were sacrificing *everything* to obtain the freedom of all women.[80]

The Charleston Equal Suffrage League promptly elected a new president to replace Frost and adopted a resolution condemning militancy in the movement. As a league and as individuals, they continued to lobby South Carolina senators "Cotton Ed" Smith and Ben Tillman, and after Tillman's death in 1918, his term replacement, William Pollock of Cheraw. Like the state league, however, the CESL deemphasized the cause of women's rights when the war came.[81]

With the death of her aunt in late 1917, Susan Frost had only limited involvement in local, state, and national suffrage matters for the duration of the movement. As coexecutor of her aunt's estate, Frost spent countless hours in settlement matters. Various scenarios for the future of the Miles Brewton House were discussed throughout 1918, with Susan Frost and her sisters ultimately encumbering themselves to take sole ownership of the Georgian mansion that had never left the hands of the original family who built it. By the spring of 1919, they were staggering from the process of evacuating their longtime Logan Street residence: "the task was stupendous," Susan Frost wrote her cousin in

California, "because we were emptying 4 L(ogan) of nearly 30 yrs. accumula-
tions, and at same time filling 27 K(ing), and at same time getting 4 L. ready for
tenants to move in right on our heels . . . besides M(ary) and I at our work all
day. I look back and wonder how we survived; it has taken wks. and will take
wks. more."[82]

Frost maintained a vital interest in the National Woman's Party and woman
suffrage, however, and as legislative chairman for the NWP in South Carolina
she occasionally found hours of time to devote to the movement in its final
stages. As always, her actions were controversial and kept her in the public eye.
Frost joined Anita Pollitzer in pressuring Senators Smith and Tillman with
telegrams, and after Tillman's death in mid-1918, his successor William Pollock.[83] With the Senate only two votes shy of passing the Susan B. Anthony
amendment by October 1918, the National Woman's Party waged an all-out
"Helping Pollock to Declare" campaign. Pollock's eventual support reduced the
majority in the Senate opposed to the amendment to one.[84]

Unconvinced that the President of the United States was doing all he could
to achieve suffrage victory, while believing that their own extreme tactics had
brought them all the closer to success and that they had to remain visible in the
face of a resurgent National American Woman Suffrage Association, the
National Woman's Party launched a new round of militancy on New Year's Day
1919. They lit a perpetual "watchfire of freedom" and proceeded to burn copies
of Woodrow Wilson's speeches emphasizing liberty and freedom in a stone urn
placed across the street from the White House. Frost and Anita Pollitzer not only
journeyed to Washington, but also, said Laura Bragg, "they were very active."
The official history of the militants, The Story of the Woman's Party, detailed
Frost's role with some precision: "Susan Frost . . . burned President Wilson's last
message to Congress in which he again spoke words without results."[85]
Although the renewed militancy brought additional arrests and jail sentences,
and the fresh spate of publicity the NWP desired, the experience did not meet
all the expectations of the Palmetto State suffragists. Pollitzer and Frost " were
greatly disappointed when the police didn't arrest them," Laura Bragg remembered; "that was at a time when in England the suffrage workers . . . were put
in jail . . . but the police paid no attention to them and I remember."[86] Actions
so controversial, occurring while the nation was engaged in global conflict in
Europe, and behavior so at odds with that traditionally expected of Southern
women, doubtless account for the few extant accounts of the Frost and Pollitzer
participation in the so-called watchfire demonstrations.[87]

The National Woman's Party continued to make news with its Suffrage
Prison Special. Beginning in February 1919, some twenty-six previously incar-
cerated militants dressed in prison uniforms and boarded a chartered railroad car
for a three-week trip to major American cities. The first stop on the tour was
Charleston. The NWP called it "the biggest mass meeting ever held . . . for any
purpose" in the old port city.[88] Susan Frost certainly never presided over a larger
gathering. The twelve hundred–seat Academy of Music was filled to capacity,

and overflow crowds taxed the military police's ability to keep street cars moving. Speakers and a suffragist singing "jail ballads" rotated between the Academy and two unplanned outdoor convocations. The Suffrage Prison Special's future stops were measured against the success of the stop in Charleston, and the national organization still heralded the event weeks later: "We are still talking about the wonderful meeting you had in Charleston for the Prison Special," NWP Lobby Committee Chairman Maud Younger wrote Susan Frost. "You certainly know how to do things there—or perhaps it is the things under your direction which go off so successfully."[89]

Although all Charlestonians could agree with the bold headlines of one of their newspapers, "Prison Special Captures City," many, including some of its civic leaders, were far less certain about what the carefully staged event meant and what it revealed about an obviously changing world. In a lengthy communication to his journalistic peer William Ball, *Charleston Evening Post* editor Thomas Waring offered perhaps the most reflective and insightful analysis of the National Woman's Party ever made by a Southern journalist. But Waring, like later recorders of history, was not sure how the militants should be remembered. "I thought you would like the tigerettes," Waring began:

> I find them exceedingly interesting and I am inclined to believe they are psychologically momentous. They seem to represent something of the restlessness and violence and daring of the times and to fit in, somehow, with the general unrest. Of course they are disturbing, too, or would be if they were a serious consideration in one's neighborhood, which they are not here. At this distance from the scene of action they are like a moving picture of the battlefield. They outshine the moderates and make the antis tiresome. They have a sense of humor—some of them—and most of them have an air and good looks. One of them, Miss Berthe (not Bertha) Arnold, has been here for a week and comes into our office nearly every day and purrs, and the cause is won for the time being. . . . This militancy has its significance, I believe, although just what it is I have not yet been able to figure out. I have always believed that the Pankhurst campaign was what finally put over the woman suffrage cause in England. . . . The militants in this country thus far have confined themselves to symbolic acts. Suppose they should go in for such things as their English prototypes did, what a world of worry they could create. They seem to think Mr. Wilson is not sincerely for their cause but is only interested in his own fortunes, and that they are bound to prove to him that his fortunes are in their keeping. Maybe they are right about some of this. For our part down here, probably an open-minded consideration of the question is denied us, as so many other intellectual luxuries, by reason of the cursed negro question.[90]

By the time the Sixty-sixth Congress convened in May 1919, woman suffragists everywhere were anticipating that the necessary votes were at hand in the Senate for passage of the Susan Anthony amendment. Two senators remained noncommittal on the question, however, including Nathaniel Dial of

South Carolina, William Pollock's replacement. Seeking to ensure a margin of safety, and now desperate for funds, the NWP again zeroed in on the state. Mabel Vernon, a party stalwart, asked Frost to arrange a parlor meeting at the Miles Brewton House, and requested several other members of the Charleston NWP to identify possible donors she could contact on her arrival. Informing Vernon that Charlestonians had been heavily bled by wartime appeals and that the proposed visit conflicted with her schedule, the lowcountry court stenographer sent a clear message about any further suffrage involvement herself, stating somewhat apologetically: "I don't like to seem selfish or self absorbed, but it is absolutely imperative for the success of my business that I devote my entire time to it just at this juncture. [I] have tremendous burdens and obligations to meet, and it takes a steady hand and an undiverted mind in order to carry out matters now before me."[91] When the long-awaited suffrage legislative victory occurred in June 1919, neither of the Palmetto State's two senators voted with the affirmative.

Historians disagree on the extent to which the militant tactics of the National Woman's Party contributed to the passage (and ratification) of the Nineteenth Amendment.[92] Both moderates and militants regarded their roles as absolutely crucial, at times even ignoring the existence of the other.[93] Frost had no doubts about whom to credit, and she believed, rather prophetically, that posterity would accord the NWP chief a large niche in the annals of feminism. Applauding the steadfastness, perseverance and unceasing energy of Alice Paul, and pledging the unending loyalty and resolve of the Charleston NWP branch to the ratification of the Susan B. Anthony amendment, Susan Frost told the National Woman's Party leader in June 1919: "Through your magnetism and personality you have gathered around you in a few years a band of workers who would follow your lead to the end of the earth. We feel confident that the name of Alice Paul will be listed on the pages of history and as the years roll on, you will be recognized as one of the world's greatest women." [94]

In South Carolina, as elsewhere, women fervently worked for ratification of the Anthony amendment. Journalist W. W. Ball observed "legions of suffragists . . . painfully excited" at the state capitol in Columbia.[95] In a region where gender roles were still rigidly defined, however, the struggle was all uphill, and only the minority were speaking, as the *Columbia State* editor astutely noted: "My observation is that a few hundred women in South Carolina, all of them good women, are eager to have the ballot and three or four thousand others when approached say 'if they want it why not let them have it?' Meantime nineteentwentieths of the women are saying nothing."[96] The battle quickly became discouraging. Describing the lower house of the South Carolina legislature as "a wild, indeterminate mass of ignorant sectionalists," NWP state chairman Helen Vaughn sent Alice Paul her remaining funds, sarcastically concluding a long epistle: "I feel now deeply thankful that I will never have to owe any debt to the S.C. legislature for my political liberty!!!!"[97] Susan Frost's response to an NWP executive revealed there was little suffrage life left in Charleston either:

"It is the height of our tourist season, when my sister and I are busy trying to make the expenses of the big home we moved into, and my office work keeps me from early to late, and Mabel is in about same fix as to time, and she and Carrie and myself are about the only ones we can count on to do anything."[98]

When the state of Tennessee ratified the Nineteenth Amendment in August 1920 and made woman suffrage a reality, the moment was both exhilarating and sobering. While "thrilled" with the victory, Susan Frost herself admitted the actuality "seems so strange after the long years of struggle. . . . Much as I was for it, it terrifies me now that it is here."[99] The League of Women Voters was created in 1920 in part to address such anxieties, educating women to their new citizenship responsibilities, and the South Carolina Equal Suffrage League disbanded to become a league branch.[100] Although it had undergone significant modification since the Civil War, the image of the Southern Lady remained very much alive in the 1920s. For those Southern women who ventured into the political arena after suffrage, maintaining the outward trappings of the old stereotype seemed essential for securing a hearing.[101]

As elsewhere, however, many women in Charleston welcomed the dawn of a new day and actively addressed social problems and feminist concerns with renewed hope and energy. The number of voters in Charleston doubled between 1919 and 1923, with women in the middle and upper classes swelling the rosters of the bluestocking wards. The expanded electorate in Charleston brought forth women who were not only less responsive to the overtures of machine politicians but whose opposition to such a system resulted in less corruption.[102] Women were added to Charleston city government commissions in increasing numbers in the 1920s, Frost among them.[103] In a history-making election in the city in 1923, Clelia P. McGowan, running despite the widely held view that "Charleston will never put in a woman" and making only one campaign speech, became the first female on the city council. She polled almost as many votes as the mayor himself. In fact, the banner headline, "Women are Victorious," virtually moved Mayor Thomas P. Stoney off the front page.[104]

Alice Paul's National Woman's Party refused to endorse the League of Women Voters' program of social feminism and education and, instead, centered its efforts on attaining an Equal Rights Amendment (ERA), first introduced in Congress in 1923. Although numerous arguments were advanced for woman suffrage in the Southern states, particularly the perpetuation of white supremacy, full-blown feminist thought may have been more widespread in the region than earlier believed.[105] Like the national organization, the Charleston NWP membership was small but included women of means, with family and professional prominence, and they were deeply committed both to woman suffrage and, after 1923, the ERA. Anita Pollitzer ultimately became chair of the National Woman's Party, and her sister Mabel headed the South Carolina branch for the better part of forty years. In her very first address to the Charleston Equal Suffrage League, Frost had argued that the most comprehensive purpose of the "woman movement" was "to raise woman to a position of equality and independence and of free service, since God gave her a soul," and the low-country professional remained a lifelong supporter of the Equal Rights Amendment.[106] Although business and historic preservation work and maintenance of the Miles Brewton House occupied much of her time after suffrage, Frost served as NWP state chair during the initial decade of lobbying for the ERA, and she resumed the position again in 1947.

Clubs and associations provided sources of stimulation and personal development for many New South women, long conditioned to their submissive role in the home sphere. They also created networks of solidarity that provided both friendship and a measure of power.[107] Frost's affiliation with the National Woman's Party put her in touch with women, many from outside the South, who were intelligent and well educated and who enlarged her horizons about women's potential and the obstacles preventing such development. As with other suffragists, Frost found close and lasting ties through her political involvement. "She is the loveliest character," Frost wrote of Mrs. Robert Gibbes Thomas, wife of a Citadel professor and, like Frost, a member of the Congressional Union advisory council:

> [She is] so intelligent, really brilliant, with a perfect fund of information on every subject, so simple and thoughtful; the pres. of the two literary societies here, and a leader in civic work; she is so lovely to me and so loyal to me in all suf. work; she is the one I wish the league to elect for its next pres., but she will not serve because she is a Penn. woman, and she says the pres. ought to be a So. woman . . . she has a great opinion of my ability as pres., and it is very encouraging to have the opinion of such a strong and loyal friend. She goes to Ranch with us a good deal and loves it as much as we do; . . . she has such wholesome views of life, and loves the out-door simple life as much as we do; suf. has done much for me, but her friendship is one of the best things it has done for me.[108]

Frost ultimately brought the same depth of commitment and frenetic energy to the restoration and rehabilitation of old Charleston that Alice Paul provided the woman suffrage and equal rights amendment campaigns. Frost used some of the same methods as the militants. She directly confronted the Charleston power structure on street-paving and zoning matters with the same vigor and fearlessness as the leader of the NWP pursued Democratic congressmen and President Woodrow Wilson. Like Lucy Burns, Frost clearly recognized that, by commandeering space in the newspaper, issues could effectively be kept alive and before the public. In her lifetime, Frost sent hundreds of letters on a host of subjects to the Charleston dailies; one editor frequently used her material "because the name had publicity value."[109] The force of Frost's convictions and outspokenness made it easy for some to dismiss her views and her causes, but the example of Alice Paul reminded Frost that perseverance and dedication could lead to victory and that one could successfully negotiate the walls that stood in the way. Through her own example Susan Pringle Frost would help fashion new contours in the role of southern women in their society. Her career took on significant new dimensions in the waning days of the woman suffrage campaign. Real estate is "the work of my heart," she confided to Nina Pringle in mid-1918; "I stand committed now to make a success of it."[110] She soon resigned as court stenographer. By November 1918 Susan Pringle Frost had rented an office on Charleston's Broad Street and confidently hung out her shingle to advertise for business.

CHAPTER 3

𝒫ATRON SAINT OF PRESERVATION

> The public thinks I made money and it makes little difference
> what the public thinks; my books will show that on almost every
> restored house sold I made big losses . . . but life is larger and
> more important than these things.
>
> Susan Pringle Frost, May 12, 1931

Susan Pringle Frost joined the speculative ranks almost a decade before she
opened an office in Charleston's professional district. Her entry into the business of buying and selling properties in July 1909 coincided with a real estate
boom that suggested Charleston's long-awaited economic awakening had
arrived.

The real estate boom that swept across both the lower Charleston County
peninsula and the suburbs north of the city of Charleston at the end of the first
decade of the twentieth century was part of the larger economic development
and business progressivism of the administration of Mayor Robert Goodwyn
Rhett. Elected mayor in 1903, Rhett was a blend of politician, scholar, lawyer,
banker, and financier, with numerous ties to the lowcountry's socially prominent. Fashioning a new business elite in Charleston, a revamped "Broad Street
faction" consisting of businessmen, lawyers, newspaper editors, and assorted
anti-Tillmanites, Rhett consciously linked his administration to existing commercial organizations while spearheading the birth of others. A Commercial
Club established by the mayor gathered data to aid in business reconstruction
and expansion, new "booster" organizations were created, among them the
Charleston Manufacturing, Jobbers and Banking Association (1905) and the
Real Estate Exchange (1907), and in 1910, the stolid Chamber of Commerce,
reputedly the nation's oldest, was reorganized. In adapting the latest business
practices to city government, Mayor Rhett blended the Old South with the
New and brought Charleston in touch with elements of the national reform
movement known as Progressivism.[1]

The "crowning achievement" of the R. Goodwyn Rhett administration
was a development project that took place virtually at Susan Pringle Frost's
doorstep, and it was a project that prompted the struggling court stenographer
to try to improve her own economic fortunes. In early 1909 the city indicated
its intention to cooperate with the West End Development Company, a private
syndicate of realtors, in reclaiming marshlands at the western tip of the

Charleston peninsula and transforming them into a beautiful boulevard adjacent to the famous Battery. The city council soon ushered in the project, authorizing building of a sea wall, filling of the nearby lots, and paving of the broad avenue around the lower peninsula.[2] Knowledge of the city council's approval of the marsh reclamation project and the development that was bound to ensue around the family home place on lower King Street proved too much enticement for the impoverished daughter of failed aristocracy to ignore. Besides, Susan Frost often declared of her investments, "It was a venture, but then I have always been venturesome."[3] With a handful of borrowed capital, Frost secured two unpretentious frame houses on a little triangle of land near the marshes at the west end of Tradd Street in July 1909.[4] Her real estate career had begun.

Other old-family Charlestonians dreamed of making money out of the mud as well, and Frost entered a real estate market that was already crowded. Thomas R. Waring, then assistant editor of the *Charleston Evening Post,* managed both his own financial affairs and those of his brother-in-law, William Watts Ball, the long-term editor of the *Columbia State* beginning in 1909. The rich speculative possibilities in lower Charleston soon prompted Waring to suggest to Ball that he consider the possibility of quitting the newspaper business altogether and take up real estate as a vocation instead of a "diversion."[5] By 1911 the Municipal Industry item of the Charleston city budget indicated that over $250,000 had been spent on west side improvements.[6] With a large number of lots ready for sale and with development in the Charleston neck, north of the navy yard, having been fueled by outgoing Mayor Rhett, the real estate market was primed for spectacular growth. The volume of real estate sales on the peninsula increased from 508 transactions in 1911 to 692 in 1912,[7] and new syndicates flourished. Many of Charleston's realty-holding companies, nurturing investments from a host of the peninsula's most influential lawyers, bankers, and Broad Street professionals, were brought together in the Hyde Corporation, capitalized at $200,000 in late 1912 by Tristram Hyde, unsuccessful candidate to succeed R. Goodwyn Rhett as mayor in the most recent municipal elections.[8]

Her father's failing health and her own financial insecurity fueled Susan Frost's entry into the real estate field and buttressed her determination to succeed despite the large number of competitors. For four years, extending the duration of the Charleston real estate boom, Frost "fished" the waters around her. She purchased several properties on the streets surrounding King Street and her home on Logan Street, and she made quick early profits. She earned almost a thousand dollars when the Charleston City Council opted for her earliest purchases, the Tradd Street homes; two lots on lower King Street deeded in May 1910, were sold two months later to the Charleston Improvement Company, bringing profits of another six hundred.[9] Miss Frost acquired lots on the nearby Isle of Palms with some of her earnings; the little "Ranch House" she erected there would later provide both a source of recreation and retreat and solitude, far from the creditors and mortgages and taxes that plagued most of her business career.[10]

Had Frost been a typical, somewhat cautious investor, she might have continued to profit modestly in real estate. Despite the general slowdown in the market after 1912, building continued at a steady pace in the northern neck of the peninsula. Borrowing money was certainly not a problem for Frost; the Pringles, Brewtons, and Frosts had always been among the most honored and trusted old Charleston aristocrats. Susan Frost was surely not averse to asking. Even during the tightness of the money market and the orderly retreat of the stock market that began in 1913, she obtained funds from two established lending institutions to go with loans from other sources, including family.[11]

As a real estate entrepreneur, Frost continually flew in the face of convention and predictability. Her fighting instinct and her will to succeed often interfered with sound judgment in a volatile real estate market. She overextended her resources early. Several of her first investments soon had liens against them; a loan taken out in 1910, to be repaid in five years, was discharged in 1919.[12] By the time she became most active in the market, it was "dull." In mid-1913 Thomas Waring wrote his brother-in-law in Columbia: "I do not look for any activity for a year at least, possibly not then. There is nothing to make a good market here but general prosperity and the general is not actively campaigning just now." Several months later Waring pronounced the market "practically dead."[13] Susan Frost chose these less than favorable times to invest more than $20,000.[14] Rather than cast her line in neighborhoods where the "bigger fish" of the real estate market had been said to "run," she pursued her dream in the blight and tarnish of old Charleston, the slum district of dirty streets and narrow alleys centering around east Tradd Street, the first settled area of the city.

The golden era for Tradd Street had been the colonial period. The first postmaster in Charleston lived on the street; so did bankers and other important civic officials. Tradd was the main artery of Charleston commerce. Merchants lived above their street level shops in quaint stucco and brick houses with iron gates and black "Carolina-tiled" roofs. Many of these dwellings still stood over a century and a half later, and virtually every house in a two block section of east Tradd Street would be catalogued as "notable," "valuable," or "valuable to the city" in Charleston's initial inventory of its historic architecture.[15]

It was a vastly different lower Charleston when Susan Frost bought her first east Tradd Street property in May 1911. The area had more African-American dwellers than white, although the spatial structure of the southeastern peninsula looked much the same in the early years of the twentieth century as it had when Frost was a child. Large numbers of African Americans lived in the many alleyways adjacent to the city's great mansions and the genteel poverty of the old aristocracy. One of Tradd Street's small structures served as a school for African-American children.[16] During the Jim Crow era, the two races coexisted, generally peacefully, under the formula arrived at by Charleston's Progressive Era leaders: "humanity but not equality, economic but not political opportunity."[17] In a city woefully behind peer urban areas in public health and sanitation well into the twentieth century, however, African Americans lived in the most squalid of circumstances, conditions Susan Frost was generally familiar with because of her father's position as city health officer. Block after block of the area Frost targeted for development suffered from blight.[18] Famous lowcountry artist Elizabeth O'Neill Verner described the neighborhood around Cabbage Row before she moved there as "seething with vermin, and great wharf rats were crossing the streets in broad daylight, and many of the houses were without water except for a spigot in the yard; when there were no bathrooms or electric lights, and other sanitary conditions were unbelievably dangerous; when typhoid fever was prevalent and bedbugs a curse."[19]

Susan Frost had a dual vested interest in the well-being of east Tradd Street. The highly visible court stenographer/realtor ultimately staked her own bid for economic recovery and long-term financial security on the revitalization of Charleston's early mercantile hub, to include several lanes, streets, and alleyways near the Cooper River. The first stage of that effort was to rejuvenate the city's oldest thoroughfare.

Tradd Street, however, was much more than an economic investment for Susan Frost. Her own roots could be traced to 61 Tradd Street, site of a three-story brick Georgian mansion built by Jacob Motte, legislator, public treasurer, and one of the three largest merchant bankers in colonial Charleston.[20] Motte's son, who inherited the property, married Rebecca Brewton, from whom Susan Pringle Frost was descended on her mother's side and in whose brother Miles Brewton's home Frost was born. The Jacob Motte house needed considerable repair when Susan Frost purchased it, but she treasured its past and the beautiful architectural features, and recalled the special effort needed to consummate the bargain: "I labored hard to buy the house to save that woodwork, coddling the not too tidy children in the house so as to gain the goodwill of the owners."[21]

Frost's understanding of the historical and architectural significance of Tradd Street was not limited to the handsome Jacob Motte residence. Her own sense of civic pride was deep-rooted. Her family history was the history of Charleston; family members had shaped the destiny of the port city over many generations. Her interest in architecture was also considerable, but her knowledge of texture and form was only gradually accumulated and she was largely self-taught. Frost's early upbringing in the Miles Brewton House developed her sensitivities to beautiful woodwork and priceless antiques. She also acquired a deep appreciation of Charleston's old ironwork and woodwork through a lifelong habit of salvaging valuable artifacts from homes threatened with demolition and storing them on the spacious grounds of the Miles Brewton House, a practice begun when an early nineteenth century home near the old Citadel was demolished.[22]

Like many others in the lowcountry, Frost also developed a heightened awareness of her heritage as a result of key publications in the early twentieth century. Harriott Horry Rutledge Ravenel's *Charleston: The Place and the People,* published in 1906, is still referred to as the volume that "reintroduced

Charleston to the world and to Charlestonians as well." The lovingly written five-hundred page compendium was published by the MacMillan Company as part of a major series of travel books.[23] Longtime influential editor William Dean Howells commended Ravenel's history to his readership in a national magazine article in 1915,[24] and the book for years remained on the recommended reading list of the popular Baedekers travel guide.[25]

Equal to, if not surpassing, the impact of Ravenel's work on Charlestonians was *The Dwelling Houses of Charleston, South Carolina,* a collaborative effort of Alice Ravenel Huger Smith and her father, Daniel Elliot Huger Smith, published in 1917. One of Charleston's most renowned artists, Alice R. Huger Smith, who was most famous for her landscapes and watercolors of the Carolina lowcountry, furnished delicate illustrations for the volume, the lines and shadows of which seemed to reflect understanding and intimate sympathy with the personal quality and individual character of the original homes. Coupled with her father's sound scholarship and notes about the old aristocracy who had lived for generations in the same location, *Dwelling Houses* became an instant bestseller and a widely treasured volume. Many date the emergence of a collective sentiment to preserve Charleston's old architecture from its publication, and the book epitomized the romanticist feeling that dominated the local preservation scene in its early years as an organized movement.[26] Frost's interest in Charleston's historic architecture had quickened well before the Smiths published their well-received book; indeed, it was the Smiths who used Frost's historic birthplace for a small volume that preceded publication of *Dwelling Houses.*[27]

Frost's sympathies for the character of Charleston, more so than her formal knowledge of its architecture, motivated her work on Tradd Street. She sensed her own identity with the larger community of Charleston. As one colleague put it: "She saw it partly through a golden haze of memory and association, not only for its buildings, and streets, and vistas, but also for those men and women she had known, or of whom she had been told, who dwelt here, and created, through a period of many generations, the town wherein she herself was privileged to dwell. . . . She never lost this personal feeling for the spirit of Charleston."[28] For Susan Frost, then, rehabilitating Tradd Street was more than a means of making a living; it was a labor of love, and the emerging lowcountry realtor ultimately viewed her project as helping preserve a portion of a tapestry that numerous generations had helped to weave, feeling "privileged to make my contribution."[29] Frost revealed both her own resolve and a pride in the Tradd Street past when she wrote journalist W. W. Ball, also a property owner in the vicinity, in June 1916: "It is one of the very oldest streets in the city, and was originally occupied only by the best people, as the fine character of the old brick houses there testify. . . . It is my firm purpose to redeem the whole street from end to end from the horrible conditions that parts of it have been in for so many years, and put it back where it was for so many years before my knowledge, that is one of the most attractive streets in Charleston, running as it does from river to river, and with fine outlooks at either end."[30]

Frost described her work on Tradd Street as "pyramiding." Taking one house at a time in the blighted area, she first cleaned, and then painted and reconditioned so as to make the house livable. Some remodeling was necessary to provide modern conveniences, but Frost felt "restoration" more accurately described her endeavors and so she placed this word on the letterhead of her stationery rather than "remodeling." In seeking to restore homes to their original beauty, she often added accessories such as mantels, an iron gate or perhaps a balcony. She stockpiled these items in ever-increasing numbers as they became highly prized around the time of World War I, and she supposedly amassed a network of contractors and plumbers who regularly apprised her of buildings containing lovely mantlepieces and woodwork that were threatened with destruction.[31] Frost's rehabilitation of Tradd Street's early structures, once described by novelist Owen Wister in their state of decay as being "like cracks in fine porcelain," sometimes yielded rare treasures such as beautifully paneled walls of cypress wood behind aging wallpaper or doors with H and L hinges, which according to legend stood for Holy Lord and were guaranteed to keep witches away.[32] If no purchaser were immediately available who could be induced to move into the neighborhood or who could be trusted to appreciate the accouterments and architecture of historic old Tradd, Frost simply bought other structures and started the process all over again.

Because her knowledge of architecture stemmed largely from that "haze of memory and association" of how the old Charleston used to be, and because she overextended herself financially in her haste to rehabilitate Tradd Street and the surrounding early East Battery commercial district, the quality of her restorations varied considerably, sometimes resembling a hit-and-miss patchwork.[33] That the reclamation did not suffer more is due to the skills of an African-American craftsman mentioned earlier, Thomas Mayhem Pinckney.

Lowcountry aristocracy achieved architectural brilliance on their plantations and in their grand mansions on the Charleston peninsula only through the tireless and often backbreaking labors of African Americans with special handcraft skills. Thomas Pinckney was but one of a long line of African-American artisans whose ancestors made up the large group of craftsmen who provided vital services to the South's antebellum aristocracy and its plantation economy. African-American artisans continued to predominate in all common and specialized crafts in Charleston throughout the late nineteenth century. There were some ten thousand African-American blacksmiths and wheelwrights in the United States at the turn of the twentieth century, and almost one tenth of those were in South Carolina.[34] For a time white bricklayers in Charleston were forbidden to form another craft union because the large number of African-American bricklayers had organized in Bricklayers' Union No. 1.[35]

Pinckney was among the most prized artisans of his day. Educated in Charleston's public schools and Clark University night school, he became a stair builder (his father was a cabinet maker) and then apprenticed with a contracting company before starting his own firm. He focused on restoration of old buildings and was particularly adept in handcarved woodwork, especially man-telpiece sunbursts. Many talented tradesmen were in his employ, and Pinckney taught his skills to numerous other African Americans.[36] Pinckney worked over a period of six years to help restore Mansfield plantation near Georgetown. The excellent condition of numerous lower peninsula homes was credited to his expertise, including the Brewton Inn, the Pirate House, all of Stoll's Alley, artist Alfred Hutty's residence on Tradd, and the home of Susan Frost's cousin Ernest Pringle on South Battery.[37] On Pinckney's death, the *News and Courier* paid homage to a "respected" artisan, one of many produced in the city, whose "industriousness and usefulness we had in honor."[38]

Pinckney became "Sue's right-hand man."[39] Frost herself was the architect, and Pinckney executed the designs. The talented artisan carved doors, mantels, stairs and moldings for numerous Frost properties on Tradd and the surround-ing streets and alleys. The volume of his work, together with Frost's financial condition, probably earned her rate reductions.[40] An evaluation of Pinckney's services in Stoll's Alley could doubtless be applied to his work on Tradd Street: "All of this work is so in scale and period that one has to be told what is not original to the house."[41] Pinckney probably experienced Frost the way black-smith Philip Simmons experienced her in repairing the iron railing at the Miles Brewton House: "she knew what she wanted and she got things done."[42] Frost admired Pinckney, however, and penned a generous tribute on his death, label-ing the artisan "a real artist and a pioneer in his work of restoration of the fine old time wood carving; others have followed but he pointed out and led the way towards the preservation of so much of our old time architecture."[43]

Frost's program for rehabilitating of Tradd Street hinged on other key fac-tors beyond her own cleaning and reconditioning. The most important of those were paving the streets and removing African Americans from the alleyways and crowded tenement buildings of the lower east side. Neither of these goals was mutually exclusive to the other or to her ultimate desires for the whole of the early eastern Battery commercial district. To achieve either depended on a vari-ety of contingencies, the most critical of which was support from the city and from fellow property owners.

In the Progressive Era, the historic preservation movement was marked by more than sheer benevolence. In both Virginia and New England, perceived challenges to Anglo-Saxon traditionalism and social and political dominance, including immigration, urbanization, and industrialism, resulted in preserva-tionists seeking to reestablish and solidify their past dominance. By erecting and preserving shrines and memorials and exalting past heroes, New England and Virginia preservationists sought both to unify propertied and leadership classes and, in turn, to uplift and educate, discipline and control those who were threats to established traditionalism and ways of life. The end result would be a "pre-served past [that] would act as a potent lever to move the present to conform to the past."[44]

Frost surely believed that her heritage entitled her to help shape

Charleston's present and its future, and she was disturbed by certain developments in modern America. Throughout much of the woman suffrage movement, Frost smoldered because "raw recruits and ignorant classes of every Nationality under the sun" would have full citizenship in a few short years while her family's role in molding the destinies of the country counted for nothing in helping her overcome the barrier of sex.[45] Although the race issue rarely figured in Frost's arsenal of suffrage arguments and she was compassionate to lowcountry African Americans throughout her life, often allowing some of the destitute to reside indefinitely in the outbuildings at the Miles Brewton House, she generally acquiesced to the inequitable Jim Crow era policies of the Charleston power structure. She believed that a gradual policy of "changing all my property fr. Negro to white" would facilitate a turnaround of lower east Charleston.

Frost did not hold African Americans totally responsible for the dilapidation around them. She regarded her own "most advanced modern ideas of sanitation" more progressive than those of the city health department, and she often blamed slum landlords for "allowing" the former colonial period mercantile and political center to deteriorate.[46] However, Frost perceived the need for a higher class clientele in the properties she restored. "I have good German tenants going into the house that I have just repaired," the lowcountry realtor wrote her California cousin in the spring of 1914; "the Negroes are so dirty and there is constant expense for water works where they live." Adding that she was negotiating for purchase of "a fine old brick house" next to the one just rented, Frost noted that "as soon as I get possession and can borrow the money I shall turn out the Negroes and fit it up nicely."[47]

Social displacement inevitably resulted from Susan Frost's policy of "turning out" African Americans, but it was the other side of the coin that was of greater concern to the struggling female realtor, who was noticeably delighted when one of the earliest inquiries about the newly renovated house at no 6 Tradd Street came from a member of the elite New York Four Hundred.[48] Susan Frost was not above appealing to the social control benefits that could accrue from her restoration work, and she found the William Watts Balls glad to sign a petition for the pavement of Tradd Street if it would guarantee different neighbors.[49]

Susan Frost faced an especially difficult battle in seeking to get the streets of Charleston paved. As late as 1904, almost half the total number of miles of roadway was dirt,[50] and the paved portion was like a patchwork quilt. Some roads were clay, gravel and oyster shells, a small portion were pyrite cinders, and some still consisted of colorful cobblestones. Only about one-third contained some sturdy material like granite blocks, vitrified brick, asphalt, or macadam.[51] Getting the area around one's doorway paved depended on whom one knew, and it was not uncommon to have Charleston's post–Civil War gentry in its state of genteel poverty opposing such improvements out of concern for increased assessments.[52]

Charleston's solution to its street paving problems was also piecemeal and varied with each succeeding administration. Although the Rhett regime first tackled the issue, its "pay-as-you-go" approach brought slow progress and heavy political influence. Greater strides were made under Mayor John Grace in the form of an abutting property owner's law that allowed two-thirds of a street's property owners to petition for surfacing and then share equally the cost with the city. Despite charges of favoritism and corruption, and complaints from uptown aldermen that their constituents could not afford the assessment, the number of miles of unimproved roadways declined in 1914, for the first time in many years, from 32.27 in 1913 to 30.97, with higher quality materials used.[53] Progress was stunted again after 1915, however, when Mayor Tristram Hyde's economic conservatism shifted the entire cost to the property owners, and the General Assembly in its enabling legislation failed to include the provision requiring the city to initiate paving projects.[54]

For weeks on end in the spring of 1916, Frost buttonholed every property owner on Tradd Street from King to East Bay and the Cooper River, gathering a petition for the Charleston City Council requesting the paving of Tradd Street. She was under no illusions, however, that the matter would be quickly expedited. The persistent realtor, in a letter to William Watts Ball, expressed her frustrations over the politics of paving Charleston's streets: "The administration and health department seem to foster those to whom they must look for reelection, and so will not force compliance with the sewerage laws and other modern methods of living, but wink at its violation when committed by those whom they think have influence in retaining them in office."[55] Frost's anxieties over the paving of Tradd Street were well founded. The petition she carried to the city council in June 1916, which passed and was referred to the Street Commission, did not bring results until almost three years later.[56]

Because her speculation on Tradd Street was so closely related to her economic well-being and because she had a considerable amount of money tied up in interest payments, Frost often sold properties quickly, at less profit than might otherwise have been the case, and moved to the next opportunity. "Life has only so many years, and I want to do so much," she wrote to a generous creditor.[57] The dreams exceeded the financial realities. Susan Frost sold or rented only two east Tradd Street properties before 1918 (two were still unsold as late as 1928), and with interest absorbing her modest profits and labor and material costs rising following the outbreak of war, she left several houses unoccupied awaiting repairs.[58] At the same time, the sweep of the ambitious realtor widened. During the same years she struggled on Tradd Street, Frost waged a one-woman battle to rehabilitate St. Michael's alley.

A block to the north of Tradd Street on Charleston's east side, St. Michael's alley prospered in the colonial period because of shipping. Later, St. Michael's was noted for housing the most distinguished of the city's antebellum lawyers including James L. Petigru, a preeminent South Carolina jurist and famed anti-secessionist. By the end of the nineteenth century, however, St. Michael's was simply another of the lower peninsula's dingy alleys. "All the perfumes of Arabia couldn't cleanse it," an unhappy father wrote his daughter after she announced her intention to move there.[59] Frost purchased three residences in St. Michael's alley in 1913 and before the end of the year had ten signatures, more than two-thirds needed, to petition the city council for paving.[60] Petigru's law office was her favorite project, however, one on which she spent large amounts of money. Her long letter to the *News and Courier* in 1941 about her preservation career proudly spoke of the Petigru project: "I kept this house intact, even to the bookcases in the library on the second floor; the front door was so far gone that the contractor refused to repair it, so I had it sent to the mill and duplicated."[61] Despite all her endeavors, Frost did not sell any buildings in St. Michael's alley until late 1918.

The United States had entered World War I by that time, and with it Frost saw additional opportunities in the Charleston real estate market. She shared those prospects with the man who would be the key to her financial buoyancy for the next quarter of a century, Irénée DuPont.

Although the Frost-DuPont blood lines crossed in the Charleston genealogical history that was often highlighted by interrelatedness among the old aristocracy,[62] Susan Frost's ties to the Delaware DuPonts emanated from the relationship of Irene DuPont, wife of the president of the giant chemical company, and Susan's sister, "Rebe." Irene DuPont's mother lived in Charleston, but Irene DuPont and "Rebe" Frost only became good friends while attending Saint Mary's School for Girls in New York City.[63] Rebecca Frost was an attendant in Irene DuPont's wedding to her cousin Irénée and ultimately gave up the primary school she operated on Logan Street to go live with the DuPonts. For over fifty years she served as personal secretary to Irene DuPont and governess and teacher to the DuPont children. "Rebe" often returned to Charleston, bringing the DuPont offspring to the Frost King Street home or to her sister Susan's little "Ranch" on the Isle of Palms.

The Frost-DuPont financial relationship originated not with real estate on Charleston's lower east side, but with the Miles Brewton House. At the time Susan Frost's aunt, Susan Pringle, died in October 1917, many heirs had fractional shares of the Georgian mansion. The three Frost sisters had claim to only two-ninths,[64] but Susan Pringle Frost had strong attachments to the Pringle House, as it was commonly called. She had been born there and had spent countless hours of her childhood amidst its gardens and within its walls, and she and her sisters cared for "Aunt Susan" in her dying days. "Rebe" Frost, now a personal secretary to Irene DuPont, facilitated discussions that ultimately resulted, in November 1918, in DuPont loans that guaranteed the three Frost sisters were sole proprietors of the Miles Brewton house.[65] With the transaction, an entire new chapter in the history of the "grand old aristocrat" at 27 King Street was ushered in; for well over a decade the Miles Brewton house was operated as a tourist home to enable the Frosts to begin to retire their debts.[66]

World War I provided a boon to Charleston's up and down economy. In letters to the DuPonts, Susan Frost outlined the specific benefits the conflict brought to the lowcountry and discussed the ramifications of those developments for her own business career. Much of Charleston's new growth was keyed to the vital role of the navy yard. Woodrow Wilson's election and his appointment of a Southerner, Josephus Daniels, as secretary of the navy, augured well for the Charleston facility, and one of the incoming president's first acts was approval of a $300,000 expenditure for a new torpedo basin at the yard. Federal funds for other harbor improvements followed, including a $125,000 lighthouse, and the harbor channel was programmed for widening.[67] During World War I Charleston's navy yard employed nearly ten thousand men, contributing significantly to the city's 20 percent wartime population increase.[68] Informing Irene and Irénée DuPont of the heavy demand for housing generated by the influx of war personnel, Susan Frost predicted the boom would be long-term and invited the wealthy couple to help both the government and Frost herself by investing in Charleston real estate. Addressing her own particular needs, Frost requested a "blanket mortgage" from the DuPonts to allow her both to consolidate her present mortgages and to make some badly needed repairs to her six unoccupied Tradd Street properties. She predicted that her contractor Thomas Pinckney could have the buildings ready for rent in two to three months.[69] The DuPonts consented.

DuPont loans helped Frost hold on to her King Street home place. DuPont mortgage credit brought the financial flexibility that, coupled with wartime housing demands on the Charleston peninsula, enabled her real estate career to expand. In July 1918 Frost resigned as court stenographer to buy, sell, and restore full time.

The next several months were the most exhilarating of her life. She rented a small office in the middle of the professional district on Broad Street and joined the Charleston Real Estate Exchange, still in its infancy. Frost earned $1,500 in commissions the first month, which she used to purchase her first automobile. "Things moved so rapidly," she enthusiastically recalled, "that one of the agents jokingly said he couldn't support his wife and baby since I had been in business."[70] In a state of euphoria Frost told chief financial benefactor, Irénée DuPont in July 1919: "Charleston is on a splendid, steady, and very healthy boom; growth in every line . . . the real est. market more active than has ever been known; everyone buying houses, both rich and poor, and splendid prices being paid. My properties on Tradd are beginning to fulfill the faith I had in them when I bought years ago."[71] By mid-1919 Frost had sold six of her own houses and several agency properties, with numerous others listed for sale in News and Courier ads.[72] Additional months of success prompted a spring 1920 announcement for the public: "Increasing business is making it necessary to seek larger quarters. I have purchased a building at 57 Broad and will move May 1, where I will continue the handling of properties for sale or rent, and will also continue in increased measure the work of restoration and preservation of the fine old residences of Charleston which have placed our city in the first rank of architectural greatness. I thank my friends for their confidence in me in the past, and will be glad to welcome them at the new stand."[73]

Frost set a precedent and scandalized her family during these several months as few women of status in Charleston history had ever done. The idea of a woman in business in the male professional district on Broad street was heretical, and several of Frost's uncles brought the point home to her.[74] The People's Building housing Charleston men of mark didn't even have female toilet facilities.[75] Frost was the first female on the Real Estate Exchange (later its first honorary lifetime member), one of the earliest two or three women to enter business in downtown Charleston,[76] and the first businesswoman with an office on Broad Street. Her only female rival in South Carolina real estate was Eulalie Salley of Aiken, who was licensed a short time before Frost.[77]

In a city where many professionals today still either walk or take their bicycles to their downtown offices, Susan Frost was one of the first women in Charleston to drive an automobile.[78] She was certainly the first to use one in her business. Her very presence in "that high-sitting car of hers" caused anxiety among neighborhood mothers. As one longtime resident recalled: "We children playing in the street around the corner from her house were cautioned to take cover when she was abroad."[79] To be chauffeured to Charleston's slum districts over uneven, ill-paved streets by a female realtor, sometimes accompanied by her pet dogs, was an experience few prospective homeowners ever forgot. Marjorie Uzzell bought her historic but rundown Orange Street tenement under such memorable conditions: "Miss Frost appeared behind the wheel of a large and ancient vehicle. She drove rapidly, never bothering to slow down at corners. Miss Sue talked all the while at top speed, occasionally turning about to my husband on the rear seat. Miraculously we arrived safely at the first house."[80] It was only years later that the Uzzells realized that theirs was probably only one of many properties on which Miss Frost relinquished personal profit to ensure that it fell into the hands of those who appreciated its place in the total mosaic of Charleston's past. For the sale of their home, "Miss Sue" received less than two-thirds the usual real estate commission.[81]

Frost's controversial presence and frenetic activity in the Charleston real estate market at the end of World War I and in the early 1920s prompted much conversation among the lowcountry gentry and no small amount of concern among the male-dominated business community. "Everyone had raised eyebrows over her real estate," recalled one longtime Tradd Street resident and Frost relative.[82] Some simply dismissed "Miss Sue" as too visionary and impractical. Preservationist Alston Deas maintained that "the business leaders thought Sue was putting money on useless property."[83] Charleston's real estate market had never been altogether predictable, however. As Thomas R. Waring told W. W. Ball at the end of World War I, "there appears to be no standard of values."[84] Although unnamed, Frost was clearly the target in Waring's June 1920 letter of concern about the Charleston economy: "From what I have been able to learn, her financial arrangements are not very stable and she has freakish views of business. She is undoubtedly a disturbing factor and her entrance into the situation gives me some anxiety. She has the "will to profit" and, if there is anything in the Nietzsche philosophy, she may get away with something. She will not succeed according to orthodox standards, but these are not days of orthodoxy."[85]

By early 1920 Frost had discharged half her financial obligations to Irénée DuPont on her Tradd Street properties. With the sale of the Frost home on Logan Street imminent and, in turn, liquidation of a significant portion of the mortgage on the Miles Brewton House, Frost believed that prospects for long-term success had never been brighter. Maintaining that her Tradd Street properties were now "the admiration of everyone," the busy realtor prepared to move into her more spacious quarters on Broad Street while plotting the *coup de grace* of her business career—reclamation of an entire block of East Bay Street buildings.[86]

Located between Tradd Street on the south and Elliot Street to the north, the quaint, colorful houses that face the expanse of the Cooper River on lower East Bay Street known as Rainbow Row have long been one of the most identifiable landmarks of Charleston. Built as merchant houses, some as early as the 1740s, the buildings originally housed some of the city's most distinguished business and political leaders. From anchoring a considerable wholesale and retail grocery business before the Civil War, East Bay declined to saloons and tenements not long after, and "slumbered for fifty years practically unchanged" until the 1920s. The row of historic buildings was so dilapidated by the second decade of the twentieth century that the Charleston City Council proposed that they be demolished and that the area be totally redeveloped.[87]

East Bay was the site of heavy speculation during Charleston's early-twentieth-century real estate boom, however,[88] and Frost developed a keen interest in the street as well. She observed that some of the congestion of the Broad Street business district was already spilling around the corner on the northern end of the block, and she wagered that restored properties could not only become part of the growth of residences on the eastern waterfront but would also be a vital link to her Tradd Street reclamation work. Citing her good showing on the Tradd Street mortgage, Frost again turned to Irénée DuPont. She requested funds to purchase six East Bay properties and explained that it was her intention to hold the package of properties for only a short time while they appreciated, with rentals taking care of interest on the purchase money loan. Relaying predictions from "one of the oldest and best known and most experienced" real estate men on Broad Street that she could expect "a barrel of money" from the deal, "Miss Sue" offered her own prognosis to the chemical company president: "It is quite the most important and best thing I have yet handled. . . . if I can now take hold of this East Bay block, I will be satisfied with what I have been able to accomplish for Charleston and incidentally for myself. . . . My future is made if I can get these properties."[89]

Frost got the block of six; the DuPonts came up with some of the funds, and local sources the rest.[90] Frost's grand financial dreams, however, were not to be realized. Prosperity associated with the war vanished just as quickly as it came. A postwar depression, lasting several years, was particularly severe for the lowcountry cotton industry and brought numerous local bank failures. Some four thousand Charlestonians eventually left the city in the 1920s, fleeing high taxes, substandard housing and generally gloomy economic conditions.[91] Journalist Thomas R. Waring wrote his brother-in-law of the dark days ahead: "Nothing much is happening here. There have been some slightly encouraging signs of business improvement. The fertilizer men have been doing a little. But we are at low ebb and I think we have a long way to go yet before we get back anywhere near to prosperity. This part of the State has a harder time before it than any other, with the boll weevil and all the rest."[92] Charleston's real estate market was hit hard by the postwar depression, dooming an already financially overextended Frost to years of fighting to meet her obligations. In late 1922, desperately trying to pry more money from her golden goose to escape mortgage foreclosure on property just north of the city limits, Frost pleaded that "it will be the last business favor I shall have to ask of any one."[93]

In contrast to the several months of exhilaration she experienced immediately after the end of World War I, Frost found the 1920s and 1930s frustrating and disillusioning, and she struggled to remain optimistic. She barely met tax and loan interest obligations. With no funds to pursue restorations, Frost hoarded woodwork and other artifacts in her rundown buildings and in the yard of the Miles Brewton House. The original balconies of nos. 83 and 87 East Bay moldered in her home for over twenty years.[94] African Americans remained tenants in East Bay Street buildings through the years to provide rental monies. Thomas Pinckney only occasionally put in workdays for the once busy realtor. In one of numerous letters expressing appreciation to Irénée DuPont for his courtesies regarding her overdue loan and interest payments, Frost gloomily reported in March 1925: "We have had three very depressed years, with few if any sales. . . . there have been practically none at all."[95]

Efforts to escape the deepening depression of the early 1920s and salvage her diminishing hopes for Charleston's lower east side prompted Frost to make numerous desperate financial appeals, particularly to the DuPonts. The increased frequency of those appeals ultimately tested Irénée DuPont's patience and created a strained relationship between him and the sister of the governess to his children. Wanting Susan Frost to succeed in her real estate career, Irénée DuPont time and time again provided important monetary backing, but Frost's unrestrained speculation and unconventional business practices left the gentle corporate executive more and more critical. Rejecting yet another Frost entreaty in late 1923, Irénée DuPont told his brother-in-law: "I am sure from Miss Frost's letters she has gotten a rather vague notion of the risks in the real estate business. She may eventually make a success of it but the probabilities are that some hard hearted lawyers will sell her out because she is behind on her interest. She certainly would have no hesitation in taking on a volume of business out of all proportion to her available capital. Of course, if she can get that capital from her friend she has used good judgement from a cold blooded business point of view, but she is likely to be left stranded some day and feel peeved at her friends."[96]

Despite the ongoing economic depression, by 1925 there were signs that the Charleston real estate market was finally rebounding. The city experienced a major cultural renaissance during the war years, and by the early 1920s artists and writers were mingling with growing numbers of winter colonists, resulting in a "cross fertilization of ideas and stirring of the spirit in many spheres of endeavor."[97] Frost saw a glimmer of hope for her own dismal economic picture in that several artists and literary figures, including DuBose Heyward and Elizabeth O'Neill Verner, made commitments to the revitalization of Tradd Street by purchasing property and maintaining residence there.[98] Hoping to capitalize on the growing number of winter visitors, Charleston's struggling female realtor focused on "train[ing] the thought of the home seeker away from the lower end of the city" by showing "beauties" all over the peninsula.[99] "Artists and architects from all over the country are coming here, with many buying homes," Frost wrote excitedly to Irénée DuPont in the late 1920s, reporting she had sold four winter homes to Northerners in the spring of 1927.[100] Throughout much of the 1920s and 1930s, however, the picture was far different for Susan Frost. There were few real estate sales; often offers that were made were simply too low to be considered seriously.

In her bid to stay solvent, Frost bartered away her dreams for restoring Charleston's early mercantile center. One by one, her buildings slipped, unrestored, into the hands of others. The first went in 1936;[101] the second, 95 East Bay Street, was sold in 1938, the first of three row houses that New York playwright and Hollywood scriptwriter John McGowan purchased. Thomas Pinckney's initial restoration work at 83 East Bay left him so "fascinated by the possibilities" that Frost "sacrificed" two other nearby dwellings to continue there. On the eve of the United States' entry into World War II, Frost was "holding on tight" to only two of the original six properties she had hoped to restore, sustained "with the selfish consolidation for my disappointment that I still hold the two best in the block."[102] Writing the *News and Courier* in February 1941 to challenge the implication of an earlier article that sale of the remainder of the East Bay Street block would achieve the consummation of her dreams, Frost conveyed how bittersweet the "miscarrying" had been: "It represented a bitter disappointment to me that I was not able to restore all my holdings, and to keep them. I have never commercialized my restoration work, or my love to the old and beautiful things of Charleston. A friend once told me that I had too much sentiment to make money and I think it is partly true. At any rate it has been a great pleasure to be able to take some small part in their restoration and [the] preservation of our old homes, and to point the way to others who were more blessed in their financial ability to carry on the work. It has been a privilege to make my contribution toward such an important and worthwhile work."[103]

Frost remained active with the Charleston Real Estate Exchange between the two world wars, both helping the exchange refine its own rules of conduct and ensuring that historic preservation matters were on its agenda. Frost favored the standardizing of rates of commission agreed to by the exchange in 1931, and she urged the body of realtors to more closely monitor "curbstone brokers," individuals operating without a city license, during the Great Depression.[104] "Miss Sue" applauded the enthusiastic support of the Real Estate Exchange for Charleston's historic district zoning ordinance in 1931,[105] and she served for nine years (1940–1949) as the exchange's nominee on the Board of Adjustments established under the zoning ordinance. When her sister Mary's health and other considerations forced her to resign from the Zoning Board of Adjustments in 1949, Frost was unanimously elected the first honorary lifetime member of the Charleston Real Estate Exchange.[106]

Riches never came to Frost, and her vision for personally restoring the streets and alleyways of Tradd and East Bay streets met with only limited success. The morass of mortgages, interest payments, and paving taxes, exacerbated by the Miles Brewton obligations, Charleston's economic distress, and her own intemperate financial management, destined Miss Frost to more losses than profits. After buying and restoring the Jacob Motte House for some $6,000 more than what she sold it for, "Miss Sue" suffered additional disappointment when the purchaser sold it out of Charleston piecemeal, "first a whole room and then a mantel [from another room]."[107] Still despairing that half her original purchase mortgage for her Tradd Street properties was unpaid when the Great Depression hit, Frost requested that Irénée DuPont allow a prospective buyer for the last of those dwellings to purchase under a gradual amortization which, though it would not enable total retirement of her past interest, would satisfy her "anxious" desire to "get out of that block."[108]

The need to profit propelled Frost into the risky Charleston real estate game; the acquisitive drive became attenuated and ultimately, to a large extent, superseded because of Frost's abiding sentiments about Charleston and its people. The ever-present commercial factor compounded the difficulties for the preservation-minded realtor, however. In contact with New England's foremost historic preservationist, William Sumner Appleton, in the early 1920s, Frost wrote of the struggle: "In this commercial day and generation it takes lots of courage and nerve to make headway on the preservation of these splendid old homes; the financial end of the game makes so much stronger appeal to the vast majority than the sentimental end, and it is uphill work."[109] Frost struggled to remain optimistic in the face of financial adversity. "I see no immediate prospect of paying out," she wrote her cousin "Nell" Pringle in March 1934, "but life is larger and more important than these things and I have tried to make the best of the losses and to turn my mind to effort to pull thro . . . and to see the good side with the trying."[110]

Frost "restored" few houses, with much of that work simply reconditioning so as to make them livable. Most of her East Bay Row buildings were sold in basically the same rundown condition under which they were purchased. Chronically in debt, hers was primarily a "holding action," awaiting better economic times and buyers who dared to move into blighted areas. But lists of rehabilitated houses or pages of real estate sales are not the appropriate yard-sticks by which to measure either Frost's business/preservation career or the value of her real estate pioneering for Charleston, a city whose economic vital-ity is heavily contingent on tourists coming to see its old homes and historic architecture.

Frost bought and held real estate for years when it was threatened with destruction, financially encumbering herself but buying time for structures threatened by decay and demolition. Hers was both an ambitious undertaking and a daring one. Frost's courage, resoluteness, and untiring enthusiasm ulti-mately served to advertise Charleston's architectural heritage and inspired oth-ers to preserve it. The city developed a preservation movement earlier than other localities did solely because of "Sue" Frost and the vision she possessed, argued Milby Burton, Charleston Museum director and preservation society president in the 1930s.[111] Having played no small role in helping to shape the contours of Charleston's historic preservation movement in the twentieth cen-tury, artist Elizabeth O'Neill Verner inevitably looked back on Frost's struggles as the catalyst for it all: "Others with vision followed, and so today we still have left to us what Philadelphia, Old Amsterdam and most other Colonial cities lost. . . . That we still live in the old neighborhoods and have preserved for posterity our beloved city, [however] is due to one woman and one woman only. . . . It is seldom that a city owes so much to one individual as Charleston owes to Susan Pringle Frost. . . . The Charleston we enjoy is a monument to one woman's vision."[112]

Acknowledged as the "Angel of Tradd" during the 1920s, Frost zealously crusaded to rehabilitate, not a single street, but an entire neighborhood of build-ings. Indeed, the pioneer realtor told one audience, "No tiny bit of this beauty in any remote section of our city is too insignificant, or too unimportant in its integral part of the whole setting, to be worth saving."[113] Frost fought to pro-tect her own properties, as well as the larger environs of the city of Charleston, from outsiders (and sometimes insiders) increasingly covetous of iron- and woodwork from an earlier era, and she assumed leadership in the 1920s for legal protection ordinances.[114] Frost was ahead of her time in envisioning saving com-munities, not as museum settings such as Williamsburg, but as places where peo-ple lived and worked throughout the year; only after World War II was a broader preservation approach than saving historic houses and villages as museums for educational purposes widely subscribed to.[115]

The neighborhood restoration approach to historic preservation initiated by Susan Pringle Frost later bore rich fruit in the work of the Historic Charleston Foundation. "It is easier to convert the doubting Thomases of the value of neighborhood restoration as a result of the work of Miss Frost," cited former Foundation director Frances Edmunds, whose revolving fund approach opened the door for revitalizing of several sections of old Charleston after World War II.[116] By the latter half of the twentieth century, private restoration programs by real estate agents would become widespread, especially as historic preservation became more and more important to community development. Such programs were novel in the early twentieth century, and those headed by women were unheard of. Frost's approach of purchasing, restoring and reselling to those who shared her interest blunted the further deterioration of Charleston's lower peninsula. It also had a direct, positive economic impact. Mayor Stoney, relaying some history of Charleston when he introduced the president of the National Association of Real Estate Boards at a 1929 gathering, boasted that the city possessed a female realtor whose activities on Tradd Street had enhanced property values by a million dollars.[117]

As a pioneer businesswoman in Charleston and in the state of South Carolina, Frost clearly made an indelible imprint on her locale. Some of the predominantly male professionals around Broad Street offered her respect,[118] many treated her as an aberration, and all felt her energy. During the years when she traveled to three states as a court stenographer, campaigned for woman suffrage, promoted other women's issues and civic causes, and helped care for a sick aunt, Frost spent countless hours getting signatures on paving petitions, lobbying municipal officials, soliciting and shepherding renters, courting potential lenders, supervising her building contractor, and laboring in the slums herself. Said one who knew Frost well, "She put so many thrills into the old real estate market that it was her competitors who gasped for breath and mercy."[119] In proving that southern women could be competitive in the often unpredictable world of business, Frost also helped open the doors of commercial opportunity for others. One beneficiary of the Frost real estate pioneering in Charleston was Elizabeth Hannahan, who, with $100 in borrowed capital, began her fifty-year career in real estate in 1933, for a time sharing an office and a partnership with the daughter of Aiken realtor Eulalie Salley on East Bay Street.[120]

Debts, not profits, highlight Susan Frost's real estate career, however. Interest, taxes, and mortgages overshadowed sales, especially in the 1920s and 1930s. Frost never maintained a bank account, and she rarely paid income taxes inasmuch as losses usually outweighed gains. "I have never had the courage to figure up the losses, but it runs into many thousands," she admitted in 1934; "the public thinks I made money and it makes little difference what the public thinks; my books will show that on almost every restored house sold I made big losses."[121] Using the latitude afforded by his Ways and Means Committee, Mayor Burnet Maybank reduced Frost's paving tax debt in 1936, citing her significant development of real estate, her restoration of many old buildings and her sacrifice of much time and energy on behalf of the city.[122]

Overcommitted with quaint little properties and so financially overextended no one would lend her money, Frost was hamstrung when the opportunity came in 1920 to save one of Charleston's most significant treasured houses. To rescue the Joseph Manigault House, the Society for the Preservation of Old Dwellings was called into being.

CHAPTER 4

A SMALL BAND OF US

A small band of us (all too few in number) have literally agonized
over the destruction of our city and have labored with untiring
zeal, and often times to the hurt of our own interest, in our
efforts to preserve her old-world beauty.
Susan Pringle Frost to *Charleston News and Courier* (c. 1928)

The spark to form a preservation society appears to have been lit when Susan
Frost approached her cousin Nell McColl Pringle over a weekend, concerned
over the proposed demolition of "the magnificent residence of Mr. Manigault
at the corner of Meeting Street and Ashmead Place."[1] Clearly brooding over
having "tied herself up so tight" with a series of real estate ventures that she had
no means to take advantage of "this big opportunity," and bewailing the men
who wouldn't trust her with more money, Frost anxiously contemplated other
alternatives. Who first suggested a preservation society be formed is unclear, and
both women may legitimately claim credit for its inception,[2] but it was the
aggressive lowcountry realtor who took center stage, issuing the notice for the
original gathering and frenetically telephoning to generate attendance.[3] And it
was Susan Frost who was unanimously chosen president of this "association"
that had no name until its third meeting. In urging "all intelligent citizens" to
attend an early mass meeting called by the group, the *News and Courier* predicted: "In setting the movement on foot Miss Frost, who has already done so
much to preserve and restore what was best in Charleston's architecture in the
past, has performed a service to the community the value of which will be recognized in increasing measure as the years pass."[4]

Like her more prominent cousin, Nell McColl possessed keen preservation
interests and a deep love of Charleston, and when she married Ernest Pringle,
Jr., she married into a family that had both shaped the lowcountry past and
sought to maintain its heritage. As a child, her husband had been involved in
one of the earliest organized preservation projects in Charleston, helping his
mother, one of the founders of the South Carolina Society of Colonial Dames,
to save a colonial era powder magazine.[5] Nell Pringle had projects of her own,
including convincing the chamber of commerce to use the old Library Society
building and persuading the King's Daughters to convert the Governor Bennett
House into their nursery. "There were so many fingers in the dike, I wondered
she had fingers left," recalled one of Pringle's daughters, using her mother's
favorite metaphor to describe her ongoing preservation agenda.[6] When Susan

Frost and Nell Pringle joined hands in attempting to rescue the Joseph Mani-gault House, they began an ill-fated adventure that would inextricably bind them, and the preservation society they created, together for over a decade.

Nell McColl Pringle likened the "Gault" house to "one of the perfect pearls on the now loosened string of architectural gems." It was designed by Joseph Manigault's brother, Gabriel, a gentleman rice planter who returned from an architectural education abroad, significantly influenced by the style and functional planning associated with the Adam brothers, to design no fewer than five buildings in Charleston, including the Bank of the United States (now the City Hall) and the South Carolina Society Hall.[7] Built in 1802–1803 in the shape of a large parallelogram, three stories high, and standing on the highest point of land within the city, the Joseph Manigault House was a monument to the fortunes of rice growing. Its interior contained a wealth of carved wood and plaster work, and the delicate carving in a ceiling atop a spectacular freestand-ing stairway created a "one of a kind view in America." A visit to Charleston would be justified without seeing anything else, stated one celebrated architect.[8]

Over time, the Manigault estate dwindled, and by the end of World War I it had fallen victim to some of the forces of modernism that were fast descend-ing on the Charleston peninsula. Automobiles, filling stations, and parking lots began to dot the local landscape, along with the earliest waves of outside visi-tors, prompting the often caustic William Watts Ball to remark: "Nothing is more dreadful than tourists, whether grasshoppers, boll weevils, or money-bagged bipeds. They will make Charleston rich and ruin her."[9] Even outsiders began to notice the threats. "A lovely structure, the Manigault house, is already neighbored by a brand new and shining gasoline filling station in the best mod-ernistic red, white and blue gasoline style. A visitor to this section is torn between the desire to cry and curse," observed the president of the American Institute of Architects on a visit to the lowcountry.[10]

The list of thirty-two, mostly women, who assembled in the spacious Pringle South Battery drawing room on April 21, 1920, read like a who's who of old Charleston aristocracy; Rhett, Prioleau, Ravenel, Cheves, and Simons joined Frost and Pringle to hear about the dangers to the city's architecture. Key figures tied to the Charleston cultural renaissance after World War I also were present, including Elizabeth O'Neill Verner and Eola Willis.[11] Etcher Alfred Hutty spoke of the value of old dwellings from the perspective of both an out-sider and an artist.[12]

Not one but three meetings were held before the Society for the Preser-vation of Old Dwellings (SPOD), now the Preservation Society of Charleston (PSOC), was officially constituted. After agreeing on dues of $1.00 a year and selecting officers, the South Battery group adjourned to rally "prominent men in the community" to gather three weeks later at the Chamber of Commerce. There Albert Simons, a restoration architect who would become a giant in Charleston preservation history,[13] spoke of the lowcountry's rich architectural heritage, and Paul Rea, director of the Charleston Museum, pledged to the new "association" the support of the museum.[14] Begging "anyone with a responsive chord" to pay heed, the *News and Courier* promoted yet another assembly, a June 26, 1920, meeting on the veranda of the Joseph Manigault House which would see ratification of a constitution and the official beginnings of Charleston's oldest preservation organization.

In trying to arrive at a title to give the "association" interested in Charleston's heritage, Frost lost one battle but won another. In one of a series of letters in the early 1920s to William Sumner Appleton, founder of the Society for the Preservation of New England Antiquities (SPNEA) in 1910, Frost confessed that she desired to have "Charleston" as part of the designation but was voted down because "the members thought it would be too long, and that Charleston was inferred."[15] The official title of the Preservation Society was no less cumbersome for the omission, however, for "Miss Sue" insisted on including "Dwelling," a word with cultural, architectural, and emotional overtones. To Frost, the Anglo-Saxon word particularly implied permanence, stability, and continuity—for these buildings of the past were not only structurally significant, but they had also housed family after family who made vital contributions to the total community.[16] Having recently made the commitment to ensure that her own home place, the Miles Brewton House, would remain in family hands through yet another generation, the term held even more cogent meaning for Frost. Formation of a preservation society with such a title was also timely, coinciding with the success of Alice R. Huger Smith and D. E. Huger Smith's 1917 book, *The Dwelling Houses of Charleston, South Carolina,* which carried warnings about the threat of "incongruous" new construction.[17]

Delighted to receive encouragement from the New England preservationist William Sumner Appleton, whose organization, like the SPOD, had modest beginnings,[18] Frost heralded the "good start" in Charleston and suggested they keep in contact: "Send me any stuff from time to time that you think would be helpful, and I will do the same to you."[19] Limited funds kept the Charleston Preservation Society from generating publicity material during its early years, but William Sumner Appleton remained generous in mailing SPNEA *Bulletins.* Frost "enjoyed and appreciated" Appleton's quarterly publication and came to regard the New Englander as a common ally in whom she could confide.

Unlike most early preservation organizations, the Society for the Preservation of Old Dwellings was not exclusively concerned with historical landmarks. Indeed, it defined its mission as safeguarding "buildings, sites and structures" of both "historical significance" *and* "aesthetic distinction." Frost's first meeting notice cited the need for a movement "looking to the restoration and preservation of the finest in Charleston's architectural past."[20] In preserving such buildings, members of the SPOD clearly understood that they would also be memorializing the life and accomplishments of their ancestors. Frost particularly emphasized the accomplishments in writing to the editor of the *News and Courier* in 1925, protesting changing the name of a lower peninsula street:

"These things (building and street names) are not without their meaning and their great value. They give tone and stability to our city. . . . Let us preserve and carefully guard what our forefathers have done that is worthy, and let us keep our city as characteristic as we can."[21]

From its inception, then, the title of the Society for the Preservation of Old Dwellings was a misnomer. A mission statement that spoke in somewhat general terms of preservation of "buildings, sites and structures" soon came to mean such specifics as churches and churchyards, streets, monuments, walls, gardens, commercial and industrial buildings, gates, and architecturally valuable artifacts.[22] One of the SPOD's most important original standing committees was that on Balconies and Old Iron Possessions.[23]

Charleston's early preservationists had good reason to be concerned over ironwork, balconies, mantels and other objects that represented the best from their craftsmen of a bygone era. By the second decade of the twentieth century, the growing number of large museums in the United States generated an often frantic search to fill empty rooms. The New York Metropolitan Museum of Art's American wing set the pace as its Committee on Decorative Arts began to search for period rooms around 1913.[24] The prosperity that accompanied World War I, coupled with the steadily increasing volume of tourists and "winter people," put Charleston at even greater risk. "The financial panic had not yet occurred and there was a tremendous amount of money," recalled one concerned preservationist; "everybody and his brother had an idea that they'd get some Charleston souvenir."[25] By the late 1920s at least three notable house interiors had been "vandalized," and the efforts of the Preservation Society were frequently undermined by those who were willing to dispose of old iron- and woodwork.[26] Frost and the SPOD ultimately viewed Charleston as a total composite of wood, stone, and iron, all of which should be saved.[27] In envisioning an entire urban landscape, architectural as well as historical, as worthy of salvage, the Charleston Society for the Preservation of Old Dwellings joined the Society for the Preservation of New England Antiquities in charting new directions for a growing national preservation movement, a movement heretofore concerned almost exclusively *only* about buildings with historical significance.[28]

SPOD viewed consciousness-raising as one of its most critical functions, one that could complement the recent cultural stirring in the city. "The public simply hasn't had their eyes open to the lovely City that is theirs," Nell Pringle told the preservation-minded audience in her drawing room in the spring of 1920; "an educational society would change their indifference almost overnight. They cannot visualize the unique beauty our shabby structures would show if put back in order." Most in need of conversion, Pringle felt, was the Charleston business community, those with a "commercial form of brain" that left them largely unattuned to aesthetic or historical interests. "What surprised me most," Pringle continued, "was the great indifference, even hostility, among business men to our classical and dignified old buildings. . . . *All* they seem to see is the lack of paint and repair in their architectural heritage." She suggested alerting the "business cult" to the potential of the tourist dollar as a way to rally their support.[29]

Although the economic benefits of preservation only gradually became a standard in the arsenal of arguments used by Susan Frost and the SPOD,[30] the relationship between the two clearly existed in the minds of Nell Pringle, Susan Frost, and other charter members of the organization. Frost envisioned a preservation movement that would be "of vital and very far-reaching importance to Charleston, possibly not in a commercial sense as some count "commercial," but certainly in a very broad sense "commercial."[31] The lowcountry realtor spelled out the interrelatedness more precisely to the *News and Courier* readership when she wrote that preservation of original street names and "our old time background" would bring people of culture and artistic taste, as well as "large means" to Charleston, "and we mutually benefit each other."[32] "To those who could not see the beauty that we saw, we urged the preservation of our buildings from a business standpoint," Frost often told audiences in giving the organization's history in later years.[33]

The immediate crisis rather than the economic benefits that would accrue from saving Charleston's historic architecture, however, was what preoccupied the little band assembled in the South Battery drawing room in April 1920. Fearful that the Manigault House was destined for imminent demolition to make way for an expanding Ford automobile dealership, Nell Pringle, on "sheer impulse," guaranteed the several thousand dollars necessary to insure a loan and title to the property. Everyone present, in turn, pledged to be responsible in the amount of $1,000, thus promising their hostess a return of everything, save her own share, for heroically "plugging the dyke." "The Society held her crushed in that dyke for twelve long years," a Pringle sibling remembered bitterly years later.[34] Acting as agent for the newly formed preservation association, Susan Frost soon negotiated the contract for the Joseph Manigault House.[35]

Frost and the SPOD projected several permanent uses for the Manigault House. Frost initially envisioned it as a "fitting museum of valuable furniture and other antiques." In the early 1920s, however, she explored with both the Civic Club and the Federation of Women's Clubs the possibility of using the old mansion as a citywide assembly hall for women's organizations. The federation favored the concept but was unable to support it financially.[36] As with her Tradd Street purchases, Frost believed that only persons of means who had an appreciation of the Charleston heritage could ensure the long-term security of the Joseph Manigault House, and until such parties were located the building would have to be repaired and rented to provide income.

Over the next two years, hopes were high for the Joseph Manigault House, despite the enormity of the undertaking. Nell Pringle and her husband, Ernest Pringle, who was the SPOD's first treasurer, deepened their commitment by underwriting the cost of improving adjacent roadways. Though burdened with the Miles Brewton House and numerous properties on the lower east side, Frost energetically pursued both consciousness-raising and fund-raising, appearing before the Young Men's Board of Trade and the Kiwanis and Rotary clubs.[37] "Give $5 or more if possible and get others to give," Frost pleaded as she told Civic Club sisters of early problems in meeting interest payments.[38] Mary Frost made an unsuccessful appeal to the Ways and Means Committee of the city council to exempt the historic property from taxation.[39]

The "Save the Manigault" movement quickly became an all uphill struggle. Mortgage, repair and operating costs exceeded income. Nearby factories were blamed for the failure to attract desirable white tenants. Bank difficulties associated with the Charleston depression of the early 1920s forced the holders of the mortgage to call in the loan. With Preservation Society financial pledges still unmet, Susan Frost unable to find lenders, and "little or no money in Charleston save that of northerners who were tourists or who had interest,"[40] Nell and Ernest Pringle bravely stepped into the breach. The two assumed debts of over $40,000 when Mrs. Pringle signed the Manigault House mortgage on March 29, 1922.[41]

The Pringles quickly moved to gain some relief from the Manigault burden. They cut their net costs in half by selling a portion of the property, the garden and the gatehouse, to the Esso Standard Oil Company. Large numbers of African-American tenants replaced whites to provide additional rental income; thoughts of any immediate repairs to the house itself were jettisoned. The spacious old mansion fell into still further disrepair as the depression continued. By the late 1920s, when the first serious reclamation work on the Joseph Manigault House began, the main building was little more than "plaster falling, piazzas sagging, each room begrimed with smoke of kerosene and cooking where whole families . . . had lived, driving nails to hold the drying clothes in the column of a mantlepiece or a door panel."[42]

In its early years, the "Save the Manigault" movement was largely a family affair involving the Pringles and the Frosts. The Society for the Preservation of Old Dwellings was an organization in name only. New recruits were few. The limited monies of the treasury were wiped out with early bank failures,[43] and economic hardship limited the ability of the small membership of the SPOD to honor its individual pledges or to generate a broader preservation appeal. Frost struggled to keep herself alive in a sea of debt. Whatever order and organization the SPOD possessed in its infancy[44] can be credited, not to its first president, Susan Frost, but to its president-to-be, Alston Deas.

The Susan Frost–Alston Deas partnership that developed was an enduring one and was of enormous benefit to the Charleston preservation community. A native of Charleston and a cousin of "Miss Sue," Alston Deas was a career army officer and was in Germany when the SPOD was formed. He returned to teach at the Citadel, and the peacetime military assignment gave him leftover hours to pursue his interests in South Carolina genealogy and the ironwork of Charleston and to volunteer some time for the Preservation Society. Deas lived across the street from Frost during these years, and the two often discussed preservation issues. It was Deas who helped "Cousin Sue" frame the bylaws and early objectives of the SPOD, and, said one observer, it was Deas who "put some organization into it."[45]

Susan Frost and Alston Deas did not always agree on preservation approaches. "We had a little difficulty with Frost in the early days because she didn't want anything taken off houses," Deas once recalled. Pointing out that valuable artifacts such as iron balconies and woodwork were sometimes jeopardized when buildings could not be saved or when property changed hands, Alston Deas moved the SPOD toward a policy of purchasing, then storing or "loaning" these endangered objects to those who would restore and protect them. Generally, however, Frost and Deas found common ground in their common cause. "We were very intimate and I was very much interested in her work and she was fond of me," Deas noted; "we always worked in great harmony." When she ultimately decided to relinquish the presidency of the Society for Preservation of Old Dwellings, Frost entrusted the mantle of leadership to Deas. Although Alston Deas soon achieved great distinction as city zoning leader and chairman of the original Charleston Zoning Commission, he frequently sang the praises of the preservation pioneer whose influence generated such significant local architectural awareness.[46]

The clouds of economic despair that hung over Charleston in the early 1920s lifted by mid-1925, bringing a fresh surge of hope and optimism to the city. "We have reorganized our Society for Preservation of Old Dwellings lately; I am getting much more Co-operation, and we are starting out very actively," wrote an obviously pleased Susan Frost in reestablishing contact with New England preservationist William Sumner Appleton. Frost also apprised Appleton of new approaches to saving the Joseph Manigault House. "We have now gotten it . . . on a lease at a very reasonable rent," the Charleston's realtor wrote, "and shall turn out the present tenants, and use the residence as headquarters for our Society, renting studios in the winter season to artists, and opening the house on an admission fee in the winter to winter visitors; in this way we will preserve it until some one comes along and buys it for a residence once more."[47]

Frost discussed another pressing issue with New England's foremost preservationist in the spring of 1925—the threats to Charleston's old iron- and woodwork. Receiving encouragement from William Sumner Appleton's response to "adopt more strenuous safeguards,"[48] the aggressive realtor took her case directly to City Hall and urged Mayor Thomas P. Stoney to have the city pass an ordinance preventing the removal of such artifacts. Stoney's corporation counsel, John Cosgrove, on being apprised of the request, maintained that the city could not prevent owners from disposing of their property as they pleased, but suggested that if Miss Frost had "a new line of thought" to propose, he would be happy to cooperate with her.[49] Thomas Stoney, whose administration played a significant role in furthering the cause of historic preservation in Charleston in the 1920s,[50] urged further dialogue; "working together," Stoney wrote Cosgrove, "it may be possible that some plan may be gotten into shape to assist her in her commendable work."[51]

That Susan Frost and Stoney official John Cosgrove were apparently unable to arrive at a workable preservation ordinance should not diminish the importance of their efforts or its significance for Frost, the Society for the Preservation of Old Dwellings, and the city of Charleston. The degree of cooperation the municipal government extended to Frost clearly demonstrates that her tenacity in her own restoration work and her consciousness-raising on behalf of the SPOD had not gone unnoticed. Moreover, the SPOD acquired additional visibility, and in working in concert, through its president, with city government in the cause of historic preservation the two groups foreshadowed the close alliances that helped bring Charleston economic and cultural success in the late twentieth century. Formal study on a historic zoning ordinance for Charleston did not begin for about five more years, with several persons ultimately responsible in some measure for its enactment. The idea of a legal mechanism for Charleston, however, with the implications it might have for a community trying to revitalize itself, was first put on the table as a result of the concerns of a lowcountry female activist who saw that valuable architecture was fast disappearing.

Amidst its ongoing appeals and fund-raising efforts for the Joseph Manigault House in the 1920s, the Society for the Preservation of Old Dwellings tried to save the Planter's Hotel, and Frost's appeal for an ordinance to safeguard the old iron- and woodwork may have been generated by concern over the threatened demolition of this landmark.[52] Built in 1806, the Planter's was the city's first hotel and catered to the up-country aristocracy, especially during the horse-racing season. The adjoining building, the Dock Street Theater, dated to 1735 and was a colonial period cultural center. By the early twentieth century, the two structures were part of the eyesore of ruins that made up Charleston's lower east side.

The Society for the Preservation of Old Dwellings sought funding from private preservation groups to save the Planter's Hotel. It also pressured such luminaries as Henry Ford to fund restoration of the Dock Street Theater. Having no success, the SPOD persuaded the Stoney administration to seal the buildings in their disrepair to await a brighter day. The new day came with the New Deal and with Thomas Stoney's successor, Burnet Maybank, who paved the way for the Works Progress Administration (WPA) to rehabilitate the Dock Street Theater and thus improve the neighborhood itself. Accolades for this successful project begin with the Charleston preservation society, however, noted one New Deal historian.[53] With the WPA project well under way, the SPOD approved a resolution that a marker be placed "in recognition of the untiring interest that Miss Susan P. Frost and Miss Eola Willis have taken in the restoration of that (Planter's Hotel) and the adjacent building."[54]

Despite its activity on behalf of the Planter's Hotel and the Dock Street

Theater, the Society for the Preservation of Old Dwellings remained focused on the Joseph Manigault House. Frost continued to seek financial backing from several sources and in May 1925 she appealed to the city Ways and Means Committee, without success, for a $200 remodeling appropriation.[55] With the depression apparently over by the middle of the decade, however, Frost moved to salvage her real estate business. It was left to the Pringle family to effect the first major rehabilitation of Manigault House.

The piecemeal process took several years, with the Pringle offspring often serving as a child labor force. McColl Pringle recalled as an eleven-year-old mixing gallons of calcimine, "used in those days because people couldn't afford to paint," and passing it up a ladder to his sister.[56] "Floors after many scrubbings with 'lye' were waxed until they shown," remembered another of the children.[57] One winter Nell Pringle, two of her daughters, and an African-American minister who lived in one of the outbuildings were joined by the author Winston Churchill and together painted the inside of the house.[58] An occasional tea to raise money usually attracted few people save the SPOD faithful. By Thanksgiving 1928, however, the Joseph Manigault House had a fresh new look and was opened to the public, with ladies in the preservation society taking turns as hostesses and collecting a small admission fee. The Ernest Pringles anxiously awaited the results of operating the first house museum in Charleston.

In the late 1920s when the Manigault House opened to visitors, tourism, though still largely confined to the spring of the year, was beginning to emerge as an important industry in Charleston, and the Thomas P. Stoney administration aggressively promoted tourism. Describing Charleston as "America's most historic city," the mayor told peninsula residents, "we have to sell the city . . . to the outside world."[59] Before his two terms had ended, Stoney had made Charleston much more accessible to the outside world, presiding over the opening of both the Ashley River Bridge (1926) and the Cooper River Bridge (1929), the Union Pier at the end of busy Market Street, and the establishment of the first air facility on James Island, reopened as the Charleston municipal airport in 1929.[60] Frost excitedly wrote Irénée DuPont of a Charleston on the rebound: "Standard Oil is proposing to build a yacht basin costing a hundred thousand dollars. . . . Artists and architects from all over the Country are coming here, and many are buying homes. . . . My judgement seems gradually being justified as to the ultimate value of Charleston property."[61]

While rapidly becoming a noticeable asset, tourism also had its liabilities, including increased traffic on the narrow streets of Charleston and the likelihood of more parking lots and gas stations, even on the lower peninsula. Charleston architecture in the late 1920s also remained severely threatened by outside collectors hoping for cheap bargains. The bit-by-bit dismantling of the showcase colonial era Broad Street residence of William Burrows, known as the Mansion House, by a wealthy New York antique dealer (the drawing room would later be totally reconstructed in a wing of the Winterthur Museum) and the loss of entire rooms of other south of Broad Street homes to museums in Minneapolis, Kansas City, and St. Louis heightened local concerns and brought about a further coalescing of preservation sentiment in Charleston. These seemingly "isolatable incidents," noted prominent city architect Albert Simons, "this business of the coincidence of the Mansion House being torn, two rooms going to Minneapolis and one room going to St. Louis in a narrow space of time, combined with Esso coming in with filling stations, right around '27–'28," was the beginning of "that movement to zoning and to saving some historic house museums."[62] The historic house that most Charlestonians fought to save in the late 1920s, however, was not the Joseph Manigault House but the Heyward-Washington House.

The Heyward-Washington House (c. 1770) was built in lower Charleston for Thomas Heyward, Jr., a signer of the Declaration of Independence. The structure became much better known, however, as "the home where Washington stayed," for the city sublet the house to provide quarters for the president on his celebrated swing down south in 1791. By the early twentieth century, one room in the house had been converted into a bakery, and the remaining contents of the house "seemed ripe for the acquisition list of some midwestern museum."[63] On hearing rumors that indeed something of the latter was about to happen, Charleston Museum Director Laura Bragg alerted Albert Simons, and the two, using a recent museum contribution from the outside earmarked for preservation, persuaded the Charleston Museum to take a six-month option on the endangered house in early 1928. Other conditions and commitments notwithstanding, the Society for the Preservation of Old Dwellings soon offered its assistance, thus becoming a vital part of "Charleston's first community restoration project."[64]

The Heyward-Washington preservation endeavor got off to an auspicious beginning precisely because it had the support of a broader segment of the Charleston cultural community than had rallied to the Joseph Manigault project and because support from outsiders was forthcoming. The tie to George Washington helped; the Society of the Cincinnati of South Carolina gave $2,500. Albert Simons, Alston Deas, Laura Bragg, and Elizabeth O'Neill Verner, all major figures in Charleston's historic preservation history, contributed valuable services and important leadership in the critical early stages of the project. Charleston's two newspapers, the *News and Courier* and the *Evening Post,* also championed the undertaking,[65] and outside money generated by the architectural connections of Albert Simons proved vital. In a few short months the preservation society and the Charleston Museum actually exceeded funds needed and made a major down payment on the Heyward House in May 1933. Laura Bragg particularly had high hopes that the entire debt could be discharged by February 22, 1932, the two hundredth anniversary of Washington's birthday, but the depression and high purchase price helped dash those dreams. Over twenty-five years ultimately elapsed, amidst endless card parties, between the time of the initial option on the Heyward-Washington House and the time the Historic Charleston Foundation, created after World War II, made the final mortgage payment.[66]

The Heyward-Washington campaign that was launched in 1928 generated some of the earliest discord in the Charleston preservation community. The Preservation Society in the late 1920s, just as it would in the late 1940s when the Historic Charleston Foundation emerged, viewed the arrival of fresh troops with some degree of concern and jealousy. Some were alarmed by the larger role the Charleston Museum had taken in the cultural life of the city after Laura Bragg took over as director in 1920 and felt that the society, not the museum, should own historic buildings like the Heyward-Washington House.[67] Seeking to squelch dissension, Alston Deas urged personal feelings be put aside in addressing the matter of endangered buildings: "It doesn't make much difference who owns it if the house stays here."[68] Frost supported this position. Ongoing financial difficulties with her real estate business and outstanding debts precluded her involvement in the Heyward-Washington project.

For the Ernest Pringles, however, the issue of the hour was not the Heyward House but the Manigault House. After a few short months of operating the Manigault House as a house museum, it was clear that despite stepped-up publicity, a modest admission fee, and "enough visitors to feel like a success," they remained locked in the vise of financial obligation, with little cause for optimism. "What we took in dribbled back into the upkeep without making a dent on taxes or even payments on the mortgage," wrote a morose Ernest Pringle to his son-in-law, a Baltimore architect.[69] Although many of the still small membership of the Preservation Society remained committed to the Manigault enterprise, the Pringles experienced nothing short of betrayal at seeing the organization they cofounded align itself with the Charleston Museum in 1928, diverting energies from what was now almost a decade-long battle to an altogether new and equally uncertain preservation gamble. Salt was poured in the open wounds when the Preservation Society made the Heyward House its headquarters.[70] "Mother was left alone in her struggle," wrote a deeply saddened Pringle daughter.[71]

The Pringle family also felt betrayed by Susan Frost.[72] The first president of the Society for the Preservation of Old Dwellings had a vested interest in the "Save the Manigault" movement, however, and never stopped promoting it. Frost also felt a keen responsibility for her cousin's being so deeply involved financially, a concern that heightened as Nell Pringle's health deteriorated.[73] In one letter of consolation over the indebtedness they both had experienced, Frost urged that they think of the larger picture: "Someday things will look brighter for us; meantime, we have both saved something of beauty and importance for Chas. and that is our only comfort."[74] Neither the Ernest Pringles nor Susan Frost were so limited in their love of imperiled Charleston architecture as to oppose other manifestations of concern about it, and both families were among the early contributors to the Heyward-Washington fund.[75]

It is ironic that, at the time the historic preservation movement was developing momentum in Charleston in the late 1920s and the city would soon frame the first historic district zoning ordinance in the United States, Susan Frost, the early moving force on the scene, had become considerably less visible. Acute financial difficulty, however, required that she give her real estate business her utmost attention. "Miss Sue" was "always just ahead of the sheriff," observed her cousin Alston Deas, who knew her condition well.[76] Consequently, Frost resigned as president of the SPOD in late 1927 or early 1928, leaving Deas in charge. At its first meeting after her resignation, the Society for the Preservation of Old Dwellings (shortly to be incorporated as the Preservation Society of Charleston) voiced grateful appreciation to its founder. The unanimously adopted resolution highlighted Susan Frost's "efficient construction work . . . in repairing old buildings and conserving the old iron details of historic dwellings whenever possible, reclaiming pieces that would have been lost to the city, and her general intelligence and whole-heartedness in her endeavors" and expressed "great satisfaction in her conduct of the society."[77]

Frost served the Preservation Society particularly well as president through the example she set. By the late 1920s, numerous renovations were being undertaken in Charleston's southeastern peninsula precisely because "Miss Sue" had dared to renovate in the severely blighted area. Frost's highly visible leadership in the "save the iron movement" that emerged in Charleston in the early 1920s fostered considerable public awareness and sensitized local government. Under Frost the SPOD adopted a policy of trying to match dealer's prices on items headed out of the city. Regretful that he could not attend a special meeting with city officials to discuss disappearing iron and wood objects, architect Albert Simons applauded the labors of Susan Frost and the preservation society in a letter that he asked be read: "In making an appeal to the artistic consciences of our visitors, asking them not to buy and export our ancient landmarks, you have adopted the most effective method of preventing, as far as possible, our annual spoliation. If it were impressed upon these collectors that we regret the loss of these things more than they can possibly profit by their possession, most of them, I am sure would refrain from this traffic. It is only when they think that these works are unappreciated, neglected and abused that they can justify their removal to better care, so it seems that your appeal to our guests implies an obligation on the part of our community to see that what we have is properly preserved."[78]

Frost waged a constant war against removal of Charleston architecture, spending untold sums of money in the process. She was relentless in her pursuit of the enemy. "Luke Vincent Lockwood bought a very nice old balcony uptown and Miss Frost wrote to him and told him he was a vandal," Alston Deas recalled about an incident that had the SPOD match Lockwood's purchase price and save the object.[79] A national magazine, in a post–World War II feature article, told the entire country of Frost's rescue habits: "Once, riding on a streetcar, she passed a house where workmen were engaged in removing a pair of beautiful iron gates from the garden wall. She stopped the car, got off, walked back to the house, found the owner and offered him $50 for the gates. Since he had expected to sell them to the junkman as old iron, he jumped at the offer. These can now be seen in the garden wall of a house which Miss Sue has restored and still owns at No. 87 East Battery."[80] The carriage houses of the storied Miles Brewton House brimmed with Frost treasures, necessitating onstreet parking of her automobile. "Miss Sue" was still at it as she neared her eightieth year, telling the *News and Courier* in 1949: "I paid a man to put a large one [cobblestone] in my car. It is still in my garden. Under present money value, a nickel is not adequate to save it from being dumped over the High Battery."[81]

Even though she had stepped down as the SPOD president, Frost was never far removed from the organization and preservation activity. She served as secretary under Alston Deas and had a hand in several successful artifact rescues that the society boasted of in the late 1920s. Frost also continued to relate closely to Charleston's preservation-minded Mayor Thomas Stoney, who was made an honorary member of the Preservation Society in 1928.[82] In negotiating over a continuing request from the Citizens and Southern Bank that it be allowed to pave with concrete instead of flagstones in front of its new building, Stoney contacted Frost at her real estate office in April 1929, soliciting her opinion and that of "Captain Deas and others who have contributed so much of their time and talent to give Charleston that distinctive air which is now being appreciated by the discriminating tourists and the intelligent local citizens."[83]

No one in Charleston history did more than Frost to keep preservation issues squarely before the public. Both outsiders and the local citizenry had to be educated, Frost felt, with perhaps the greater enemy in the 1920s being the one within. Frost also believed that the success of outside appeals depended on the depth of commitment within Charleston itself. In exhorting Charlestonians to join the society, the Broad Street realtor often pointed out the larger benefits of their support: "Your (one dollar) fee will help in our work; but your influence, and your sympathy with us would be of far greater value to us and to the cause for which we stand."[84] As the threats to Charleston's old architecture increased in the 1920s, so did the urgency and eloquence of the Frost preservation appeals: "If we would make it very plain to them that we value the beauty of our city, her stately homes and hand carved woodwork, and hand wrought iron work, and that we are not willing that they should be sold out of our city, we would find that these visitors would in time join with us in saving our city, and our labours would be greatly eased. Let us not barter away our birthright. We have something that few cities in this new-world country have; let us safeguard it by concerted effort. Now is the time. Tomorrow will be too late!"[85]

In her efforts to get others to catch the preservation vision, Frost as well as the membership of the SPOD often used anti-Williamsburg rhetoric. Charlestonians were among the first to marvel at the enormous restoration project funded by John D. Rockefeller, Jr., when it was completed, but certain ironies did not escape lowcountry preservationists. "While Mr. Rockefeller was so busy restoring Colonial Williamsburg, his boys were ripping down our old-est houses to make way for his oil company pumps," observed unofficial Charleston historian Sam Stoney.[86] Frost, who surely knew of the Rockefeller venture if she had not seen it, in distinguishing between reconstructing and restoring for a *News and Courier* audience, remarked: "we do not have to recon-struct as at Williamsburg, only to restore what we already have in such profu-sion from one end of the city to the other."[87] The founder of the SPOD insisted that Charleston should remain a "living organism" where residents could live and work amidst the historical beauty that surrounded them and not a "museum piece" such as Williamsburg. Another Frost letter, written near the end of the Manigault House struggle, focused on the vital integrity she saw missing from the Rockefeller venture:

> The aim of the Society for the Preservation of Old Dwellings has not been to have a series of Williamsburgs dotted along the coast, but that wherever beautiful architecture of an earlier period is found, no matter where it is located, to pre-serve it as and where it stands if it is worth preserving . . . not recreated but restored; not torn down and rebuilt everywhere, but restored just where earlier builders built it . . . . Should we not as the first and most important step, restore lovely old houses in the locality of dump heaps with the hope and expectation that as time goes on the dump heap will be removed and homes continue to give shelter to our people and object lessons of beauty to our visitors and our chil-dren.[88]

By the early 1930s, despite the national depression and the ongoing uphill struggles to save the Manigault and Heyward-Washington houses, the Charleston historic preservation movement experienced some of its most encouraging signs. The threat to Charleston architecture was even attracting national attention. Of enormous portent for the future, Charleston's historic zoning ordinance of 1931 created an "Old and Historic Area" of some 138 acres in the southeastern corner of the peninsula. "Historic places and areas of his-toric interest" would now be protected, with any changes to their exterior or any new construction in the district to occur only with approval from a newly created agency, the Board of Architectural Review. At about the same time, and again in part owing to Albert Simons's influence, the American Institute of Architecture created a Committee for Safeguarding Charleston Architecture, with both national cultural leaders and Charlestonians, including Preservation Society President Alston Deas, as part of the group.[89]

The Manigault property was far removed from the "Old and Historic Dis-trict," however, and the Ernest Pringles saw little change in their personal preservation struggle, despite a "formal opening" of the house by the Preserva-tion Society in early 1930 and changing exhibitions throughout the spring. By the end of 1931, the Pringles' total financial obligations were greater than at any time since they had taken over the mortgage from the SPOD.[90] With the failure of his fertilizer business and the collapse of the bank in which he was a stockholder, Ernest Pringle announced he could no longer carry the Joseph Manigault estate.[91]

The year 1932 was one of desperation, with the "Save the Manigault House" movement finally attracting some larger community support. In his search to find a "Lorenzo the Magnificent to underwrite such a project," Simons even proposed having Standard Oil Company buy the rest of the property and show the house to any visitors who purchased five gallons of gasoline from their station on the front lawn.[92] Milby Burton, who became Preservation Society president during the year, joined the outgoing chief executive, Alston Deas, in contacting wealthy potential benefactors in New York and elsewhere known to have a fondness for the lowcountry.[93] Charleston newspapers, particularly the *Evening Post* of Thomas R. Waring, chairman of the newly created Board of Architectural Review, publicized the critical situation, and the Preservation Society held more card parties in the hope that small profits might buy time until there was better news. Although the fight was lost well before the year began, the last months of the Manigault House crusade demonstrated that an expanding core of talented professionals was interested in the old city and suggested why so many other preservation stories there had different endings.

Aware that others had now joined the fight, Frost urged the Ernest Pringles to hold on: "I feel that the eyes of the public are being centered now on the Manigault House and the time when you will be relieved is not very far off, and if you could keep up the interest with the help of the door receipts until we can get somebody to take over the property."[94] Willing to forego any attempt to reclaim taxes, paving costs, and operational expenses if a buyer could be found for the cost of the mortgage, Nell Pringle's husband explained a last-ditch scenario to his son-in-law: "The investment is $50,000, and the object will fail if some little help does not come. My wife proposes to move to and live in the Manigault House, if plumbing and the most necessary heating equipment be installed, and $1500 a year to be provided, to care for taxes, $300, and the $1200 needed for interest on the mortgage. Probably $3000 or less in all will enable her to put her plan into effect. She will then assemble there the best pieces of her own furniture, and those of my sister, who will be asked to lend them, and the house will become a shrine for those interested in Colonial architecture and Colonial furniture."[95]

While she attempted to revive the sagging spirits of Nell and Ernest Pringle, Frost desperately tried to rally the local public and to spark last-minute outside interest in the Manigault House. Warren Laird, dean of the School of Fine Arts at the University of Pennsylvania, acknowledged to Albert Simons that he was strongly moved by a letter from "Mrs. (or Miss) Frost," but, like most architects, had little money to give to such worthy enterprises.[96] In one of her angriest and most passionate appeals, a letter to all Charleston newspapers on April 7, 1932, Frost recounted the valiant twelve-year struggle of the Pringles and the SPOD and singled out the architects of the country such as Laird who had frequently praised "this beautiful specimen of Georgian style" but who had failed to collectively rally and help save it. "Every time that we allow one of these stately mansions of the past to go into oblivion," "Miss Sue" admonished, "we are taking just one more terrible step towards destroying the old-world beauty and charm of our city and are transforming it gradually from the artistic to the commonplace."[97] The busy realtor mailed some two hundred copies of her editorial to carefully targeted audiences, including a host of architects, selected guests from the Miles Brewton House register, and the entire membership of the Yeamans Hall Club, a private millionaire's winter colony.[98]

No miracles were to occur, however, and as the reality of financial disaster and a failed preservation crusade settled around Nell and Ernest Pringle, Susan Frost bared her soul to her relatives. The curse of debt, the pain of business failure, the struggle to overcome adversity, the depths of despair—Susan Frost had known them all too, and as she reached out to comfort them, a flood of memories came rushing back: "I am reminded of the early morning, about seven o'clock, November 5, 1895, when Father drove up to Capt. Charles Pinckney's residence to take the final step in assigning all he had in favour of his creditors. . . . My father went through such trying business losses. . . . I have had such a struggle myself."[99] Promising the Pringles to "make restoration" for a portion of their losses, should she ever be in position to do so," Frost focused on "the good side of the trying": " Life is full of mysteries and it takes strong faith and courage to go thro., but it is also full of joy and happiness; I know you and Ernest have suffered from the experience of the Manigault House, but I have always felt in the end you would not regret it, in spite of all the trials, you are still holding on to one of the most distinguished homes in the city." [100]

Preservation Society president and Charleston Museum director Milby Burton, not the Ernest Pringles or Susan Frost, was the hero in the last act of the Manigault House drama. The mortgage was foreclosed in early 1933, with destruction of the property all but certain. With help from editor Thomas Waring, Burton, in a series of letters and conferences, persuaded a native of Beaufort who was the heiress of the Great Atlantic and Pacific Tea Company (A&P), the Princess Pignatelli, to buy the house at auction (the selling price was $3,001) and then donate it to the Charleston Museum. A few years later, Burton succeeded in getting the Standard Oil Company to return (without cost) the unique gate house in front of the structure. As he had done with the Heyward House, Milby Burton persuaded the South Carolina legislature to give the Manigault property a tax-exempt status.[101]

At a monthly meeting in the Heyward-Washington House in the spring of 1933, the Preservation Society of Charleston closed the books on the drama that had lasted almost thirteen years. Its thanks to Nell Pringle for carrying the Manigault property for so many years came in the form of a resolution: "Whereas one of the principal architectural monuments of the city of Charleston has been but lately saved for the city and the nation and Whereas the preservation of that monument, the Joseph Manigault house, depended for many years on the steadfast faith, the renewing hope, and the continuous sacrifice of one devoted woman. Be it resolved that we, the Society for the Preservation of Old Dwellings, do hereby and herewith render our most hearty thanks to Mrs. Nellie McColl Pringle, not only in our own names, but for all those others of the city, of the state, and of the country at large who have at heart the interest of the future in the art of the past."[102] The book never closed for the Ernest Pringles, however. They remained forever haunted by the irony of a property dedicated as a memorial, not to the indefatigable Nell Pringle, but to the heir to one of the greatest grocery chain fortunes in U.S. history.[103]

The failure of Charlestonians to rally totally behind the Joseph Manigault House project and the inability of a larger, more vigorous historic preservation movement to emerge in the city in the 1920s and early 1930s troubled Susan Frost, the Preservation Society, and area cultural leaders and remained a subject of concern and discussion for years. Despite all the advertised perils and calls for public involvement, the Preservation Society itself experienced little growth in its first decade of existence. In 1932, when the "Save the Manigault House" movement finally reached a white heat, Milby Burton recalled that a member of his staff had to be brought in from the Heyward House garden to break a seven-seven tie and elect him president of the Preservation Society.[104] After several frustrating years of fund-raising activity, Burton concluded that the problem was not lack of funds but simply lethargy and disinterest.[105] Albert Simons long remained pessimistic about both the Heyward House and the Manigault House because of Charleston's "heavy financial burden for the support of many cultural institutions far out of proportion to her comparatively small white population."[106]

Constantly wrestling with the issue in the 1920s, wondering why so few shared her vision, Frost concluded that the problem was "the enemy within our gates." Part of the difficulty, she believed, was the high property taxes in the city, which prompted many to lighten their financial load by tearing down old buildings.[107] Although she appreciated the "deference and courtesy" extended the SPOD by antique shops and studios who checked with her before disposing of old wood- and ironwork, she could only react with horror and disbelief on occasions such as when she learned that the city council had plans to sell a balcony to a visitor for $500.[108] "Miss Sue" pleaded long and hard for the united front that could save Charleston's endangered historic architecture. As Frost observed in the late 1920s, the fight was often a lonely, grueling battle: "Our work and burden are tremendously increased by the fact that we not only have to fight those from outside, but even those of our own household, from within, if we are going to save the great beauty of our city. A small band of us (all too few in number) have literally agonized over the destruction of our city and have laboured with untiring zeal, and often times to the hurt of our own interests, in our efforts to preserve her old-world beauty."[109]

The debate was joined at the national level with the publication of a highly controversial article by journalist Edward Twig in *Forum Magazine* in early 1940.

Twig, who had lived in Charleston for varying lengths of time over several years, labeled the city "The Great Myth": "There is no such place as the utterly beautiful, charming, gracious old city that the romantics, the wishful thinkers, the fablists say there is. Remote from that great day of hers is the real Charleston— poor, uncourtly, apathetic, and having as little to do with her own brilliant past as she has with the American present. . . . She is like an old woman who has lived too long, disfigured with age, forever dying, yet always still alive."[110] Twig wrote of a poor city, where the only rich were "the damyankees who have come because of the legends," and a locale stagnant because of its own "overpowering self-hypnotism and conceit." The only meaningful restoration, Twig concluded, was that done by outsiders "who so desperately want the mythical Charleston to exist." He suggested that preservation locally was little more than a sham battle, fought so that a "down-at-the-heels" city could receive new life's blood from the tourist dollar.[111]

Frost alone escaped the searing indictment of Edward Twig, although he feared that she, too, was fighting a losing battle. Observing that the preservation fight being waged on the peninsula at the time he wrote, a struggle to save the walls of the medieval-like jail, was only for commercial reasons and that Charlestonians would "tear the whole city down . . . for a project big enough," Twig concluded: "Few were the genuine lovers of Charleston's past and her relics who begged that this ancient landmark be kept for its own sake. One lady who loves Charleston and is the Society for the Preservation of Old Dwellings has waged a continuous and valiant fight for beautiful or desolate ruins. Time will defeat her, too."[112] Journalist Twig had struck a sensitive nerve as was still evident when *Forum* announced two issues later: "The Editors regret that space is unavailable this month for further discussion of the Charleston crisis. If possible, the battle will be joined once more in the April issue."[113]

Nell Pringle, too, had seen a Charleston capitulating on preservation matters because of materialism and forces of modernism. "We once had a beautiful civic soul . . . and fair ideals . . . and old honor," she penned in her short story of "Susan Snow" and the Manigault House, but those were submerged under "the needless trample of commercialism creating a motory, modern place of grease and cheapness." Nell Pringle greatly admired the bravery and stamina of her cousin Susan Pringle Frost, the inspiration for her autobiographical piece, who had tried so hard to awaken "a city that was lulled into contentment by money in her hands, by moving pictures, jazz and motors." In seeking to instill appreciation of the enduring values of an earlier civilization, Frost often attacked the same elements of modernism that the fictional "Susan Snow" battled.[114]

At work when preservation was not fashionable, when the fresh winds of hope and the cultural renaissance of the World War I era had been upstaged by more economic despair, the Society for the Preservation of Old Dwellings fought enormous odds in its first decade of existence. It found funds scarce, obstacles great and workers few in the unsettled times of the 1920s. Though not unattuned to economic benefits that might accrue as a result of their labors, most of the SPOD's early membership belonged to the romanticist school of the historic preservation movement, and they sought to restore to the low-country a picturesque past of beauty, charm, and architectural richness such as that depicted by artist Elizabeth O'Neill Verner.[115] The Society for the Preservation of Old Dwellings never had money partly because it treated every endangered artifact as a valued part of the whole and, like Susan Frost and Nell Pringle, impetuously encumbered itself.

From today's preservation perspective, and in light of the far-reaching neighborhood restoration projects in Charleston in the 1950s through the 1970s, we can easily dismiss the artifact-gathering and house museum campaigns of the Society for the Preservation of Old Dwellings in the 1920s as limited, unimaginative, largely unplanned, crisis-activated ventures. To do so is to ignore the magnitude of the threats to Charleston architecture, to diminish the persistence and courage of a captain and a few disciples who might easily have capitulated in face of all the roadblocks and limited support, to minimize the degree and quality of leadership a woman provided a southern community which, like most, operated within a male-oriented power structure, and to overlook the significant new initiatives Susan Frost and Charleston provided to an expanding preservation movement.

By the early years of the twentieth century, Southern women like Susan Pringle Frost had clearly emerged, in their clubs and associations, as forces for social betterment in their towns and villages. Ties to families long active in the political and cultural life of the city, connections much in evidence in the Pringle drawing room in 1920, made Southern women's involvement in the public sphere more palatable. In perhaps its key role in the 1920s, that of consciousness-raising, the Society for the Preservation of Old Dwellings, despite scant encouragement and limited resources, kept alive a vision. Once the Charleston preservation movement began to gain headway, it built and broadened from a base Susan Frost and the SPOD had set in place. In recognizing that the tourist trade was an increasingly vital industry in the lowcountry by the 1930s and 1940s, Charleston civic leaders and the local citizenry more fully grasped the importance of the persistence and perseverance of Susan Frost, Nell Pringle, and the little band of preservation activists who formed the SPOD. In a 1935 editorial titled "Who Saved the Old Houses?" the *News and Courier* observed that "the Charleston architecture which is widely complimented would be all but vanished if Miss Frost and her associates had not refused to be discouraged."[116]

In saluting Susan Frost and her small core of troops, however, such editorials rarely, if ever, commented on the displaced and on what happened in their lives. For her part, Frost remained preoccupied with her own tenuous survival struggle and with whether there would be boarders enough at the Miles Brewton House during tourist season to allow her to make any headway on her debts to the DuPonts. While Charleston's grande dame of historic preservation appeared a bit more sensitive to those "turned out" of lower Charleston as the movement gained momentum in the 1930s and 1940s,[117] aside from offering temporary residence in her own carriage house Frost promoted no permanent solutions to their problems.

Although she hardly brought great organizational skills and order to the preservation society she led, and although her own restoration programs and fight to hold on to the Miles Brewton House severely taxed her energies and her resources, Frost earned a major niche in Charleston preservation history. She possessed a large vision, believing the city's entire historical fabric to be worthy of rescue; in envisioning Charleston as a "living city," not a Williamsburg-type museum community, and in advocating that the buildings be saved, not because of what happened inside but because of broader architectural and cultural importance, Frost was no less a preservation pioneer in her region than the visionary William Sumner Appleton was in New England.

Frost clearly realized that preservation might be integrated into community planning, and in her fierce leadership of the "save the iron" movement in the 1920s she boldly promoted municipal protection laws. One "lively" SPOD meeting in mid-decade was given over exclusively to reviewing how European cities had legally preserved their monuments.[118] In pressuring Mayor Stoney to promote passage of a protective ordinance in 1925, Frost forced consideration of the very type of mechanism for which Charleston later became famous. The *News and Courier* recognized the connection, observing that the historic district zoning ordinance of 1931, the first of its kind and later widely endorsed by the National Trust for Historic Preservation as the most viable way of preserving the unique character of threatened urban centers, was "a sequel to the pioneering of Miss Frost and those who worked for her."[119]

Having vigorously promoted protective preservation legislation, Susan Pringle Frost became the most vigilant watchdog over it during the first quarter century of its existence.

CHAPTER 5

$\mathscr{P}$RESERVATION WATCHDOG

> I hate to be the one to always complain . . . but someone has to
> do it. . . . It might hurt my business but I do feel someone has to
> do this otherwise our Zoning Ordinance will be of no account.
> Susan Frost to James O'Hear September 26, 1934

At the time Charleston was making its mark among the nation's municipalities
with its historic district zoning ordinance, Susan Pringle Frost was deeply preoccupied with her own trials. In addition to the burdens of the Joseph Manigault House she shared with Nell and Ernest Pringle, Frost and her sister Mary
had their own challenges closer home. Each new spring tourist season brought
renewed hope that the two could make some headway in their obligations to
the DuPonts on the Miles Brewton House by opening the mansion to visitors,
while sister "Rebe's" continued employment as governess to the DuPont offspring guaranteed that the perpetually unfulfilled pledges of debt retirement
would not mean immediate mortgage foreclosure. In the spring of 1931, Susan
Frost was also attempting to end her years of speculating on Tradd Street. "I
have had such a struggle; I am very anxious to get out of that block," the
Charleston realtor wrote to Irénée DuPont, guardedly optimistic, despite her
financial morass, that the pending offer on her last dwelling, at 23 Tradd Street,
would meet with her Delaware benefactor's approval: "Of course this will not
give me the cash to pay the past interest I owe you, and I neglected to discuss
this in my last letter. The last time I had a prospective buyer you very kindly
agreed to let me carry over this interest a little longer. I have the interest all figured out, but am not in a position to pay at this time, at the same time I am
reluctant to let this chance of selling go by as it is the last unsold house that I
reclaimed on Tradd Street. . . . I do not feel anything will be gained from my
standpoint by holding the property at a higher price, but, of course, I have to
do as you desire me to do in the matter of the mortgage."[1]

Despite the national depression, Susan Frost remained more hopeful about
her East Bay Street holdings, especially with signs of a growing tourist industry
in the lowcountry. Frost believed that by retaining her properties a few years
longer she could realize the "clean-up" that some of her business colleagues predicted. The DuPont chief executive received yet another update for his files:
"Those properties in my name, but on which Irene holds mortgage, will yet
surprise you. They constitute what is considered by Northern visitors and local
people as the most attractive block in the city under its present development,

being within a stone's throw of the waterfront. I feel sure as soon as this depression lifts that I will be able to sell at a good price or to restore them myself. I would prefer the latter course, but shall do what is best for the mortgage and the development of the city."[2]

Coping with her own tribulations, however, did not prevent Frost from following with great pleasure the progress of Mayor Thomas Stoney's administration as it moved over a two-year period, 1929–1931, to fashion a comprehensive zoning plan to protect the city's many old buildings. Frost applauded the resolve of the mayor, who after hearing that Standard Oil Company had plans to erect a filling station in the very heart of old Charleston told city lawmakers in October 1929: "It is not a question of whether Council can afford to zone Charleston but whether Council can afford not to zone Charleston."[3] Once the zoning process was complete, Frost became one of the most enthusiastic defenders and monitors of the historic ordinance enacted.

Charleston's city fathers had been quietly moving toward zoning since the mid-1920s, both because they had been sensitized to endangered architectural treasures by Susan Frost, Alston Deas, and the Society for the Preservation of Old Dwellings, and because members of Stoney's administration, including the mayor himself, aggressively investigated the experiences of other municipalities in types of zoning. With the exception of a weak law in New Orleans, there was no other preservation precedent in the country, but Stoney's port development commissioner Roy MacElwee, gathered data from several cities in the 1920s, including New York, Cleveland, and Norfolk, Virginia, and in the process became an unsung hero in fashioning a Charleston ordinance.[4]

Holder of a Ph.D. degree, Roy MacElwee talked to Charlestonians about zoning as early as 1925 and on several occasions touted the possibilities in a national journal devoted to municipal affairs, the *American City*. One article offered a thorough review of preservation efforts in Charleston throughout the decade, highlighting the pioneer work of Susan Frost, whom MacElwee labeled "the Angel of Tradd Street." "Zoning, superzoning and advisory services" were necessary to continue the preserving, restoring and rebuilding begun by Frost, the port commissioner maintained,[5] and after getting the support of Preservation Society president Alston Deas, the two convinced Mayor Stoney to appoint a temporary Planning and Zoning Commission in 1929. After thorough outside review, Commissioner MacElwee later submitted his own zoning ordinance to the group, chaired by Deas. Although the complexities of the issue and the lack of precedents to follow ultimately necessitated outside professional assistance, Alston Deas always maintained that Charleston's early breakthrough in zoning was due to "the suggestions and determined effort" of the city's port commissioner.[6]

As Preservation Society president in the late 1920s, Alston Deas played no small role, however, and Susan Frost kept in regular contact with her cousin as his committee did its work. Deas himself determined what areas of the lower peninsula would be affected by a "tentative" ordinance, drawing the street boundaries and compiling a list, with descriptions, of what buildings should be saved. With but a few modifications, the historic district zoning ordinance later drafted by professionals hired by Mayor Stoney, the Morris Knowles firm of Pittsburgh, would follow along the lines sketched by Deas.[7] An article in the *New York Times Magazine* within days after several public hearings and the Charleston City Council's ratification of a comprehensive zoning plan suggested the uniqueness of the zoning proposal: "While other American cities have zoning laws designed to conserve light, air, and the public health and comfort, and to preserve residential sections from the invasion of business, Charleston has just set up a zoning arrangement designed to preserve that distinctive architectural quality in the old South Carolina city which is its historic heritage and which is now recognized as one of the principal assets of the town."[8] The president of the American Institute of Architects labeled the Charleston design "the most progressive ordinance ever adopted in America."[9] Preservation legislation in other parts of the country was known generically for many years as "The Charleston Plan."[10]

The nation's first historic district covered slightly less than 150 acres in the southeastern corner of Charleston. The overall ordinance was administered by a planning and zoning commission and the city engineer. A board of adjustment had the authority to interpret the law and grant variances. Any proposed new buildings and any proposed alterations to the exterior of structures in this special zone had to be approved by a board of architectural review, a citizen committee that served without compensation. Violation of any part of the zoning ordinance of 1931 was a misdemeanor, punishable by fine or imprisonment.[11]

The process of enacting a major new governing ordinance revealed what Susan Frost had painfully discovered during the years of trying to rescue the Manigault House and save Charleston's old iron- and woodwork—the level of awareness of architecture was low, with the majority of the citizenry, for the most part, simply uninterested in historic monuments and aesthetically significant structures. Public meetings on the zoning ordinance were sparsely attended. "Experience has told me that the public does not want to be bothered with architectural propriety," Charleston's premier preservation architect, Albert Simons, explained to an outsider inquiring of the city's new ordinance.[12] Simons also observed a low level of understanding on the city council, despite several readings of the ordinance and sessions with the outside professional firm. "None of them understood it," he noted, "but considered it politically harmless and evidently popular and passed it."[13] Simons gave countless hours of free advice on building materials, paint colors, and architectural authenticity to homeowners on the lower peninsula; the entire historic district of Charleston, to some extent, emerged as a grand design from his drawing board.[14]

At the outset Susan Frost did not have a clear understanding of all that the new zoning law embraced, nor was she certain about how the 1931 ordinance affected her own business. She quickly sought clarification from the knowledgeable Simons. While still maintaining her real estate office on Broad Street,

Miss Frost had long found it convenient to conduct business in the spacious sur-roundings of the Miles Brewton mansion on King Street. Several conferences with Albert Simons and James O'Hear, chairman of the Zoning Commission, resulted in the realtor's being allowed to print on her stationery letterhead the location of her "studio" at the Miles Brewton House, with other rules to take effect should she make a change.[15] On learning of Frost's concern over restau-rants in the newly designated special district, Simons spelled out enforcement procedures and the vital necessity for public support of the ordinance "con-ceded by authorities to be the best in the land": "The enforcement of the Zon-ing Ordinance is not in the hands of the Zoning Commission but in the office of the City Engineer and the Building Inspector. They can only enforce the Ordinances as far as public opinion demands or will permit. The support and cooperation of the public in maintaining our Zoning Ordinance . . . is the only safeguard to insure that it will function as intended."[16]

Frost soon familiarized herself with all aspects of the Charleston zoning law; the process took only a short time. With the surfacing of opposition once the change took effect, the lowcountry realtor became a frequent speaker on behalf the ordinance and those who implemented it.

Frost's earliest concerns about possible zoning violations focused on con-ditions on Church Street. By the early 1930s, the tenement district made famous as Catfish Row in DuBose Heyward's *Porgy* (1925) was the site of sub-stantial new commercial and residential development. An occasional letter to the editor bemoaned the displacement of African Americans and loss of "the original atmosphere of the neighborhood,"[17] but the greater concern locally was the encroachment of business onto the lower peninsula. Witnessing the open-ing of two new restaurants and a hat store, Frost viewed with dismay a new commercial section in the making and soberly forecast to Albert Simons: "With this opening of shops in Church Street it will not be long before it will rival King Street."[18] Throughout 1934 Susan Frost continued to closely monitor the Church Street scene, regularly peppering Zoning Commission chairman O'Hear and city engineer J. H. Dingle with her views. "I hate to be the one to always complain about this," Frost wrote after hearing of still more retail activ-ity on the lower east side, "but someone has to do it. I am afraid it will put me in bad with some of the ladies who try to open these places in Church Street. It might hurt my business but I do feel someone has to do this [*sic*] otherwise our Zoning Ordinance will be of no account."[19]

Many on the Charleston peninsula resented the zoning ordinance as an invasion of their property rights, and, like Susan Frost, Albert Simons soon became discouraged at being unable to generate greater appreciation of the city's old architecture. "I feel sure it will take a long time to develop a body of public opinion sufficiently strong to make our work really effective," he wrote at the end of 1932.[20] Throughout the 1930s Simons and the Board of Archi-tectural Review modified their expectations, increasingly confining their activ-ity to "the prevention of atrocities rather than an effort to educate public taste."

Writing to a representative of the Vieux Carre Property Owners Association of New Orleans seeking to gain from the Charleston zoning experience, Simons described the retreat process and the strategy necessary for survival in the early years: "The Board of Architectural Review has not folded up nor surrendered but, like Fabius Maximus or Chiang Kai-shek has from time to time executed strategic retreats. We have always avoided a pitched battle, fearing to bring the ordinance into court where an unsympathetic jury might send the ordinance to the guillotine for interfering with the godgiven right of every man to make all the money he can, no matter how much of a mess he creates in the process."[21]

Critics of the Charleston historic district ordinance also maintained that social control rather than social benevolence was the driving force behind the law. Frost knew of some "intelligent people" who believed its purpose was to segregate the races,[22] but in an early spirited defense she answered a challenge, not from African Americans, but from a representative of the Charleston laboring classes.

The challenge arose when the president of Charleston's Central Labor Union, Aloysius Flynn, objected to the Zoning Board's rejection of a permit to build apartment houses on the boulevard adjacent to the Battery. Flynn believed that the decision deprived Charleston's labor force of jobs and newcomers of housing, and he criticized the Preservation Society for having supported the decision. The labor leader wrote in protest: "God gave to the Southern end of our city, which was further enhanced by the entire taxpayers of the city, regardless of whether you lived in Wards No. 1 and No. 2 or No. 11 and No. 12, a residential section, facing, or adjacent to the Atlantic Ocean and the Ashley River and swept by the ocean breezes; and we consider that the laboring man has as much right to live below Broad street as has the capitalist."[23]

Frost wasted no time in defending both the zoning ordinance and the Preservation Society. In her own letter to the editor, she reviewed the history of the municipal regulation, citing examples to suggest that the law was being consistently enforced. The concerned realtor maintained that the development of "modern life" and business activity necessitated cities' regulating business in relation to residential sections, and she assured readers that the purpose of such policy was not to discriminate. Her civics lesson went further: "It [the zoning ordinance] was not designed to promote a particular line of business activities such as building, neither does it deal solely with human beings and not at all with social orders. It deals largely with architectural values as related to human interests. It was planned primarily to protect the residents in all parts of the city from unsightly, noisy or otherwise objectionable business projects." Frost concluded with her own vote of confidence for Charleston's municipal officials: "The members of the commission, and the board of adjustment have an important and a difficult task, and they are carrying out the duties of their office with fairness and ability, it seems to me."[24]

Aside from covering only a small percentage of Charleston's old architecture, a major defect of the Charleston historic district zoning ordinance was the

inability of the Board of Architectural Review to stop the demolition of buildings. The limitation became increasingly noticeable during the Great Depression. In the summer of 1933 alone, at least thirty buildings on the peninsula
were razed by Charlestonians seeking to escape taxes or reduce tax liability.[25]
The problem was exacerbated when then Mayor Burnet Maybank, seeking to
spur investment and perhaps also to alleviate some of the city's pressing housing problems,[26] authorized subsidizing builders of new homes by tax exemption
for two years.

Critical of this proposal and Mayor Maybank's acceptance of New Deal
monies for construction of low-rent apartments, and very much aware that
Charleston's aesthetic significance was now a commercial asset "of almost ines-
timable value," the *News and Courier* went on the attack. In a series of six articles written in the fall of 1933 and in such editorials as "Renovate the Old
Houses" and "Utilize Old Buildings," the lowcountry newspaper offered an
alternative solution to the Maybank approach—a series of tax incentives for
holders of old buildings, including exemption of levies on those restoring property and no tax relief should structures be torn down.[27] The *News and Courier*
held up a model for its readers: "the reclamation of virtually the whole of Tradd
street from Meeting to East Bay from a slum district to one of the most interesting and desirable residence sections of the city—an accomplishment due
chiefly to the pioneer work of Miss Susan P. Frost—is a shining example of
what can be done."[28]

Promoting preservation as a means of attracting tourists and increasing
municipal revenue became widespread in the lowcountry in the early 1930s. In
its selling of historic Charleston, a rejuvenated Preservation Society, though not
abandoning its patriotic appeals and its ruminations about Old World beauty,
spoke more and more of the economic benefits that would accrue. By the late
1920s, over forty-seven thousand visitors were coming to Charleston annually,
spending some $4 million.[29] The initiation of the Azalea Festival in April 1934
dramatically accelerated the numbers, and at some point in the depression
decade over a quarter of a million tourists were generating the single largest
source of revenue for the city's coffers.[30] Not everyone considered tourism an
unmitigated blessing, however. Although he saw positive benefits for the Board
of Architectural Review and for zoning, Albert Simons ultimately became leery
of the fair-weather preservation fanaticism generated by tourism and told a
New Orleans preservationist:

> At the present time presidents of banks and of the Chamber of Commerce and
> of Rotary and of whatnots are all fanatical for preservation. Like all converts, they
> are more Royal than the King, more Catholic than the Pope, and want to pre-
> serve everything that is owned by somebody else, whether good, bad or indiffer-
> ent. Should the tourist trade lapse, their interest would evaporate. However, this
> popular approbation for the preservation of antiquities, even though based on
> mercenary considerations, should strengthen the hand of the Board of Architec-

tural Review in carrying out the purpose of the Zoning Ordinance. We rather feel that if the ordinance goes unchallenged in the courts for a long enough time, it will acquire a sort of validity by squatters' rights.[31]

Languishing throughout the 1920s with little more than two dozen members, the PSOC experienced considerable growth in numbers, if not in funds, during the Great Depression decade. Twenty-three new members were reported at the December 1933 meeting;[32] membership totaled some three hundred by 1937.[33] The larger preservation army placed increasing emphasis on the economic gains resulting from their work, with one of its charter members, Elizabeth O'Neill Verner, a particularly visible figure. Verner was both artist and preservationist, and by the late 1930s her numerous exhibitions, lectures, and publications, especially her 1939 edition of *Prints and Impressions of Charleston,* had resulted in national recognition for both herself and her native city.[34] One of her most eloquent public appeals underscored the economic value of saving old buildings then being demolished:

> . . . as each one of these quaint structures is demolished Charleston becomes a poorer city. We are making less of an appeal to the traveling public and losing the money which these tourists annually leave behind. Instead of presenting pointed roofs, over-hanging balconies and time-colored buildings, the eastern section of the city resembles a disorderly brickyard. This appeal as America's Most Historic City is the only characteristic Charleston has of its own that cannot [sic] be duplicated. . . . (I appeal) to the city at large who advertises the historic as an asset, and then destroys the very flavor of the past, thereby vividly recalling the killing of the goose that laid the golden egg.[35]

Although Frost served as honorary vice president for life in the Preservation Society after 1934, hers was more often an active role, occasionally substituting for an absent president, sometimes presenting programs on the history of the organization, and always speaking her piece regarding zoning and Charleston's endangered historic architecture.[36] At home in the middle of the summer of 1935, when most lower peninsula Charlestonians had long since fled to the cooler climate of the western North Carolina mountains, Frost hammered out another letter of concern. "I do so as a pure and simple act of public duty," she proclaimed, "and not because in this hot weather I enjoy staying at my typewriter to protest against what seems so obvious by such needless destruction of one of our loveliest spots, nor because I am not fully aware of the danger I put myself in of wearying the public with my much speaking, but solely because I deem it a serious public duty in the interest of protecting the architectural value of our city, to raise my voice in protest when these questions arise, and not to sit by idly and cowardly and take the course of least resistance, which is far easier."[37]

Despite advertising "the business standpoint" of preservation by the mid-

1930s, Frost remained committed to the larger view of preserving the beauty of an entire architectural canvas and getting others to catch the same vision. She also remained deeply disturbed about "the enemy within our gates" and about continuing demolitions. Acknowledging, nearly two decades after the formation of the Society for the Preservation of Old Dwellings, that some progress had been made, Frost pressed for continuing vigilance: "I think the public does appreciate our effort and value our work, but I also think we stand in great need of a Mussolini to protect our buildings of value when such unnecessary destruction can still take place such as above referred to on State Street. . . . But do we really need an outsider to point the way? Have we no sense of the values of life? No conception that beauty in all its forms and wherever found is part of the spiritual universe, and that when we destroy it, we destroy some of the real values of life? . . . Our hope is that it will not take another seventeen years for our own people to catch this vision of the loveliness of our city which strangers in our midst so well endorse and appreciate."[38]

With tourists generating more and more revenue in the lowcountry throughout the 1930s and the ties between saving old architecture and tourism more evident, Charlestonians developed a fuller appreciation of the preservation pioneering of Susan Pringle Frost, whom they affectionately knew as "Miss Sue." Her "staunch leadership," resourcefulness, persistence, and perseverance were increasingly extolled by the press and municipal officials. In its editorial of April 4, 1935, titled "Who Saved the Old Houses?" the *News and Courier* lamented that had the campaign of this "moving spirit" of the SPOD been "in its flush" twenty years earlier, the home of South Carolina patriot Henry Laurens and other landmarks might also have survived.[39] A feature story in the same paper in the late 1930s on "Miss Sue's" busy life admitted that success had not always attended her efforts, "but it is certain that by her endeavor in this Society and by the direction that she has given her real estate business, Charleston has preserved many old buildings that would not have been appreciated had she not seen their possibilities and worked for their preservation in a practical and business-like manner. . . . in her enthusiasms and ambitions she is younger and more vital than many another business woman who has not her enlarged vision and perspective."[40] In reducing some of her municipal indebtedness in 1936, Mayor Burnet Maybank offered the city's thanks.[41]

While monitoring the historic district zoning ordinance and the larger preservation picture throughout the 1930s, Frost also kept a wary eye on the impact of the New Deal in the South Carolina lowcountry. With New Deal programs affecting private enterprise, states' rights, and the race question, and with its particular threats to historic landmarks both in and around Charleston, Frost joined the chorus of critics who chastised Franklin Roosevelt, Harry Hopkins, and Mayor Burnet Maybank who was closely tied to New Deal politics.

Maybank was somewhat unique among Democratic leaders in the South in his consistent loyalty to the New Deal and President Roosevelt. That support stemmed from both kindred political philosophy and political ambition, and it resulted in Maybank's holding three state posts that aligned him with the New Deal at the same time that he was mayor of Charleston.[42] Determined to shore up the city's finances and generate vitally needed civic improvements, and sensitive to the human tragedy left in the wake of the depression, Maybank aggressively sought a share of whatever federal aid was available. His use of federal work relief netted the city long-overdue health, educational, and recreational facilities for both whites and African Americans and significantly contributed to his own solid base of political support.[43]

A vocal minority of Charlestonians, however, led by the *News and Courier* editor, William Watts Ball, were staunch critics of the New Deal. They especially denounced its pro-labor policies, its intrusion into the private sector, and its efforts to better conditions for African Americans. Within two months after Roosevelt's inauguration, Ball became the first Southern journalist to withdraw support from the new president, and by the summer of 1933 the *News and Courier* had declared war on FDR and his legislative program.[44] Throughout the decade, Ball had a loyal follower in Frost.

Frost and Ball had much in common. Only five years apart in age, both had ties to old Charleston, Ball having membership in the exclusive St. Cecilia Society because his father did,[45] and both were active in St. Michael's Episcopal parish. The two also shared elitist conceptions of Charleston's place in the state and in Southern history. Although Frost and Ball had been rival real estate speculators in the early part of the twentieth century, each was anxious to see the blighted lower peninsula recapture some of its prior brilliance. Moreover, as editor of the illustrious old *News and Courier,* Ball was both sympathetic and generous to Frost and her historic preservation agenda. Ball's increasingly segregationist views in the 1940s strained their relationship,[46] but both agreed on the excesses of the New Deal and both supported Wendell Willkie in the presidential election of 1940. Frost labeled Ball a "modern prophet who foretells and forthtells," and greatly admired his editorial courage.[47]

The New Deal measure that most aggravated Frost and Ball was the TVA-type electrical power project on the Santee and Cooper rivers. Ball saw the specter of socialism behind the public power issue, and when he first learned of the project, the conservative journalist called it a "sweet dream" designed to "make every day Sunday" in South Carolina.[48] To Frost the power project, spearheaded by Burnet Maybank and vital to his political career,[49] was a more immediate disaster, a human tragedy that would force people who had lived and worked their land in the river basins for generations to give up their homes and seek a livelihood elsewhere. At the same time, vestiges of another era— plantations, old churches, and homes of patriots—would all be washed away. Frost was ultimately more strident on the Santee-Cooper project than the *New and Courier* editor. Eventually, she justifiably accused the man she had once described as "a staunch advocate of all that is fair and righteous in the daily life of the State and City"[50] of playing politics on the controversial measure.

South Carolina's little TVA got beyond the dream stage in the spring of 1934 when the state legislature created the South Carolina Public Service Authority, a state agency empowered to borrow funds from federal agencies to construct and operate a hydroelectric power and navigation system in the Santee-Cooper basin in the coastal plain. Prospects for relieving depression unemployment gave the concept broad appeal (six to eight thousand jobs were projected), but it was also sold as a vehicle to generate economic recovery by accelerating the rate of industrial growth and providing cheap electrical power to the state's farms. The construction proposal remained in limbo for several years as the courts heard three injunction suits on behalf of three South Carolina private power companies. However, when the Supreme Court declared the Tennessee Valley Authority constitutional in early 1938, obstacles to the lowcountry power project would soon be removed too.[51]

Firm opposition to South Carolina's power project came from many quarters other than private business, and those protests did not abate until late 1939 when construction was well underway. Plantation owners, who were more Northern than Southern, offered powerful objection, their hunting preserves seriously threatened. Those voices blended with those of conservationists, who felt that flooding the delta threatened certain wildlife with extinction; they also blended with those of preservationists and the historically oriented who reverenced plantations like Medway and "Rice Hope" and the homes where Generals Francis Marion and William Moultrie had spent their youth. Political and economic conservatives, charging socialism and reckless spending, were also part of the noisy din of critics.[52] Seeking to thwart the opposition early before it could mount too serious an offensive, Burnet Maybank convinced William Watts Ball that the industrialization generated by power projects in Tennessee and Alabama threatened to destroy the Carolinas, and he received pledges, which Ball honored throughout the thirties, that the Charleston editor would not write anything to threaten establishment of the Santee-Cooper Authority.[53]

W. W. Ball's change of position on the Santee-Cooper project both befuddled and angered Susan Frost. Frost suspected Ball of furthering Maybank's gubernatorial ambitions, and she accused the editor of "either maliciously or ignorantly misrepresenting" the human suffering that would accompany uprooting of landowners. Frost conveyed her "decidedly letdown" feeling to the journalist whose reasoning she found "so far below your usual standard of thought and of policy": "I cannot bring my mind to see wherein lies the connection between what is spent and wasted in other states by the federal government and what we are willing to demand shall be wasted in our state on useless projects by the squandering of the taxpayer'[s] money; if the government wantonly lays waste land in Maine and Florida with projects that are afterwards abandoned, why should we have to pursue the same course? . . . I have never heard anywhere that two wrongs make one right, and if it is wrong to squander the hard earned money of the taxpayer on useless projects in one state there is no law nor reasoning by which it can be right in another state."[54] By the late thirties, the lowcountry realtor believed both scandal and profiteering to be associated with Santee-Cooper and wrote Ball that it was "the most iniquitous thing perpetrated on a helpless people by a group of politicians and money grabbers."[55]

In her intense opposition to the controversial South Carolina public power project which she saw threatening historical homes and monuments, Susan Frost joined forces with conservationists, often predicting doom for virgin forests and wildlife. In seeking to rally the conservation world, Frost turned to the prominent naturalist and lowcountry apologist, Herbert Sass.

For many years on the staff of the Charleston *News and Courier,* Sass both wrote its history and that of the city of his birth.[56] Herbert Sass was also a champion of natural resources and his "Woods and Waters" column was widely read. Related to the Frost sisters by virtue of family ties to Rebecca Brewton Motte, Herbert Sass wrote a glowing foreword to "Miss Sue's" history of her home place, *Highlights of the Miles Brewton House.*[57]

In a lengthy response to the entreaties of Susan Frost on the South Carolina power project, Herbert Sass confessed to much "heart-searching" and was especially troubled that many homes of historical value would be destroyed. Sass argued, however, that highway builders and pulp mills were more of a threat to the forests of the lowcountry than the controversial delta power project, and maintained wildlife might actually benefit and the landscape be improved. The possibility of economic revitalization weighed heavily with the naturalist: "our people. . . are so much in need of something to take the place of our vanished resources—our indigo, our rice, our sea island cotton, our phosphates—that I didn't feel justified in opposing this enterprise even though there be considerable doubt of its efficacy," Sass wrote Miss Frost. Herbert Sass had considerable empathy for those he knew who would be affected, however, and agreed with his Charleston relative that he would not mourn should the European war abort the New Deal undertaking.[58] The latter did not occur, and Susan Frost, like most other Santee-Cooper critics, ceased her battle as construction moved on apace.

The New Deal emphasis on slum clearance and public housing also touched off a storm of controversy in Charleston and arrayed local historic preservationists against Mayor Burnet Maybank and Washington politicians. Many longtime Charlestonians were uneasy over the social implications of such programs, especially after Secretary of the Interior Ickes's announcement of September 27, 1935, that a loan of $1,150,000 for construction of a public housing project for blacks in Charleston had been approved, while a second application for an apartment complex for whites had been set aside for further study.[59] When the Federal Housing Authority slum clearance proposal of March 1938 endangered several historic landmarks located in a single block on the peninsula, the Charleston preservation community jumped into the fray.

Burnet Maybank labeled the Magazine Street area a "cesspool of horrors." Historic preservationists spoke only of the treasures: "Few, if any cities, have three such handsome buildings, located in one such block, as the jail, Jenkins'

Orphanage, and the medical college," said Susan Frost in identifying the objects of concern.[60] Frost and the Preservation Society conducted an intense but short-lived campaign on behalf the Medical College,[61] and a major battle over the Jenkins' Orphanage for African-American children was averted after the Charleston Housing Authority took over the building, with the orphanage moving to a new location. However, the fight to save the old jail, with its high walls and turret towers, would be joined long after Mayor Maybank had departed the lowcountry for the governor's chair.

Those who fought battled for both the jail and the jail wall. "A history of Charleston lives in that wall," proclaimed Preservation Society President William Means, who accused the city of "Fiddling as Rome Burns": "The wall is not beautiful. It probably has no artistic or architectural merit, but neither has the mummy of King Tut-ankh-amen, yet it is very valuable. . . . While there is no Nero among us, there are thousands of fiddlers. . . . If we are not able to pass on to future generations what we have so easily acquired, we will be pointed out by our descendants as a generation fiddling while Rome burned."[62] Many regarded the enemy in the jail controversy as the New Deal. "Is there to be no end to the legalized vandalism perpetrated by Uncle Sam in the city of Charleston, and in the name of progress?" questioned a former PSOC president?[63] Susan Frost begged the *News and Courier* editor for space for a letter that "might carry some little weight, unless it should happen that the public is tired of my earnest efforts to save our historic landmarks."[64] Heavily dependent on the tourist trade by the late thirties, Charleston businesses became more vocal in identifying with preservation causes and joined in appeals to keep the jail wall intact.[65] The contest was even brought to the attention of a national audience.[66] A resolute Mayor Henry Lockwood, successor to Burnet Maybank, made his position clear—"I stand for the preservation of anything in Charleston that will attract more people to our city"—and successfully pledged to hold on to a portion of the wall.[67]

Another preservation controversy erupted in Charleston during the extended fight over the jail wall, brought about when brief but devastating tornados struck the lowcountry in September 1938. Some of the city's famous landmarks sustained heavy damage, and New Dealer Harry Hopkins quickly issued WPA funds for relief and rebuilding.[68]

Instead of repairing the extensively damaged roof and interior of the Charleston City Hall, Mayor Burnet Maybank decided to completely remodel and expand the structure, and major exterior renovations were sanctioned by city council. Alston Deas promptly charged the chief executive with violating the Old and Historic District Zoning Ordinance.[69] Day after day, for well over a month, the mayor felt the hostility of the local citizenry against altering the form of one of Gabriel Manigault's architectural masterpieces. "To change its exterior proportions would destroy its value just as surely as to paint a new uniform upon General Washington would destroy the value of the Trumbull portrait," protested journalist/conservationist Herbert Sass.[70] Letters of disapproval echoed from others of the Charleston cultural community.[71] Repairing her own heavily damaged slate roof at the Miles Brewton House, Susan Frost also took time to join the parade of critics.[72] Burnet Maybank finally quieted the bitter public controversy by acceding to "the people's wishes" and approved only essential repairs to the original structure.

Approaching the age when most people retired as World War II neared, Susan Frost relentlessly continued to restore her own property while pressuring public officials to preserve its architectural past. In late 1937 a series of letters to Mayor Maybank and City Engineer J. H. Dingle told of new loans and the near completion of restoration of two small English brick houses on Bedon's Alley off Tradd Street and invited the two to pay a visit. Reminding the two that the Preservation Society had been successful a few years earlier in persuading the city to keep the cobblestone paving on Chalmers Street just north of the commercial district, the lowcountry realtor urged the city engineer to use similar paving on Bedon's Alley. When the public official hesitated, citing high costs and unavailability, Frost informed the mayor she had an ample supply of the stones which originally came to Charleston as ballast in vessels engaged in the cotton trade. A terse communication to Dingle from his superior attested once more to the success of Charleston's noted businesswoman in relating to the city's male power structure: "Please have a few cobblestones hauled to Bedon's so this street can be repaired as soon as possible." The *News and Courier* soon advertised an open house at one of Frost's Bedon's Alley properties.[73]

Long an unofficial monitor of the Charleston zoning ordinance, Susan Frost became an official watchdog in June 1940 when she agreed to serve on the Zoning Board of Adjustments (BOA), having been nominated by the Charleston Real Estate Exchange. She served for almost a decade. Despite pressing family matters and increasing age, Frost's tenure was marked by a high degree of conscientiousness and civic responsibility woven around her usual candor and frequent bluntness. The BOA reviewed requests and issued permits for minor modifications of the zoning ordinance. None of the five-member board was more versed on the streets and thoroughfares of the peninsula than Miss Frost, and her knowledge of the history of individual structures in the Old and Historic District brought a valuable dimension to the deliberations of the group. On one occasion when an important meeting of the Preservation Society precluded her joining the BOA, Frost asked the city engineer to serve as her proxy, and she submitted a lengthy letter that set forth the issues and her position on several zoning requests.[74] She followed a similar procedure when she left for summer vacations in western North Carolina. In faithfully upholding the letter and spirit of the zoning law, Susan Frost was not averse to stepping on toes, even those of her social class. "I am opposed to allowing Mrs. Rutledge at 44 South Battery to build that little house she spoke of," Frost told BOA chairman T. W. Perry on the eve of one annual hiatus, "and would not vote for it if present; I see no reason at all for making an exception. It is in one of our choicest residential areas, where the rules protecting against over-crowding by violation of the Zoning Ordinance should be strictly enforced; so many of our lovely gardens have been cut up for building lots before the Ordinance went into effect, that we must protect those that are left. Therefore if this matter comes up after I leave, I would appreciate it if you would cast my vote according to these principles."[75]

The war years themselves were not kind to the aging Susan Frost. Few visitors and boarders brought revenue to the Miles Brewton House. Doubling her energies to make sales in a real estate market affected by war did not always bring success, either. "You can see how quiet things are except for war work," the lowcountry realtor wrote her California cousin in January 1943 in a lengthy epistle; "we take it one day at a time; there is nothing else to do."[76] The death of two servants within a two-week period in late 1942, one who had been with the household for fifteen years, resulted in only one replacement, and left Susan Frost muttering about the impact of "war fever" on "the servant question."[77] Much more devastating was the death of her sister Mary in mid-1943. Months after she died, "Miss Sue" was still depressed, hoping to regain "some of my old time courage and zest in life." Gardening provided only a small measure of solace, and to assuage her guilt over having not taken greater interest in her deceased sister's compilation of family history, Susan Frost joined with sister "Rebe" in guaranteeing publication of Mary Pringle Frost's *The Miles Brewton House: Chronicles and Reminiscences.* The endeavor proved a great palliative, and once she rushed her own companion volume, *Highlights of the Miles Brewton House,* into print in 1944 the seventy-year-old proprietor of the famed King Street mansion considered her obligation to future Pringle/Frost generations completed.[78]

For both the city of Charleston and the growing preservation community within it, World War II was a different story. The economic revitalization generated by rapid expansion of the Navy Yard and the Charleston Shipyard and Drydock remained long after armed conflict ceased. Pursuing initiatives begun in the late thirties to correct deficiencies in the 1931 zoning ordinance and protect a wider range of historically and architecturally valuable houses than just those on the lower end of the Charleston peninsula, Robert N. S. Whitelaw, aggressive director of the Carolina Art Association, spearheaded the first city-wide architectural survey in the United States. Simultaneously, Whitelaw's special Civic Services Committee conducted an intensive wartime preservation educational campaign, highlighted by a 1942 exhibit at the Gibbes Art Gallery titled "This Is Charleston" and two years later the publication of the survey results in an illustrated book of the same name. At the end of the war, undaunted by the failure to get modifications of the original historic district zoning ordinance and to also achieve a comprehensive parking plan for Charleston City, and convinced that the Preservation Society alone could not meet the challenges of postwar growth, Whitelaw issued a call for a new preservation organization.[79]

Robert Whitelaw's call for fresh and visionary new preservation soldiers occurred at a time when Charleston's oldest such group was celebrating a mile-stone. A quarter of a century old in 1945, the Preservation Society of Charleston (still referred to by many as the Society for the Preservation of Old Dwellings) commemorated the occasion at the Heyward-Washington House with an address by its founder and first president, Susan Pringle Frost. "Starting with very few members and almost no financial backing, the society has nonetheless been in the forefront of all movements looking to the preservation of our land-marks, both private and municipal, both residences and public structures," Frost told her audience. While admitting that some architectural "gems" had been lost, the preservation grande dame applauded years of activity and steadily increasing influence that were now paying great dividends for the city. The pio-neer preservationist observed with great pride that what was once a small band had swelled to an army of several hundred, with many of those "influential men."[80]

As Robert Whitelaw and architect Albert Simons saw it, however, numbers were part of the problem. "It was a membership organization," said Whitelaw of Charleston's earliest preservation group; "its president changed every few years and it just hadn't been active."[81] Simons, a member of Whitelaw's blue-ribbon survey committee, maintained the approach and scope of the PSOC was both too narrow and unsuited for the times. "Just fixing up one or two houses for museums certainly was not solving the problem," he observed; "we found at the time that we ought to go out and accomplish some widespread preservation work . . . houses to be lived in, and adaptive use for other buildings that are not residences."[82] Robert Whitelaw envisioned complementing the grass-roots, con-sciousness-raising activities of the Preservation Society with a revolving-fund foundation that would purchase, rehabilitate, and resell buildings worthy of preservation. Whitelaw's brainchild, incorporated in 1947 as the Historic Charleston Foundation (HCF), would, under the forceful leadership of Frances Ravenel Smythe Edmunds, dramatically widen the sweep of neighborhood restoration and focus a whole new wave of national attention on Charleston in the several decades after World War II.[83]

Somewhat fearful of being preempted in a world that been solely theirs since the end of World War I, Susan Pringle Frost and her Preservation Society demonstrated considerable anxiety when the Historic Charleston Foundation surfaced. "They had a feeling that here was a dictatorship coming about . . . and they'd be swallowed," observed Helen McCormack, whose planned address before the PSOC was cut short by heated debate about the new group.[84] "The Preservation Society's feelings were rather hurt, but they had no reason to be," recalled Charleston Museum Director Milby Burton, who maintained the orga-nization he once headed had become too myopic in its approach.[85] Alston Deas also remembered talk of a "rival society coming up" within the organization Susan Frost founded and admitted being drawn to the HCF because it was a "more vigorous and more business-like" group.[86] After its initial scare abated, the Preservation Society recovered its composure and soon acknowledged that, while each organization followed "different roads to their heaven," both were laboring for the common good.[87]

With tourism resuming after World War II and reaching unprecedented levels in the lowcountry by the late 1940s, and the Charleston peninsula still feeling the effects of dramatic wartime growth, the postwar years saw heightened debate over business development, eradication of slum areas and new housing, and the ability of the Charleston zoning ordinance and those who enforced it to meet the challenges of the time.[88] Some argued for spot zoning, many argued against it. While the Zoning Commission had consistently opposed such action, longtime zoning champions like Albert Simons believed past policy and present day needs were incompatible, and he argued the time had come to bring in outside experts and redraft the code. Citing several problems needing solution on the peninsula, including suitable location of multistory apartment houses and doctors' offices in the residential district, advance planning for the development of marginal land along the Ashley River, and improvement of the northern approaches to the city, architect Simons concluded: "In the 17 years since the present ordinance was compiled and adopted, great changes have occurred in the city so that many of the provisions which were then wise and beneficial now require modifications. . . . The long over due solution to these and other problems will require more time and thought than the members of the Zoning Commission can be expected to give."[89]

Despite her advancing age, Susan Frost remained the ever-vigilant zoning watchdog in the face of new threats to the landscape of old Charleston. When a developer announced plans in late 1948 to erect a fourteen-story apartment building squarely in the heart of the peninsula, his attorneys requesting rezoning, "Miss Sue," with typical zeal, jumped into the fray. Council chambers were clogged for the public hearing, many fearful that, if spot zoning were granted, it would be an "opening wedge" which would render no residential area safe. Susan Frost, still a member of the Zoning Board of Adjustment, applauded the developer, often a tour guide for winter visitors, but not the development project, asking the builder to consider his own feelings should his stately residential area suddenly experience construction of a multistory apartment building. In a ringing speech at the public hearing, the doyen of Charleston preservationists asserted that any amendment to the zoning ordinance would be "a calamity" that may as well result in the entire code's being "thrown overboard," and she begged the council and Zoning Commission to use "sound judgment and protect the past glory of our city."[90]

The performance was vintage Frost. Typically in her later years Susan Frost stirred up opposition to development projects or threatened buildings by writing letters to the newspapers and speaking at public forums. Indeed, the name of Susan Frost was regularly called forth, her courage and foresight held as exemplary, in rallying Charlestonians to arms in preservation battles after World War II.[91] "She was a very old lady by then," Frances Edmunds recalled, "but her reputation was such that her influence was great . . . (especially) on young people in the community."[92] Occasionally Frost spoke out and wrote letters to the editor because others asked, but her language and the intensity of her arguments suggested she probably would have been at the podium or typewriter soon anyway. Threats to the landscape of her beloved Charleston were simply too serious a matter on which to keep quiet, even as she moved toward her eightieth birthday. "One by one we are destroying our landmarks," she wrote in 1947, distressed because of "imminent danger" to the series of quaint rectangular brick buildings on Broad Street known as "Lawyer's Row": "when all are gone we will have a mediocre city overrun with ugly modern buildings. . . . I hope this protest may have some influence against destroying in the future any of our old architecture."[93]

While the work of Robert Whitelaw and the blossoming of the Historic Charleston Foundation captured many of the historic preservation headlines in the lowcountry in the late 1940s and early 1950s, the past achievements of Susan Frost were more publicized than ever. No less than five major articles focused on "Miss Sue's" career between 1946 and 1952, including one that appeared in the national periodical *Independent Woman* and an Associated Press story that was distributed to daily newspapers in the Carolinas and Georgia. Projections for inclusion of Frost in articles in two other national magazines, the *National Geographic Magazine* and the *Saturday Evening Post,* did not materialize.[94] Sometimes other stories highlighting recent Charleston history paid homage to its preservation pioneer, and the local press extended birthday greetings yearly to "Miss Sue" with some commentary about her role in sparking a movement that had ultimately become widely accepted.[95]

Susan Frost resigned from the Board of Adjustment of the Zoning Commission in March 1949 because of the illness of her sister "Rebe," but she continued as the preservation conscience for the city for several additional years until she was past eighty. The last fight she participated in was one of the fiercest ever waged on the peninsula—the five year struggle, 1948–1953, to save the Charleston Orphan House and the Orphan House Chapel. The latter, dating to 1802 and one of the handful of local buildings designed by celebrated Charleston architect Gabriel Manigault, became the emotional battle zone. The contest became particularly strident when Sears Roebuck and Company, with plans for a new store, appeared to renege on early expressions of sensitivity to the two historic landmarks.[96]

Soon after hearing of the proposed demolition, Susan Frost fired a personal letter to Sears chairman General Robert Wood and began her customary process of rousing the local citizenry. "I wonder if people who advocate the destruction of this type of building have ever considered that there are many things in life of greater value than business structures," she caustically wrote to the *News and Courier* in May 1948.[97] Frost played particularly heavily on the spiritual versus the commercialism/materialism dichotomy that seemed inherent in the struggle over a place of worship. Likening the Orphan House Chapel to a sacred shrine, the preservation society founder challenged the giant of the business world with such biblical injunctions as that of King Solomon to the Hebrew people—"Remove not the ancient landmarks which thy fathers have set"—and God's warning to Moses as he approached the summit of Mount Sinai: "Take off thy shoes from off thy feet for the place whereon thou standest is Holy Ground."[98] Still trying to halt the razing several days after it had begun, Susan Frost recalled the "Save the Manigault" movement, the inspiration for organizing the Society for the Preservation of Old Dwellings, and reminded natives once more that tourists came to Charleston because of its old architecture, not its modern stores.[99] Seeing signs of optimism for countless other buildings needing redemption in the many cries of distress raised on behalf of the Orphan House Chapel, the *News and Courier* challenged Charlestonians to support the "splendid work" of the SPOD and its founder, Miss Susan P. Frost, as well as the fledgling Historic Charleston Foundation.[100]

The quarter of a century following enactment of the zoning ordinance in 1931 were among the most significant in Charleston preservation history. Its pioneering law, despite the limited size of the historic district, provided the legal mechanism to regulate new construction on the lower peninsula and monitor exterior changes to its old architecture, and other cities were soon seeing the benefits of such codes. By the early 1940s, with the completion of the first city-wide architectural survey and the publication of *This Is Charleston,* others could see what Susan Frost already knew: that entire sections of Charleston contained architecture that was worthy of preservation. A new generation of preservation leaders brought organizational and planning abilities to the movement, complementing the emotional and at times romantically sentimental views of many of the fiercely dedicated early partisans. By the end of World War II Charleston had a preservation leadership cadre twice the size of similar groups in other cities.[101] The creation of the Historic Charleston Foundation, with its Revolving Fund for Area Rehabilitation, effectively augmented the public awareness thrust of the Preservation Society, eight hundred members strong by the time of the Orphan House battle,[102] and augured well for the future of historic preservation on the peninsula.

At the time Susan Frost became seriously ill in 1955, historic preservation was still not totally part of the mainstream in Charleston, however. Despite the efforts of Frost and other key members of the SPOD in the 1930s and 1940s in widening the arguments for historic preservation to include the financial benefits, the economic viability of preservation was not fully embraced as a community value until the 1970s.[103] Defects in the 1931 zoning ordinance did not begin to be successfully addressed until the late 1950s, and in 1966 the city finally expanded the original historic district and endowed the Board of Architectural Review with tighter control over demolitions.[104]

Susan Frost found many enemies to historic preservation in Charleston throughout the depression and World War II. Sometimes the adversary came from the outside—the corporate developer, the artifact collector, or, in the case of the New Deal, the federal government itself. Quite often, however, the enemy was located within city walls. Occasionally it was municipal policy makers, sometimes entrepreneurs ignoring the zoning ordinance or seeking ways to circumvent it, and frequently vandals and wreckers either uneducated to the significance of the unique architecture around them or simply acting on their own needs or whims. Be they internal or external, Susan Frost had little tolerance for despoilers of historic Charleston, and sooner or later all felt her wrath.

Most often her passion was expressed through letters to the editors of the Charleston dailies. At virtually any hour of the day or night "Miss Sue" sat at the typewriter and, using her two finger approach, committed a rush of feelings to paper. Her language, often brusque and blunt, was purposefully designed to incite, and it frequently did. Susan Frost proselytized on the streets and at civic meetings, on the telephone and in her car. Journalist T. R. Waring, Jr., remembered "Miss Sue" as "a sort of Tugboat Annie personality . . . fast-talking in the Charleston patois and accustomed to pushing causes."[105] Her cause célèbre was historic preservation, and she exercised a bulldog-like determination in serving as architecture sentinel and zoning overseer in Charleston for over a quarter of a century. She was unwavering in her mission to save entire neighborhoods from forces that threatened them. As a conscience for the historical and architectural integrity of the Charleston that once was, Susan Frost played arguably her most valuable role.

By the end of the five year battle over the Charleston Orphan House and Chapel, Susan Pringle Frost had observed her eightieth birthday, and the Miles Brewton House was rapidly becoming the only world she knew. "Let others take up the fight to preserve our ancient landmarks," she wrote during the conflict with Sears Roebuck, as if to acknowledge an end to her own active role.[106] Stiff fingers allowed fewer and fewer letters to spring from her ancient typewriter, and she finally gave up driving, muttering all the while about increased traffic and the difficulties of parking. In early 1948 Frost reluctantly sold her beloved Isle of Palms "Ranch" getaway. Two years later, after sixty-five years in the family, the Frost retreat at Saluda, North Carolina, was sold. "I had a birthday yesterday and friends came to see me and brought presents; I think it is time now tho. to stop counting b. ds. or having parties," the octogenarian penned in one of her last missives.[107] After years of activism with historic preservation and women's issues, Susan Frost now seemed content to settle quietly into the comforting confines of the old family home.

CONCLUSION

Susan Pringle Frost did not go "gentle into that good night." Relentless crusaders never do. The renowned Charleston realtor sold her Broad Street office after her sister Mary's death but continued to conduct business from the basement of her King Street residence.[1] She soon outfitted another space, the back porch of the Miles Brewton House, with necessary essentials—a typewriter, telephone, and comfortable chair. Even in the dead of winter, Frost would answer a letter or two from the back porch and then would return to the warmth of a gas stove in the "cozy corner" at the end of the great entrance hall, where she maintained another telephone, radio, and reading table. The upstairs porch office also allowed quick access to the steady stream of seasonal visitors who came to tour the inner recesses of the mansion on the lower peninsula. Until the late 1940s, Frost accepted boarders whom she served three meals a day. "I get up at 6 and on the go all day until about 9 in evg. when Winsie and I turn in for the night," she wrote in one of her regular mailings to cousin Nina on the West Coast, including as she often did a reference to her favorite dog.[2] Nothing gave Frost more pleasure in her later years than opening the doors of the Miles Brewton House to tourists, who provided her a captive audience with whom she could hold forth on the old family home, historic preservation, or other issues of interest.

Although increasingly confined to the Miles Brewton House, Frost nevertheless continued to champion her favorite causes. In addition to historic preservation and women's issues, these included, particularly in her later years, better treatment of African Americans and ending cruelty to animals.

Frost had always argued that, in caring for the needy, there should be no discrimination on the basis of color.[3] She supported the goals of the Charleston Interracial Committee, which dated back to the early 1920s.[4] During World War II, unlike most Southerners, especially those of her social class, Frost came to believe that sacrifices abroad entitled blacks to better treatment at home. Deeming it unfathomable that, at the same time blacks and whites were fighting together in the battle zones of Europe and Asia, South Carolina legislators were considering a bill to segregate buses, Frost told the *News and Courier:* "We wonder when and where this segregation of races will end. If we Anglo Saxons cannot sit next to a Negro in a bus or stand alongside him in looking at an exhibit which displays the God given talents to mankind, how under heaven will we manage when all reach the higher life where there shall be no segregation, where each will stand in the last day on his or her own individual merits and not on the hue of the skin?"[5]

The aging preservationist also became less forgiving of those she believed to be causing racial tensions. In the fall of 1943 she told William Watts Ball point-blank that his "incessant editorial hammering" on "the Negro question" resulted in "more harm and encourages more Race hatred." She admitted to not understanding "how one of your great intellect and superior talent should harp so continually on the matter."[6] On record as preferring a black to a white playground in proximity to her home, Frost publicly invited a querulous white homeowner to the Miles Brewton House to discuss the matter further, adding, "I have certain convictions and am not afraid to express them publicly or privately."[7] "Miss Sue" often attended evening services at an African-American church,[8] and as late as the early 1950s she allowed poor blacks, for a dollar a month, to live with her servants and their children in the adjacent carriage and coach house.[9] Although Frost's racial views never created as great a controversy on the peninsula as that surrounding Judge J. Waties Waring in the late 1940s, she was, said journalist Thomas R. Waring, Jr., "clearly ahead of her time on civil rights."[10]

Other than historic preservation, the topic Frost most often addressed in her many letters to the editors of Charleston's dailies was more humane treatment for animals. The plight of dogs and birds most distressed the Miles Brewton proprietor, whose back porch housed an exotic ornamented bird feeder and whose house history ended with a special section detailing the lives of each of six dogs (including one named Ashley Soluble Guano), all memorialized with gravestones in the mansion gardens.[11] Cockfighting also bothered Frost; so did dog pounds (she hated the term), horse racing (she urged a cousin to form a Society for the Prevention of Horse Racing) and homeless animals. A longtime member of the Society for the Prevention of Cruelty to Animals, Frost solicited funds for local shelters and campaigned for junior branches in the public schools.[12] A regular reader of the *News and Courier* columns of naturalist Herbert Ravenel Sass, "Miss Sue" submitted her own articles to such national journals as *Humane Magazine* and *Animal Magazine*.[13] The present-day animal rights activists had a godmother in Susan Pringle Frost, who was known to accost those adorned in fur coats with the words "you are wearing an animal."[14]

Frost also avidly followed politics in the late 1940s and early 1950s, although her allegiance nationally was forever changed after the FDR years. On learning shortly after Franklin Roosevelt's death that State Senator Oliver Wallace proposed to name the new bridge to Sullivan's Island in Roosevelt's honor and that another *News and Courier* reader was advocating a national holiday to honor the former president, Frost became incensed: "I sincerely hoped that the country would be forever rid of his memory and of all the harm he had done our Country; but as two gentlemen at my home recently told me that it would take a hundred years to overcome the damage to the Country by his Administration and as I firmly believe the same to be true I could not expect to live to see the Country restored to normalcy. We can hope, however, that his name will in time be forgotten instead of being memorialized. If we must have a name for the aforesaid bridge, let it be one of the founders of the Country, one among those who founded and built up the Country instead of destroying and dragging it down."[15] The Truman administration did not endear itself to Frost either, and in 1952 she informed her cousin that she had joined the Charleston City/County Citizens League, a group vowing to restore "clean, honest, competent government" and supporting conservative Republican Senator Robert Taft of Ohio for president.[16] Frost fondly remembered that her aunt Susan Pringle had once hosted the congressman's father, William Howard Taft, at the Miles Brewton House. In endorsing Robert Taft for president, "Miss Sue" maintained that Dwight Eisenhower would have served his country "far better" had he retained his military command. She said she was yet to be persuaded that "it is fit or becoming" for a man of high military rank to become prominently involved in national politics.[17]

Church was always central to Frost's life. When old age no longer permitted her to drive the short distance to St. Michael's Episcopal Church, the rector paid regular Sunday morning visits to her home to administer the sacraments. Frost greatly respected the church attended by her ancestors, but such veneration did not preclude "Miss Sue" from making her presence felt as much at St. Michael's as anywhere else in Charleston. Frost was perhaps the first woman to speak out on critical church policy matters. She championed vestrywomen for the staid Episcopal congregation on the corner of Meeting and Broad long before elders allowed them to take office, and her outspoken involvement in the controversy to establish free pews earned her a rebuke from the senior warden.[18] "Sue Frost didn't challenge convention for the sake of challenge," recalled a native related to the outspoken critic, "but because of injustices and inequities."[19]

Sequestered at the Miles Brewton House, Frost remained blunt and opinionated on a wide variety of topics until her death. Until he retired from the *News and Courier,* William Watts Ball was a regular recipient of Frost's position statements. One letter thanked the lowcountry editor for his fight, "mild tho. it is," against the pensioning of public school teachers; then she moved on to another education issue, support of expansion of the University of South Carolina.[20] "Miss Sue" opposed postwar atomic weapons testing in the Pacific, and capital punishment ran counter to her belief in the scriptures.[21] As a veteran female driver, Frost testily resented disparaging comments about women's abilities on the streets and highways.[22] She spoke out against divorce time and again.[23] The "Miss Sue" who was cared for by a cousin in her last few years was still a "Miss Sue" who typed late into the night.[24]

Frost's eccentricities were legend in Charleston. She daily gardened in her bloomers in the dawn hours. Regulars on the Battery were not unaccustomed to seeing her giving her dogs an automobile ride in the early evening hours, and tales abounded about her driving and "the car with hiccups."[25] Prize-winning lowcountry author Julia Peterkin once roughed out a short story based on an episode about "Miss Sue," who with "racing engine" and "grinding clutch" returned late from a second Sunday church service to find her sister worried because drunken sailors were asleep in the carriage house garage.[26] Any longtime native knew something of "Miss Sue" and her peculiarities. She was, said one, "one of our real characters."[27]

Charleston reverences its older ladies, however, and it regards with affectionate humor those who flaunt convention. Natives aspire to achieve such a venerated estate. Artist Elizabeth O'Neill Verner, in *Mellowed by Time,* maintained that such types are part of the charm of the city: "Charleston delights in her characters—their utter disregard for the conventional, their determination to live as they please, to act as they please and to dress as they please. There is little of the stereotyped anywhere. Not only do we have our outstanding eccentrics, but every group is composed of sharply drawn individuals. Charleston is rife with stories about them; there is always the hope that, if one lives long enough, and is courageous enough, one may some day be considered one of Charleston's characters."[28] A current Charleston-educated novelist agreed, concluding of those on the peninsula: "These are a people who prize eccentricity the way the Chinese formerly valued women with small feet."[29]

Charleston prized Susan Pringle Frost all the more as she neared death in the late 1950s, having been bedridden for several years, and it continued to heap honors on its grande dame of historic preservation. Along with revered author Josephine Pinckney, the Federation of Women's Clubs admitted Frost into its Hall of Fame in 1959. A year earlier, the Preservation Society conferred lifelong honorary membership on its founder. Proclaiming it "an honor richly deserved," the *News and Courier* suggested how others might pay homage: "She helped to save our city as a gracious and dignified place in which to live. If Charlestonians want to do full honor to Miss Frost, the best way to do so is by working with zeal against urban blight, ugliness and bad zoning which destroy a city. Not to be forgotten is the importance of investing in neighborhoods which need only a little interest and restoration to bloom again."[30] In a flattering late 1958 article, "Susan P. Frost Put Sentiment First to Become Benefactor to Charleston," a *News and Courier* staff writer told the now-familiar Frost restoration story once more and identified numerous projects of the famed realtor that had been listed as "worthy of mention," "valuable," or "noteworthy " in the city's pioneering architectural survey in the early 1940s.[31] Accolades soon poured in all over again. On October 7, 1960, at the age of 87, "Miss Sue" of Charleston died at 27 King Street in the house where she was born. She had wanted to die there.[32]

Frost's career reveals much about the history of reform, voluntarism, and changing roles for women in the United States in the late nineteenth and early twentieth centuries. Her story also tells us much about a region and a nation in a state of flux. Frost was part of the Victorian generation of "new women" who blended traditional virtues with activist social roles and, in the process, developed enhanced perceptions of self and gender and a keen sense of mission. Like many members of this group, Frost was white, Anglo-Saxon, upper class, a city dweller, better educated than average, single, and, like many unmarried women, employed outside the home, albeit in a profession (real estate) dominated not by women but by men.[33] She was also involved, like many of her class and sex, in the expanding network of female voluntary associations in the Gilded Age/ Progressive Era. For many women, as for Susan Frost, involvement in single-sex networks like women's clubs and a suffrage league opened the door to a new identity and provided an avenue through which to enter and affect public affairs.

Southern women, however, found the road from pedestal to politics more circuitous than their national counterparts and fraught with pitfalls and controversy. The "woman question" preoccupied the nineteenth and early twentieth centuries, but for Southern males, and many females, the answers to queries such as: about whether a woman should enter college, become a professional, or attend club meetings and speak in public (or, heaven forbid, vote) were still quite clear cut. Her pompous Uncle William Bull Pringle admonished Frost to avoid becoming "a real estate man" and to be content like other Victorian ladies who "fill their natural mission in life."[34]

Nevertheless, forces in a modern industrialized and urbanized society served to solicit the activism of the new woman. The new woman was aided by the residue of an old ideology, often referred to as the "cult of true womanhood," which gave women first claim to rightness and monitoring of the culture as well as legitimized single-sex association. Women notably demonstrated their ability to organize social movements and to effect political change by operating in the public sphere in two major nineteenth-century crusades—abolition and temperance.[35] Women also evidenced considerable talent for public service during the Civil War in the ranks of the Sanitary Commission, in the hospitals of the North and South, and as "government girls." By the dawn of a new century, ever increasing social problems impacting on the home, children, health, and sanitation generated a need for women to be "social housekeepers." Home and community thus became inextricably bound together.

Women were everywhere on the Progressive Era landscape, and the involvement of women in progressive reform marks the high-water point of women's engagement in American politics.[36] In the South women's clubs became major tools for social change, with many such groups possessing the fervor and commitment of the Waco, Texas, Woman's Club whose motto was "If we rest, we rust."[37] Susan Frost was part of a remarkable group of Charleston women, including the Poppenheim and Pollitzer sisters, Clelia McGowan, Mary Vardrine McBee, and Mrs. Julius Visanka, who through activism in politics and such local groups as the Federation of Women's Clubs and the Civic Club left an indelible positive imprint on Charleston education, public health, city beautification, child welfare, and other social issues vital to the Progressive reform movement.[38] In the course of dealing with society's problems, women began to focus more intently on their own condition, especially as they fought to get the one reform deemed essential to the success of municipal housekeeping—woman suffrage.

Both the Progressive movement and the women's movement of the early twentieth century embodied ironies and paradoxes, however, and Frost's career embraces some of those same complexities. Turn-of-the-century feminism struggled with recognizing both sexual equality and sexual difference, individual freedom and sex solidarity, gender consciousness and the elimination of gender roles. Most new women of the Progressive Era possessed an ideology that centered more around female distinctiveness than sexual equality, and by the 1890s this was the thrust of the suffrage movement as well.[39] The middle class makeup of the suffrage movement ensured that, in no small way, it would be a crusade to perpetuate the influence, ideas, and distinctive character of its constituency. Suffragists of the lineage of a Susan Frost were not so much concerned about a genuinely pluralistic society as they were about generating social and feminist change and, as educated and professional women, having a substantial say in the process. Indeed, most Progressive Era reformers did not seek to bring about radical societal change; rather they tried to get control of changes that were already taking place in American life.[40] In the South this ensured that the race issue would be at the heart of the suffrage question. The new women of the New South, then, were concerned about trying to be both traditional and pathbreaking, about being true both to the white South's conservatism and to progressive ideals. As such, they looked both forward and backward. Their strategies for change, however, came more from the top down than from the grassroots up and often smacked of a middle-class value system.[41]

Frost's historic preservation career, like her feminism, was quite distinctive, with many of her preservation concepts well ahead of the day when they would be fully tested and in great favor. She pioneered as one of the earliest women licensed by the state of South Carolina to sell property, and hers was among the initial private restoration programs by real estate agents in the United States. Frost's one-woman crusade to eradicate the blight and revitalize Charleston's lower east side was unique and courageous. Her commitment to restoring entire neighborhoods of old houses as part of a functioning community was more sweeping than the innovative preservation work of noted New Englander William Sumner Appleton,[42] and foreshadowed architectural controls and historic district zoning, approaches widely adopted only after World War II, as a means of preserving the unique character of urban centers. Locally, Frost opened the eyes of Charleston's city fathers to the benefits of legal ordinances for restoration purposes in her "save the iron" campaign in the 1920s. In addition the concept of neighborhood restoration that she planted was later successfully implemented by the Historic Charleston Foundation in its revolving fund program.

Frost's preservation endeavors are marked by paradox, however, and she herself was often a bundle of contradictions. Frost was part of an expanding preservation movement nationally, a movement generated by upper-class women with time on their hands who formed such patriotic and historical associations as the Colonial Dames and the Association for the Preservation of Virginia Antiquities to preserve their own culture in the face of the challenges presented by immigration and modernization. Although Frost's historic preservation initiatives helped set in motion a campaign that brought new life to the streets of lower Charleston and ultimately economic vitality to the entire city, they also brought displacement to a group of residents—especially African Americans—who had known no other home than the alleys and backyards of the lowcountry peninsula. That process continued after World War II as the historic district kept expanding and the Historic Charleston Foundation reclaimed neighborhoods north of Broad Street.

Although few of the neighborhoods of the lower east side would likely have been left to save without the heroics of Charleston's unorthodox female realtor, by the time of the critical preservation fights in the 1920s, 1930s, and 1940s, Frost was no longer an active element in the battle. Although she was a preservation cheer leader and zoning ordinance watchdog between the two world wars, leadership had passed to others of the lowcountry's renowned cadre of preservationists, especially Alston Deas, Robert Whitelaw, Milby Burton, and Frances Edmunds, who were much more adept at day-to-day planning and execution of detail. Frost was, in no small way, imprisoned by her own financial mismanagement and overextension by the time there were enough leaders and followers to implement her grand vision. Despite her crusade to save the whole of the Charleston's townscape, most of the energies and minuscule resources of the Society for the Preservation of Old Dwellings in its fledgling years were spent in holding on to two highly significant historic structures—the Joseph Manigault and Heyward-Washington Houses. The SPOD kept its focus narrow, and its potential was limited.

Utilizing the same array of modern transportation and communication means that many Progressive Era reformers relied on to spread the word and mold favorable public opinion, including the automobile, telephone, typewriter, a business office, and the growing market for newspapers and magazines, Frost persevered in her crusades to bring about change. Her simplistic but deeply rooted religious faith left her confident that, no matter what the hardship, "With the help of God I will leap over the wall." The example of Alice Paul, courageous and undaunted in times of hardship, also inspired and comforted her, and like Paul, Susan Frost rarely took "no" for an answer. After the 1938 hurricane that struck the lowcountry, Frost wrote to John D. Rockefeller, Jr., requesting a thousand dollars to repair damage to the Miles Brewton House. Undismayed by his response that commitments to Williamsburg precluded such assistance, she wrote again a short time later asking for two thousand.[43] In her lively description of Southern women, writer Sharon McKern might well have had Charleston's unique "Miss Sue" in mind when she wrote: "The southern woman is resilient, courageous, emotional, charismatic, adaptable, energetic, given to wild flashes of insight and to mercurial moods as well as bold histrionic flourishes. . . . Her greatest charm comes from her idiosyncratically wayward ways—her freewheeling independence, her irreverent candor, her *yahoo* readiness to thumb her nose at convention—and her unparalleled penchant for survival."[44] Never one for understatement, Susan Frost would have agreed she was all of the above.

Susan Pringle Frost was caught between two generations and between two impulses: patrician and social agitator. She was both a modern woman of the New South and a carryover from another era. Although she grew up in a South that told its womenfolk that only work in the domestic sphere was acceptable, this daughter of impeccable lineage also came of age in a world undergoing significant change. At the same time that she remained true to two key tenets of the cult of the Southern lady, piousness and purity, Frost made a mockery of the submissiveness and domesticity components.

Paradoxically, then, Susan Pringle Frost earned her greatest fame in preserving the visible remainders of a culture that afforded women little opportunity for self-development and accomplishment, while acting in a totally unconventional fashion as an activist in the public sphere long denied women in the South. Few American cities have been so positively affected by such unorthodox behavior. No marker attesting to the overall preservation accomplishments of Frost exists amidst the extraordinary network of eighteenth- and nineteenth-century architecture of lower Charleston, and perhaps none is needed. After all, like the renowned English architect, Sir Christopher Wren, her monuments are all around her.

NOTES

INTRODUCTION

1. Nancy Woloch, *Women and the American Experience* (New York: Alfred A Knopf, 1984), 224.

2. Anne Firor Scott's pioneer works provide in-depth analysis of the culturally defined image of the lady and the actual realities of women's lives. See particularly her article "The 'New Woman' in the New South," *South Atlantic Quarterly* 61 (Autumn 1962): 417–83, and *The Southern Lady: From Pedestal to Politics 1830–1930* (Chicago: Univ. of Chicago Press, 1970).

3. An insightful essay by Anne Goodwyn Jones on the origins and historical function of the concept of Southern womanhood and its evolution can be found in *Encyclopedia of Southern Culture,* ed. Charles Reagan Wilson and William Ferris (Chapel Hill: Univ. of North Carolina Press, 1989), 1527–30.

4. Frank R. Frost, "Some Memories or Last Summer's Clouds," 1922, Frost Family Papers, South Carolina Historical Society (hereafter cited to as SCHS), Charleston, South Carolina.

5. Susan Pringle Frost, "Jottings: Memories of My Father—A Tribute," May 26, 1948. I am greatly indebted to Richard N. Côté of Mount Pleasant, South Carolina, for furnishing me a copy of this document. "Jottings" can be found in the Alston/Pringle/Frost Papers, SCHS.

6. Frances R. Grimball, "Miss Frost Restores Houses, Fights for Women's Rights," *Charleston News and Courier* (hereafter cited as *NC*), February 1, 1946.

7. Letter, F. L. Frost to Mr. Pringle, June 15, 1871, as contained in Mary Pringle Frost, *The Miles Brewton House: Chronicles and Reminiscences* (Charleston: Walker and Evans, 1939), 142–43.

8. Ibid.

9. Francis LeJau Frost graduated with distinction from the Medical College of South Carolina in 1859.

10. George C. Rogers, Jr., *The History of Georgetown County, South Carolina* (Columbia: Univ. of South Carolina Press, 1970), chronicles the death of this industry that produced wealth and fame for the state. Patience Pennington [Mrs. Elizabeth W. Allston Pringle], *A Woman Rice Planter* (Cambridge, Mass., 1961), offers a loving tribute and recounts her own heroic endeavors to save the dying rice industry. Lawrence S. Rowland, "'Alone on the River': The Rise and Fall of the Savannah River Rice Plantations of St. Peter's Parish, South Carolina," *South Carolina Historical Magazine* 88, no. 3 (July 1987): 121–50, offers a look at the heretofore largely neglected tidal-culture rice plantations of the lower Savannah River in the extreme southwest corner of South Carolina. For the personal frustrations of Frank Frost and postwar rice planting/harvesting, see the Rebecca Frost letters, *The Miles Brewton House,* and Richard N. Côté, *Rice and Ruin: The William Bull Pringles and the Death of the South Carolina Rice Culture, 1822–1884* (forthcoming).

11. Susan Pringle Frost, "Jottings," recalled inconveniences for the family resulting from her father's frequent attendance of slaves who were ill. See also Rebecca Pringle Frost, letter to her sister Susan, June 1869, *The Miles Brewton House,* 136.

12. Susan Pringle Frost, "Jottings."

13. Several persons furnished valuable information in helping me develop a reasonably complete family tree for the ancestry of Susan Pringle Frost, including Margaretta Childs, Mrs. W. T. Hart, Alston Deas, and Mrs. Edward Manigault. I am particularly indebted to M. Jennie McGuire for her assistance in constructing family lines on the Frost side. The Reverend Thomas Frost was the great-grandfather of Frank R. Frost, and "Some Memories" contains valuable ancestral history. See also Mary Frost, *The Miles Brewton House.* The Reverend Francis LeJau's missionary career can be found in Michael J. Heitzler, *Historic Goose Creek, South Carolina, 1670–1980* (Easley, S.C.: Southern Historical Press, 1983).

14. For a complete Pringle family history, see the *South Carolina Historical Magazine* 22:25–33; 16:21–30, 93–112; 50:91–100, 144–55. See also Mary Pringle Fenhagen, "Descendants of Judge Robert Pringle," 62 no. 3 (July 1961): 151–64; 62, no. 4 (October 1961): 221–36.

15. The early immediate descendants of Miles Brewton and their endeavors can be found in A. S. Salley, Jr., "Col. Miles Brewton and Some of His Descendants," *South Carolina Historical and Genealogical Magazine* 2 (April 1901): 128–43, and Côté, *Rice and Ruin.*

16. An historic sketch of Rebecca Motte can be found in the Daughters of the American Revolution Chapter Book, 1929–1932, Eola Willis Papers, SCHS. The Charleston Chapter of the DAR was named for Motte.

17. M. Jennie McGuire, "Elizabeth Frost of Antebellum Charleston, South Carolina," June 1988, paper in possession of author.

18. See series of late 1908–early 1909 letters of Susan Frost to Mrs. J. J. Pringle, Alston/Pringle/Hill Papers, SCHS.

19. Pioneering works by, among others, Margaret Hagood and Rupert Vance, pointed to the unique nature and power of the family in the social networks of the region. More recently, social historian Carl Degler, *Place over Time: The Continuity of Southern Distinctiveness* (Baton Rouge: Louisiana State Univ. Press, 1977), maintained that "roots, place, family and tradition are the essence of identity" in the South, with its unique appeal in part stemming from "the human warmth and security of its commitment to family and kin." Brief scholarly essays and current bibliography on such topics as "Family," "Community," and "Sense of Place" in Wilson and Ferris, *Encyclopedia of Southern History,* offer additional background on the images and realities of Southern distinctiveness and the role of family in Southern existence.

20. Jean Friedman, *The Enclosed Garden: Women and Community in the Evangelical South, 1830–1900* (Chapel Hill: Univ. of North Carolina Press, 1985), argued that kin networks and the rural church and its discipline went a long way toward preserving traditional roles for women after the Civil War, thus delaying feminist reform in the region until the late nineteenth century. Friedman contended that in both the temperance and woman suffrage movements, membership came from neighborhood kinship groups whose motivation was to preserve community values. I am indebted to Jean Friedman for a copy of her paper, "Piety and Kin: The Limits of Antebellum Southern Women's Reform."

21. Susan Frost, "Jottings."

22. Ibid.

23. Mary Frost, *The Miles Brewton House,* 78.

24. Orville Vernon Burton, author of *In My Father's House Are Many Mansions: Family and Community in Edgefield, South Carolina* (Chapel Hill: Univ. of North Carolina Press, 1985), contributed insightful essays on "Fatherhood" and "Motherhood" to Wilson and Ferris, *Encyclopedia of Southern Culture.*

25. The parents of Susan Pringle Frost believed they should teach the great truths of the Christian faith to their children because Sunday School was intended for parents whose children did not have the same advantages as the more fortunate in society. See Frost, "Jottings."

26. Ibid.

27. "Jottings" contains limited details on the Susan Frost's years at the Murden/Sass private school on Legare Street.

28. Prominent planter and cotton factor, later a noted executive in the Charleston fertilizer business, Theodore D. Jervey, *The Elder-Brother* (New York: Neale Publishing Co., 1905), 34, recalled in his autobiographical novel about post–Civil War "Ellenton" that dips at the bathing house, a "hideous, ramshackle structure which was an eyesore to any one whose aesthetic sense of the beautiful was at all developed" and which was always crowded, "entailed an expenditure out of all proportion to the pleasure gained," and he found jumping from the rafts "far more satisfactory and decidedly more attractive."

29. Susan Frost, "Jottings."

30. For the role of Charlestonians in the settlement and long-term development of Flat Rock, North Carolina, see Sadie Smathers Patton, *A Condensed History of Flat Rock: The Little Charleston of the Mountains* (Asheville: Church Printing Co., n.d.). By the early 1830s, lowcountry planter Charles Baring and Charleston lawyer and judge Mitchell King owned thousands of acres of land stretching from the center of Flat Rock to near where the town of Hendersonville would be located. Edward Read Memminger, son of the secretary of the treasury for the Confederate States, wrote his own history of the community, *An Historical Sketch of Flat Rock* (privately published by his daughter, original in hands of The South Caroliniana Library, University of South Carolina, Columbia). Frank R. Frost, "Some Memories," offers recollections of vacations spent in Catawba Springs, Morganton, and Hendersonville.

31. Susan Frost, "Jottings."

32. Ibid.

33. See Catherine Clinton's overview of the myths and realities of maiden aunts in Southern history in Wilson and Ferris, *Encyclopedia of Southern History,* 1553–54.

34. Mary Frost, *The Miles Brewton House,* 75–82; letter, Susan Pringle Frost to Nina Pringle, October 1, 1917, Pringle Family Papers, Bancroft Library, University of California, Berkeley (hereafter cited as Pringle Papers).

35. Mary Frost, *The Miles Brewton House,* 76.

36. Ibid., 16–20, 75–78. Susan Frost, *Highlights of the Miles Brewton House* (Charleston: Susan Pringle Frost, 1944), 45, indicates that her aunt Susan derived "much pleasure" from being able to help meet tax obligations with proceeds from her flower sales and that she occasionally bought additional pieces of furniture for the Pringle House as well. Letters, Susan Frost to Nina Pringle, January 18, 1921; May 24, 1921; and July 21, 1921, Pringle Papers, trace events leading to the opening of the Charleston Flo-

ral Company, a joint enterprise of Miss Frost with an Englishman, Robert Millican. Reflecting something of the shaping influence of her Aunt Susan Pringle, Susan Frost confessed to her favorite cousin, July 21, 1921: "I have always wanted to go into the florist business." A cousin, Margaretta Childs, remembered Susan Frost as an "energetic gardener" who regularly rose at six, donned her bloomers, and toiled for an hour in the formal gardens behind the 27 King Street mansion. Data furnished by Mrs. Childs to author, May 20, 1981.

37. Susan Frost, *Highlights*, 56–57, maintained that Theodosia Burr Alston "no doubt often stayed" at the Miles Brewton House, inasmuch as her married life was spent on one of the Alston plantations near Georgetown, South Carolina. On the presumed death at sea of Theodosia Burr Alston and the reputed "Nag's Head portrait" of her that later surfaced, see Côté, *Rice and Ruin*, 43–47.

38. Letter, Margaretta Childs to author, May 20, 1981.

39. Frank R. Frost, "Some Memories," 41.

40. Jervey, *The Elder-Brother*, 390.

41. Walter Fraser, *Charleston! Charleston!: The History of a Southern City* (Columbia: Univ. of South Carolina Press, 1989), 310.

42. Ibid., 303.

43. The politics of race ultimately brought U.S. troops to Charleston in September 1876, with several blacks and whites killed in outbreaks of violence surrounding Wade Hampton's election. See Fraser, *Charleston!* 298–300. For details of Frank Dawson's career, murder, and the ensuing trial, see Fraser, 298, 319–22.

44. Frank R. Frost, "Some Memories," 35.

45. William Courtenay's reputation resulted from the rehabilitation of Charleston after the devastating earthquake of 1886. Courtenay's achievements are addressed in Fraser, *Charleston!* 303–19, and in "William A. Courtenay Ranks with City's Greatest Mayors," *NC*, December 15, 1952. In a letter to the *NC*, June 30, 1940, Susan Frost, in defending the controversial John Grace as one of the best administrators Charleston ever had, acknowledged but a hazy recollection of all the good Mayor Courtenay had accomplished for Charleston.

46. E. Merton Coulter, *George Walton Williams: The Life of a Southern Merchant and Banker, 1820–1903* (Athens, Ga.: Hebriten Press, 1976), 250. Williams was a businessman instrumental in the revitalization of Charleston after the earthquake of 1886. When Grover Cleveland was married in the White House two years after his first election, Williams was one of a group of Charlestonians who sent the new First Lady a wedding present of a large solid silver vase with gold interior lining. Frank Dawson of the *News and Courier* observed, on Cleveland's retirement from office in 1889, that "no place in the United States would welcome him more cordially than Charleston." Many actually thought the outgoing president might retire there.

47. Coulter, *Williams*; Susan Frost, "Jottings."

48. Robert Rosen, *A Short History of Charleston* (San Francisco: Lexikos, 1982), 113; John Joseph Duffy, "Charleston Politics in the Progressive Era" (Ph.D. diss., Univ. of South Carolina, 1963), 14; Fraser, *Charleston!* 339, observed that in Ward 3, one of Charleston's most prestigious, there were 917 blacks and 1,512 whites at the turn of the century, while in Ward 11, the ratio was reversed, with 2,591 whites among 5,921 blacks.

49. Fraser, *Charleston!* 290.

50. By 1880, the insane of both races were strictly segregated at Charleston's Roper

Hospital, and the complexion of local politics changed, with the black leaders of the Reconstruction era being replaced by whites. The Courtenay regime's budget cuts in the early 1880s impacted much more significantly on blacks than on whites. Fraser, *Charleston!* 307–8.

51. Mamie Garvin Fields (with Karen Fields), *Lemon Swamp and Other Places: A Carolina Memoir* (New York: Free Press, 1983), 45–48.

52. Ibid., 52–57; see also Jervey, *The Elder-Brother,* 68, and Fraser, *Charleston!* 284.

53. Susan Frost, "Jottings."

54. Susan Frost, *Highlights,* 60–67. The children in a series of photographs of were identified as "descendants of the family servants who have served the household for seven generations."

55. For an incisive look at the role of such antebellum institutions and the experiences of some of the young ladies who attended them, see Steven M. Stowe, "The Not-So-Cloistered Academy: Elite Women's Education and Family Feeling in the Old South," in *The Web of Southern Social Relations,* ed. Walter F. Fraser, Jr., R. Frank Saunders, Jr., and Jon L. Wakelyn (Athens: Univ. of Georgia Press, 1985). Charleston regularly dispatched her finest daughters to Saint Mary's, and Susan Frost was preceded at the school by her sister Mary. For a history of the institution itself see Katherine Batts Salley, ed., *Life at Saint Mary's* (Chapel Hill: Univ. of North Carolina Press, 1942), especially 88–89. I am indebted to former Saint Mary's president, John T. Rice, for furnishing information about the tenures of Mary and Susan Frost.

56. Salley, *Life at Saint Mary's,* Stowe, "Not-So-Cloistered Academy." In the letters of the young women he studied, Stowe found clear evidence of independence of mind and a dominant theme that emphasized neither family obligation nor intellectual inclination but "contentment and delight with sisterhood" (96).

57. Susan Frost, "Jottings."

58. Thomas R. Waring, Jr., "The Grand Old City of the South," *New York Herald Tribune,* April 6, 1930, 14–15, 22. Waring offers an insider's look at what is largely a private and generally unpublicized event that socially defines "the elect and the elite" of Charleston. See also Frost, "Jottings."

59. Fraser, *Charleston!* 326–27, indicates that property damage to Charleston from the violent storm reached $1,160,000. An estimated two thousand African Americans drowned when a huge wave swept over the islands from Hilton Head to John's Island.

60. Tom W. Shick and Don H. Doyle, "The South Carolina Phosphate Boom and the Stillbirth of the New South, 1867–1920," *South Carolina Historical Magazine* 86 (January–October 1985): 1–31, convincingly argue that the surviving lowcountry planter class and its urban allies, the cotton factors and merchants, could indeed effectively respond to new opportunities for economic development, but the boom was promoted less for enthusiasm for the Henry Grady–type vision of industrial progress than out of "desperation to escape, or stave off, the decline of a shattered economy."

61. Shick and Doyle, "The South Carolina Phosphate Boom," 11, 24, 26. By 1888, Charleston fertilizer supplied approximately one-fifth of the total domestic market in the United States. The Ashley Phosphate Company was capitalized in 1881 with investments totaling $100,000, and in 1883 it was one of the ten most successful fertilizer companies in Charleston County. By 1910 nearly 60 percent of U.S. fertilizers were consumed in the South Atlantic states.

62. Fraser, *Charleston!* 326–27.

63. Susan Frost, "Jottings."

64. Letter, Susan Frost to Ernest Pringle, Jr., December 2, 1931, Joseph Manigault House papers, SCHS.

65. Grimball, "Miss Frost Restores Houses."

CHAPTER 1: "WHILE THE PEBBLE HAS BEEN DROPPED . . ."

1. Scrapbooks, 121, Hemphill Family Papers, Manuscript Department, Perkins Library, Duke University, Durham, North Carolina. James Calvin Hemphill was on the Board of Directors of the South Carolina Interstate and West Indian Exposition and was manager of promotion and publicity. Six large scrapbooks in this collection contain clippings reporting on the progress and organization of the exhibition.

Numerous periodical articles touted Charleston's hopes for economic revitalization and proclaimed all the marvels of the South Carolina Interstate and West Indian Exposition of 1901–1902. See, for example, T. Cuyler Smith, "The Charleston Exposition," *Independent* 54 (January 16, 1902), 142–51; James B. Townsend, "A Great Southern Exposition," *Cosmopolitan* (March 1902): 523–34; George Kennan, "The Charleston Exposition," *Outlook* 70 (March 22, 1902): 713–718; "Charleston and Her 'West Indian Exposition,'" *Atlantic Monthly Review of Reviews* (June 1902): 58–61; Lillian Betts, "Sunny Days at the Exposition," *Outlook* 71 (May 10, 1902): 120–24; "The Charleston Exposition," *Scientific American Supplement* 53 (April 12, 1902): 21996; 46 (February 22, 1902): 21886. A more recent account, written for popular consumption and containing photographs from the fair, is Jamie W. Moore, "The Great South Carolina Inter-State and West Indian Exposition of 1901," *Sandlapper* (July 1978):11–15.

2. *Exposition,* 503. A complete set of the *Exposition,* the official organ of the South Carolina Interstate and West Indian Exposition, can be found in the Eola Willis Papers, SCHS.

3. *NC,* December 9, 1949. This lengthy late-in-life letter to the newspaper offers the most complete account of Frost's work as private secretary to Bradford Gilbert.

4. Ibid.

5. Scrapbooks, 18, Hemphill Papers.

6. Ibid.

7. Separate institution building and the resultant benefits for U.S. feminism are developed by Estelle Freedman in her seminal article, "Separatism as Strategy: Female Institution Building and American Feminism, 1870–1930," *Feminist Studies* 5 (Fall 1979): 512–29. See also Virginia Grant Darney, "Women and World's Fairs: American International Expositions, 1876–1904" (Ph.D. diss., Emory Univ., 1982).

8. Anne Firor Scott, *The Southern Lady,* 157–58. William Stephenson, *Sallie Southall Cotton, a Woman's Life in North Carolina* (Greenville, N.C.: Pamlico, 1987), is a brief biography of this significant Southern clubwoman.

9. *NC,* May 23, 1902.

10. *NC,* February 6, 1902; *Worcester (Mass.) Post,* October 2, 1903. The latter is one of several news clippings contained in the Miss Henrietta A. Kelly file, SCHS, that focus on the possibility of resurrecting the silk culture in the state. In the same file, note "Silk Culture Is Woman's Work," *Charleston Evening Post,* n.d. See also the *Exposition,* 146, 237, 275, 283 and 465; Willis Papers, SCHS; and *NC,* February 1, 1902, and March 17, 1902.

11. *Yearbook, City of Charleston,* of 1902, 31–32.

12. Frances R. Grimball, "Miss Frost Restores Houses, Fights for Women's Rights," *NC,* February 1, 1969; *NC,* October 8, 1960; Charlotte Walker, "Crusade," *Charleston Evening Post,* March 14, 1952.

13. Letter, Thomas R. Waring, Jr., to author, September 16, 1980.

14. An interview with Mrs. Edward Manigault, Charleston, South Carolina, June 22, 1983, revealed that Henry Augustus Middleton Smith was a cousin of Susan Frost. William Brawley's second wife was Mildred Frost, whom he married in 1907 after the death of his first wife.

15. Letter, Susan Frost to Elsie Hill, June 30, 1915, Reel 17, National Woman's Party Papers, Library of Congress, Washington, D.C. (hereafter cited to as NWP Papers, LC).

16. Letter, Susan Frost to "My Dear Cousin Bessie," November 4, 1908, Allston/Pringle/Hill Papers, SCHS. After her husband's death, Elizabeth Allston Pringle managed Chicora Wood plantation from 1879 to 1918. In the years immediately preceding Susan Frost's visit, Pringle had published excerpts from her diary in the New York *Sun* under the name "Patience Pennington." *Chronicles of Chicora Wood,* published posthumously in 1922, offered valuable descriptions of the intricate workings of a rice plantation.

17. *Yearbook* of 1904, 7–13.

18. Letter, Susan Frost to Elizabeth Waties Allston Pringle, February 5, 1909, Allston/Pringle/Hill Papers, SCHS.

19. Letter, Susan Frost to Lucy Burns, July 9, 1915, Reel 17, NWP Papers, LC.

20. "Historical Society Honors a Leader," *NC,* August 5, 1957. South Carolina Historical Society 1988 publication notice, in conjunction with the Reprint Company, Publishers, of three volumes of historical writings of Judge Smith: *The Baronies of South Carolina* (reprinted from a book of that title published shortly after the author's death in 1924), *Cities and Towns of Early South Carolina* and *Rivers and Regions of Early South Carolina.*

21. Interview with Mrs. Edward Manigault, July 14, 1981.

22. Letter, Susan Frost to Hon. T. T. Hyde, December 6, 1916, Hyde Papers, Charleston City Archives (hereafter cited to as CCA), Charleston, South Carolina.

23. Interview with Mrs. Edward Manigault, June 22, 1983.

24. Letter, Frost to Hyde, December 6, 1916, Hyde Papers, CCA; *NC,* June 30, 1940.

25. Letter, Susan Frost to Editor, *NC,* August 12, 1952. Frost's objection was a religious one: "only God can give life and only God should take it."

26. Conclusions reached from author interviews with Mrs. Edward Manigault, July 14, 1981; March 10, 1982; June 22, 1983. Rebecca Frost was godmother to a prostitute, Annie Gordon, who worked in Florence, Sumter, Charleston, and Augusta between 1914 and 1917. A collection of Annie Gordon's letters can be found in the Alston/Pringle/Frost Papers, SCHS. I am indebted to Richard Côté for this reference.

27. Doyle W. Boggs, "John Patrick Grace and the Politics of Reform in South Carolina, 1900–1931" (Ph.D. diss., Univ. of South Carolina, 1977), 48, 184.

28. John J. Duffy, "Charleston Politics in the Progressive Era" (Ph.D. diss., Univ. of South Carolina, 1963), 53.

29. Ibid., 53–54; Charleston *Yearbook* of 1905.

30. *Yearbook* of 1905.

31. Letter, Susan Frost to Elizabeth Waties Allston Pringle, 1908, Allston/Pringle/Hill Papers, SCHS.

32. Letters, Susan Frost to T. T. Hyde, January 4, 1916; March 3, 1916; August 8, 1916; December 6, 1916; Hyde to Frost August 9, 1916; December 7, 1916, Hyde Papers, CCA.

33. Duffy, "Charleston Politics," 206.

34. *NC,* June 26, 1940.

35. Comments from Margaretta Childs to author, May 20, 1981. I am indebted to Mrs. Childs for making me aware of the Grace letter and for responding to numerous other inquiries about her legendary cousin "Sue." In the June 30, 1940, letter to the *NC,* Frost praised Mayor Grace for "looking after the lowly as well as the well-to-do."

36. Letter, Susan Frost to *NC,* June 30, 1940.

37. Ibid.

38. Boggs, "John P. Grace," 154; Charleston *Yearbook,* 1921, xxviii, xxxiii; Susan Frost, letter to the editor, *Charleston Evening Post,* November 4, 1921; *NC,* June 30, 1940.

39. Letter, Susan Frost to Nina (Cornelia Covington) Pringle, January 22, 1912, Pringle Papers. Beginning in 1909, Frost wrote the first of over three hundred letters to her cousin who was two years younger. The relationship was an especially close one, and Susan Frost often revealed her innermost feelings about matters professional and personal to her West Coast relative. Nina's father, Edward J. Pringle, was a son of William Bull and Mary Motte (Alston) Pringle and left Charleston in 1853 to practice law in San Francisco.

40. "I had another effusion fr. my juror the other day," Frost wrote to Nina Pringle, September 16, 1912, Pringle Papers; "he sends them at long intervals; the first was seven years ago; then another two years after that, and this last just recent." The earliest of the Susan Frost letters to her cousin, written July 25, 1909, has Frost begging, "please don't follow Hess' example and get married and leave me, and don't get old, for there is so much that I wish you to do with me, and husbands and old age spoil all the fun." Again to Nina, December 4, 1911, "I am a coward about getting old, I dread it so much." In a letter, May 18, 1911, Susan Frost admitted to her California relative a growing sensitivity about her increased weight: "I have heard so much about how fat I am; everyone that meets me starts a block off to exclaim on my size, so that I feel as if I must look like a house on legs."

41. Letter, Susan Frost to Nina Pringle, December 4, 1911, Pringle Papers.

42. Ibid., February 22, 1912, Pringle Papers.

43. Letter, Susan Frost to Mrs. M. T. Coleman, July 15, 1915, Reel 33, NWP Papers, LC.

44. Letter, Susan Frost to Nina Pringle, December 4, 1911, Pringle Papers.

45. Ibid., March 26, 1913, Pringle Papers.

46. Susan P. Frost, "Woman Secure in Business World," included with letter of Frost to Nina Pringle, August 1, 1916, Pringle Papers.

47. Letter, Susan Frost to Nina Pringle, July 7, 1916, Pringle Papers; Frances R. Grimball, "Old Charleston Lives Again in Houses Rescued by Miss Sue," *Independent Woman* 25 (October 1946): 300. Frost regarded the Business and Professional Women's Club as one of the finest organizations in Charleston.

48. Letter, Susan Frost to Nina Pringle, January 13, 1916, Pringle Papers. Though acknowledging that she never took "any part or stock in those things, and always wondered how others could do so" and that she did not intend to do any soliciting or work to win the Buick automobile being offered as first prize, Frost was clearly pleased with the 12,140 votes she garnered.

49. Marjorie Mendenhall, "Southern Women of a 'Lost Generation,'" *South Atlantic Quarterly* 33 (October 1934): 350.

50. Anne Firor Scott, "The 'New Woman' in the New South," 481. Scott's scholarship is the starting point for insights into Southern clubwomen. See her chapter "The Lord Helps Those" in *The Southern Lady*, 134–64. A recent up-to-date synthesis of major scholarly work on this topic and nearly every aspect of Southern women and their history can be found in Anne Firor Scott and Jacquelyn Dowd Hall, "Women in the South," in *Interpreting Southern History: Historiographical Essays in Honor of Sanford W. Higginbotham*, ed. John B. Boles and Evelyn Thomas Nolen (Baton Rouge: LSU Press, 1987), 454–509. For other data on Southern women's organizations, the author is indebted to Martha H. Swain for a copy of her paper, "Organized Southern Women as a Force in the Community," presented at the Symposium on Women in Southern Society, University of Richmond, 1984. Margaret Ripley Wolfe, "Feminizing Dixie: Toward a Public Role for Women in the American South," in *Research in Social Policy: Historical and Contemporary Perspectives,* ed. John H. Stanfield II (Greenwich, Conn.: Jai Press, 1987), 190–94, contains observations on what she labels the first generation of Southern feminists. For a contemporary account of women's club activism, see Mrs. A. O. Granger, "The Effect of Club Work in the South," *Annals of the American Academy of Political and Social Science* 28, no. 2 (1906): 248–56. For broader perspectives on clubwomen as a force in the national community, see Karen Blair, *The Clubwoman as Feminist: True Womanhood Redefined, 1868–1914* (New York: Holmes and Meier Publishers, 1980).

51. Darney, "Women and World's Fairs," 145, 148.

52. *NC*, December 3, 1901; February 3, 1902; *Exposition,* 284, 565.

53. *Exposition,* 565.

54. Papers of Louisa and Mary B. Poppenheim are located at the Perkins Library, Duke University, and reveal much family history. Files of the Civic Club, SCHS, contain that group's minutes and artifacts as well as much useful information on the City Federation of Women's Clubs. Clipping files on Mary B. and Louisa B. Poppenheim were secured from SCHS. See also Barbara J. Ellison, "Louisa Poppenheim: 'Citizen of Charleston,'" *NC*, July 12, 1964. Microfilm copies of the *Keystone* are available through Greenwood Press, *Perspectives on Women and Women's Rights,* Series II. For information on the earliest membership in the Federation's Hall of Fame, see *NC*, October 21, 1959. Louisa Poppenheim helped organize state women's club federations in North Carolina and Virginia and served as president of the South Carolina Federation of Women's Clubs and as honorary vice-president of the General (National) Federation. Other aspects of her club involvement are highlighted in the *South Carolina Clubwoman* 4, no. 3 (March 1948). Mary Poppenheim had a long record of service to the United Daughters of the Confederacy, holding the position of president general from 1917 to 1919. She was the author of *Heroes in Grey* and an editor of *South Carolina Women in the Confederacy,* and she was one of the first three women elected to membership in the South Carolina Historical Society.

55. Ruth Ensel Rubin, "Pioneer Charleston Civic Club to Disband: Organized in 1900," *NC*, April 24, 1955; *Yearbook,* The Civic Club of Charleston, 1910–1911, 1941, Civic Club papers, SCHS.

56. The Charleston City Federation of Women's Clubs, 1899–1924, Civic Club of Charleston papers, SCHS, 8, 12–15, 17, 20–23; Ellison, "Louisa Poppenheim." Federation members regularly pressured the mayor, city council, jailor, and chief of police to add

police matrons, and a club member once pretended to collapse inside the walls of the jail to dramatize the issue.

57. Mayor R. G. Rhett appointed five members of the Civic Club to the Playground Commission in 1911, and by the early 1920s the club had members on the City Park Board and the Charleston Home Board as well. Both the salaried director and the voluntary chairperson of the Juvenile Welfare Commission were women during the Grace years.

58. On Carrie Pollitzer and the admission of women to the College of Charleston, see J. H. Easterby, *A History of the College of Charleston* (New York: Scribners, 1935), 189–92; Hartley Hall, "Liberation Pioneer Led College Coed Movement," *NC,* March 14, 1970; and obituary notices in *NC* and *Evening Post,* October 25, 1974. On Mabel Pollitzer and the City Betterment Committee, see minutes, City Betterment Committee of the Civic Club of Charleston, 1913–1917, Mabel Pollitzer Papers, SCHS; Anita Pollitzer's role in the woman suffrage and Equal Rights Amendment crusades can be seen in the National Woman's Party Papers, LC, and through the NWP publication *Equal Rights* (Washington: National Woman's Party, 1923-present). She headed the NWP in the late 1940s. See also "Anita Pollitzer, Suffragist, Dies," *New York Times,* July 5, 1975. Clipping files on the Pollitzers can be found at the SCHS.

59. The Civic Club began with only fifteen members. Christie, Mary, and Louisa Poppenheim were joined by their mother, while "Rebe" and Mary Frost were part of the original group. "Rebe" Frost was an early treasurer. *Yearbook,* the Civic Club of Charleston, SCHS, contain its rosters.

60. Letter, Susan Frost to Nina Pringle, January 22, 1912, Pringle Papers.

61. Minutes, Civic Club, Civic Club papers, SCHS.

62. Fraser, *Charleston!* 371; Charleston *Yearbook* of 1923.

63. Telephone interview with Philip Simmons, June 12, 1983. Simmons, a noted Charleston African-American craftsman, stated that he had heard that Miss Frost "at one time just about owned the Jenkins Orphanage."

64. Minutes, Civic Club, February 26, 1919, Civic Club papers, SCHS.

65. Following its cultural renaissance in the World War I era and the renewed interest in Charleston's architecture and historical past in the 1920s and 1930s, many on the peninsula sought to publicize Charleston through a major festival. For some twenty years, from 1934 until the early 1950s when it fell apart, the Azalea Festival served this role. Various other proposals were debated by civic leaders in the interim before the highly acclaimed arts festival, Spoleto, modeled on the Italian Spoleto Festival, was initiated by Gian Carlo Menotti in 1977.

On May 28, 1919, the Civic Club of Charleston rearranged the order of its meeting to hear a proposal of Miss Maude Gibbon to afford locals the opportunity to hear "the best music by the best artists." Her plan called for a series of twelve concerts, eight to be given by "the foremost musical artists of the world" and four by "the best musical talent of Charleston." All concerts would take place on Sunday afternoons. They would be conducted under the auspices of a club comprised of all Charlestonians who would pay membership fees ranging from $3 to $17, thus guaranteeing their own entry to all performances. Later Civic Club minutes reveal nothing further about Miss Gibbon's plan.

66. Easterby, *History of the College of Charleston,* 191. Private interviews of Constance B. Myers with Carrie and Mabel Pollitzer, Winthrop College Archives, Dacus Library,

Rock Hill, South Carolina, detail the process of raising the necessary funds for admission.

CHAPTER 2: "BY THE GRACE OF GOD . . ."

1. Barbara B. Ulmer, "Virginia Durant Young: New South Suffragist" (M.A. thesis, Univ. of South Carolina, 1979), 40–47, 50–57, 103–5. Although there were fifteen suffrage clubs scattered around the state as late as 1900, few had dues-paying members, and Virginia Young's reluctance to share leadership offset early suffrage strides in the state.

2. The suffragists themselves referred to the years 1896–1910 as "the doldrums." No new woman suffrage states were won, only six referenda were held (none was successful), and the Anthony amendment languished. Still indispensable in the long years of the suffrage drive is Eleanor Flexner, *Century of Struggle: The Woman's Rights Movement in the United States* (Cambridge, Mass.: Belknap Press of Harvard Univ. Press, 1959). Accounts by the National American Woman Suffrage Association of the woman suffrage movement in South Carolina can be found in Elizabeth Cady Stanton et al., eds., *History of Woman Suffrage*, 6 vols. (New York: National American Woman Suffrage Association, 1922), 6:579–84.

3. Anne Firor Scott, "Historians Construct the Southern Woman," in *Sex, Race and the Role of Women in the South,* ed. Joanne V. Hawks and Sheila L Skemp (Jackson: Univ. of Mississippi Press, 1983), 108. The emergence of the "new woman in the New South" can be traced through others of Scott's significant conference papers and journal articles, available under single cover as Anne Firor Scott, *Making the Invisible Woman Visible* (Urbana and Chicago: Univ. of Illinois Press, 1984).

4. A. Elizabeth Taylor, "South Carolina and the Enfranchisement of Women," *South Carolina Historical Magazine* 80, no. 4 (October 1979): 298–99. Professor Taylor, a pioneering scholar in the field of women's history, published numerous articles and one book detailing suffrage activity throughout most of the Southern states. Several of her articles are listed in Scott, "Historians Construct," 256–57. The first president of the New Era Club was the wife of a former governor of South Carolina.

5. Edward T. James, Janet Wilson James, and Paul S. Boyer, eds., *Notable American Women 1607–1950.* 3 vols. (Cambridge, Mass.: Belknap Press of Harvard Univ. Press, 1971), 2:309–10. In her autobiography Kearney referred to the WCTU as the liberator of Southern women.

6. *NC,* February 3, 1902.

7. Stanton et al., *History of Woman Suffrage,* 6:583. The significance of this Virginia activist is evaluated in Lloyd C. Taylor, Jr., "Lila Meade Valentine: The FFV as Reformer," *Virginia Magazine of History and Biography* (October 1962): 471–87.

8. Minutes, Charleston City Federation of Women's Clubs, 1899–1924, SCHS, Charleston, South Carolina.

9. For coverage of British suffrage militancy, Pankhurst tours to the United States, and the exposure of American suffragists to the revitalized movement in England, see Sidney R. Bland, "Techniques of Persuasion: The National Woman's Party and Woman Suffrage, 1912–1920" (Ph.D. diss., George Washington Univ., 1972).

10. Flexner, *Century of Struggle,* 262.

11. Bland, "Techniques of Persuasion"; Flexner, *Century of Struggle,* 256–85.

12. *Charleston Evening Post,* March 1915, article contained in Pringle Papers.

13. *NC,* April 2, 1914. Frost sent a copy of this her first suffrage address to her California cousin. See Frost letter to Nina Pringle, April 3, 1914, Pringle Papers.

14. Letter, Susan Frost to Nina Pringle, February 10, 1915, Pringle Papers.

15. *NC,* October 24, 1915.

16. Letter, Susan Frost to Nina Pringle, May 14, 1915, Pringle Papers.

17. Letter, Frost to Pringle, October 22, 1914, Pringle Papers.

18. Letter, Susan Frost to Nina Pringle, January 15, 1915, Pringle Papers.

19. Florence, South Carolina, newspaper clipping, dated March 3, 1915, Pringle Papers.

20. Clipping accompanying letter, Susan Frost to Nina Pringle, January 16, 1915, Pringle Papers.

21. Minutes, South Carolina Equal Suffrage League (hereafter cited as SCESL), South Caroliniana Library, Columbia, South Carolina.

22. For fuller involvement of Mabel and Carrie Pollitzer on civic and women's issues, see Constance Myers, interview with Mabel Pollitzer, September 5, 1971, Winthrop College Archives, Dacus Library, Rock Hill, South Carolina; Myers, interview with Carrie Pollitzer, September 26, 1973.

23. Minutes, SCESL, May 15, 1914.

24. Letter, Susan Frost to Nina Pringle, May 14, 1915, Pringle Papers.

25. The suffrage histories of the Congressional Union (the National Woman's Party after 1917) have all been written by former members. These include: Doris Stevens, *Jailed for Freedom* (New York: Boni and Liveright, 1920); Inez Haynes Irwin, *Story of the Woman's Party* (New York: Harcourt, 1921); Caroline Katzenstein, *Lifting the Curtain: The State and National Woman Suffrage Campaigns in Pennsylvania As I Saw Them* (Philadelphia: Dorrance and Co., 1955).

26. *NC,* June 28, 1915. For full details of Elsie Hill's trip to Charleston and some of the controversy surrounding the visit of an official whose organization sympathized with the British suffragettes, see Records of the National American Woman Suffrage Association, Box 48, Manuscript Division, Library of Congress, Washington, D.C. (hereafter cited as NAWSA Papers, LC).

27. *NC,* June 28, 1915.

28. Letter, Susan Frost to Mrs. M. T. Coleman, July 15, 1915, NWP Papers, LC; Myers, interview with Carrie Pollitzer, Winthrop Archives.

29. *Suffragist,* July 3, 1915, 3. Letter, Susan Frost to Mrs. Coleman, July 15, 1915, NWP Papers, LC. The deputation was composed of suffragists from Charleston, regardless of whether or not they were members of the ESL, with signatures being identified as "Charleston suffragists and suffrage sympathizers." The *Suffragist* listed some thirty-five Charlestonians as being among the petition signers.

30. Letter, Susan Frost to Mrs. Coleman, July 15, 1915, NWP Papers, LC; letter, Susan Frost to Elsie Hill, June 30, 1915, Reel 17, NWP Papers, LC.

31. Letter, Alice Paul to Susan Frost, July 29, 1915, Box 32, NWP Papers, LC.

32. Letter, Lucy Burns to Susan Frost, July 2, 1915, Box 31, NWP Papers. For an assessment of the generally overlooked role of Lucy Burns in the CU/NWP suffrage struggle, see Sidney R. Bland, "'Never Quite as Committed as We'd Like': The Suffrage Militancy of Lucy Burns," *Journal of Long Island History* 17, no. 2 (summer/fall 1981): 4–24. See also the biographical sketch in Barbara Sicherman and Carol Green, eds., *Notable American Women: The Modern Period* (Cambridge, Mass.: Belknap Press of Harvard Univ. Press, 1980), 124–125.

33. Letter, Susan Frost to Mrs. M. T. Coleman, July 15, 1915, NAWSA Papers, LC.

34. *NC,* June 28, 1915.

35. Letter, Susan Frost to Alice Paul, July 21, 1915, Reel 17, NWP Papers, LC. Jewish members, including Carrie and Mabel Pollitzer, constituted roughly one-fourth of the CESL organizational committee. Frost wrote Alice Paul that "something was owing" to her Jewish constituency because "they have been so lovely and loyal to me."

36. Letter, Susan Frost to Elsie Hill, June 30, July 6, 1915; Frost to Lucy Burns, July 6, 7, 10, 1915; Frost to Alice Paul, July 21, 1915; Elsie Hill to Lucy Burns, July 18, 1915; Burns to Hill, July 20, 1915, Reel 17, NWP Papers, LC.

37. Letter, Alice Paul to Susan Frost July 15, 1915, Reel 17, NWP Papers, LC.

38. Letter, Lucy Burns to Elsie Hill, July 22, 1915, Reel 17, NWP Papers, LC.

39. Letter, Lucy Burns to Vivian Pierce, July 22, 1915, Reel 17, NWP Papers, LC.

40. Letters, Susan Frost to Nina Pringle, September 26 and October 15, 1915, Pringle Papers.

41. A Frost letter to Nina Pringle, dated November 2, 1915, Pringle Papers, was one of many throughout her life that addressed a money crunch and her source of hope: "I have been doing some high financing ever since the war, but 'by the help of God I will leap over the wall'; don't you like that quotation fr. Psalms?" When she was most vexed with Susan Frost during convention planning, Burns confessed to Elsie Hill "that [Frost's motto] is the only thing she has ever written that has appealed to me." Burns to Hill, July 20, 1915, Reel 17, NWP Papers.

42. Letter, Lucy Burns to Alice Paul, September 8, 1915, Reel 19, NWP Papers, LC. Still not completely sure she could count on Frost, Burns also asked Hill, "Do you think she would do this and do it well?" (letter, Lucy Burns to Elsie Hill, September 30, 1915, Reel 19, NWP Papers, LC).

43. Letter, Susan Frost to Virginia Arnold, October 11, 1915, Reel 19, NWP Papers, LC.

44. Letter, Susan Frost to Nina Pringle, October 15, 1915, Pringle Papers. This election, legendary in Charleston, saw Governor Richard Manning dispatch military units to the peninsula in an effort to preserve order, but shooting resulted during the confusion and tension of the recount, and a *News and Courier* reporter was killed. A fuller account of the 1915 mayoral election in Charleston can be found in Doyle W. Boggs, "John Patrick Grace and the Politics of Reform in South Carolina, 1900–1931" (Ph.D. diss., Univ. of South Carolina, 1977), 85–101.

45. *Suffragist,* November 27, 1915, 8.

46. Letter, Alice Paul to Susan Frost, November 20, 1915, Reel 21, NWP Papers, LC.

47. Letter, Susan Frost to Mrs. M. T. Coleman, July 15, 1915, NAWSA Papers, LC.

48. Letter, Susan Frost to Nina Pringle, December 20, 1915, Pringle Papers.

49. Ibid.

50. Letter, Susan Frost to Nina Pringle, March 30, 1916, Pringle Papers.

51. April 1916 Charleston news clipping, Pringle Papers.

52. Letter, Susan Frost to Nina Pringle, February 20, 1916, Pringle Papers.

53. Charleston news clipping; letter, Susan Frost to Nina Pringle, March 30, 1916, Pringle Papers.

54. Minutes, SCESL, October 27, 1915; November 23, 1916.

55. Mrs. Robert Gibbes Thomas, wife of a professor at the Citadel, joined Susan Frost as the only two tidewater women holding state office. Both were also members of the CU Advisory Council in 1915. See minutes, SCESL, November 23, 1916.

56. Susan Frost told her California cousin (letter, March 24, 1917, Pringle Papers) that she had survived the previous two months knowing she would soon be relieved of the CESL presidency, but that the league suspended the constitution in order to give her a "rising, unanimous vote" for reelection, refusing to accept any response but yes.

57. Taylor, "South Carolina and the Enfranchisement of Women," 301.

58. Ibid., 305.

59. Following extended court battles, Mrs. Catt received the first of several payments that would total approximately $1 million in early 1917. For details of Catt's "Winning Plan" and its impact on the final suffrage victory, see Flexner, *Century of Struggle,* 289–92.

60. The National Woman's Party represented a fusing together of the Congressional Union and the Woman's Party, the CU affiliate in the western states where women had the right to vote. The merger process is detailed in Irwin, *Story of the Woman's Party.*

61. *Suffragist,* March 17, 1917, 7. A. Elizabeth Taylor compiled extensive state-by-state surveys of woman suffrage work throughout the South, but her studies largely ignored any efforts of the CU/NWP. For a scholarly overview of key leaders and strategies and accomplishments of suffrage organizations in the South, see Marjorie Spruill Wheeler, "New Women of the New South: The Leaders of the Woman Suffrage Movement in the Southern States" (Ph.D. diss., Univ. of Virginia, 1990). For the book of the same title, see Wheeler, *New Women of the New South* (New York: Oxford Univ. Press, 1993).

62. Letter, Doris Stevens to Alice Paul, April 4, 1917, Reel 41, NWP Papers, LC; letter, Amidon to Paul, April 5, 1917.

63. "The Woman's Party Advances in the South," *Suffragist,* April 21, 1917, 8.

64. For detailed examination of NWP militancy and the rationale behind it, see Bland, "Techniques of Persuasion."

65. Sidney R. Bland, "Fighting the Odds: Militant Suffragists in South Carolina," *South Carolina Historical Magazine* 82 (January 1981): 32–43.

66. "The South Salutes the Suffrage Sentinels," *Suffragist,* June 9, 1917, 4 and 8.

67. Letter, Susan Frost to Nina Pringle, June 21, 1917, Pringle Papers.

68. *Suffragist,* July 28, 1917.

69. Telegram, Lucy Burns to Susan Frost, August 18, 1917, Tray 44, NWP Papers, LC.

70. *Suffragist,* September 22, 1917; October 27, 1917; December 8, 1917.

71. Letter, Susan Frost to Woodrow Wilson, October 30, 1917, as cited in the *Suffragist,* November 10, 1917, 5.

72. Myers, interview with Laura Bragg, March 27, 1974, Dacus Library, Withrop College Archives.

73. Letter, T. R. Waring, Jr., to author, May 16, 1983.

74. Selby Paul, "Two Sisters Come to Charleston," July 20, 1953, article contained in McBee biographical files, Charleston Public Library, Charleston, South Carolina. Mary McBee recalled the visits of Elsie Hill, Alice Paul, and Inez Milholland, often an NWP parade herald, as well as the huge crowds that flocked to see suffragists on tour in their prison uniforms in early 1919.

75. Myers, interview with Mabel Pollitzer, Winthrop Archives, noted that Alice Paul and Mabel Pollitzer were especially close, both having been born on the same day, January 11, 1885.

76. Myers, interview with Laura Bragg, Winthrop Archives. Anita Pollitzer had a brief tenure as head of the National Woman's Party in the late 1940s.

77. Myers, interviews with Bragg and Pollitzer, Winthrop Archives. Laura Bragg remembered suffragists on the peninsula as "just a group of ladies that met at different houses" whose activity was mostly "oral talk. Eternal talk." Mabel Pollitzer recalled that there were "twenty-four or thirty" women at the first suffrage meeting in the city and that few more than that number kept the movement alive.

78. Detailed proceedings of the split of the Charleston Equal Suffrage League are contained in the National Woman's Party Papers, Reel 53.

79. Letter, Anita Pollitzer to Pauline Clark, December 13, 1917, Reel 53, NWP Papers, LC.

80. Reel 53, NWP Papers.

81. Columbia *State,* January 26, 1919, clipping contained in Anita Pollitzer Papers, SCHS.

82. Letter, Susan Frost to Nina Pringle, May 8, 1919, Pringle Papers.

83. Anita Pollitzer, "The Awakening South," *Suffragist,* June 22, 1918.

84. For details of the "Helping Pollock to Declare" campaign see Bland, "Fighting the Odds," 41–42.

85. Irwin, *Story of the Woman's Party,* 399.

86. Myers, interview with Laura Bragg, Winthrop Archives.

87. Laura Bragg's recollections and Inez Haynes Irwin's single sentence in her chapter "Burning the President's Words Again" are the only known accounts of Susan Frost's militancy in Washington. Given the volume, breadth and personal nature of the correspondence between Frost and her California cousin during the years 1910–1920 (an average of more than one letter a month, usually several typed pages, detailing virtually all the social and professional activities of the Charleston court stenographer/realtor), it is unlikely such a definitive deed for the cause of woman suffrage would not have been chronicled. No stories of either suffragist's Washington involvement appeared in Charleston newspapers.

88. *Suffragist,* March 1, 1919.

89. Letter, Maud Younger to Susan Frost, April 23, 1919, Reel 70, NWP Papers.

90. Letter, Thomas R. Waring to William Ball, February 15, 1919, William Watts Ball Papers, Perkins Library, Duke University, Durham, North Carolina (hereafter cited as Ball Papers).

91. Letter, Susan Frost to Mabel Vernon, May 24, 1919, Reel 71, NWP Papers.

92. Radical vanguards have historically paved the way for moderate reforms, and the NWP both sharpened debate on the suffrage question and pushed the moderates to greater action. Flexner, *Century of Struggle,* gave each group credit. Anne Firor Scott and Andrew Scott, *One Half the People: The Fight for Woman Suffrage* (Philadelphia: J. B. Lippincott Co., 1975), 41, maintained that the militant tactics did more good than harm and that "nervousness about what the radical women might do next encouraged both Congress and the president to make concessions and to embrace the conservative suffragists as the lesser evil. William L. O'Neill, *Everyone Was Brave: A History of Feminism in America* (Chicago: Quadrangle Books, 1969), argued, as do many historians, that World War I "added a few strings to the suffrage bow."

93. The six-volume *History of the Woman Suffrage Movement* published by the National American Woman Suffrage Association is, in actuality, a history of that organization's role in achieving the ultimate victory.

94. Letter, Susan P. Frost, Kate McIver, Mabel Pollitzer, and Sophie Brown to Alice Paul, June 19, 1919, Reel 72, NWP Papers. William O'Neill, *Everyone Was Brave,* 126,

argued that Alice Paul was "the only charismatic figure generated by the feminist movement in its salad days." In recent years, an Alice Paul Centennial Foundation, Inc., in conjunction with the Smithsonian Institution and the Arthur and Elizabeth Schlesinger Library on the History of Women in America, created an Alice Paul Memorial Fund. Its efforts resulted in the purchase of Paulsdale, Alice Paul's home in Mount Laurel, New Jersey, a property listed on both the National and New Jersey Register of Historic Places.

95. Letter, W. W. Ball to Thomas R. Waring, January 15, 1920, Ball Papers.

96. Letter, W. W. Ball to James F. Byrnes, January 23, 1920, Ball Papers.

97. Letter, Helen Vaughn to Alice Paul, January 20, 1920, Reel 76, NWP Papers.

98. Letter, Susan Frost to Mabel Vernon, January 25, 1920, Reel 76, NWP Papers.

99. Letter, Susan Frost to Nina Pringle, August 21, 1920, Pringle Papers.

100. Minutes, SCESL.

101. For an examination of the public activities of Southern women in the decade after ratification of the Anthony amendment, see Anne Firor Scott, "After Suffrage: Southern Women in the 1920s," in Scott, *Making the Invisible Woman Visible,* 222–43.

102. Boggs, "John Patrick Grace," 193.

103. See various copies of *Yearbook,* city of Charleston, as well as the yearbooks of the Civic Club of Charleston. In addition to serving on the Juvenile Welfare Commission and the Bath House Commission, Susan Frost served on the Charleston Arts Commission as a result of appointment by Mayor Thomas Stoney in 1925.

104. Charlotte McCrady, "Former City Councilwoman Still Active," Charleston *Evening Post,* June 1, 1955.

105. Marjorie Spruill Wheeler, in a paper, "Beyond Suffrage: Southern Suffragists and the Campaign for Women's Rights," presented at the 50th meeting of the Southern Historical Association In Louisville, Kentucky, November 1, 1984, made this case quite strongly. She concluded: "From the 1890s until the end of the suffrage movement in 1920, their (the suffragists) prime objective was recognition of woman's status with full rights and privileges."

106. *NC,* April 2, 1914.

107. Kathryn Kish Sklar, "Hull House in the 1890s: A Community of Women Reformers," *Signs* 10 (1985): 657–77, examined the extent to which the political power and range of activities of this group of reformers flowed from their collective life as co-residents and friends.

108. Letter, Susan Frost to Nina Pringle, February 15, 1916, Pringle Papers. For a discussion on the types of friendships that evolved within the National Woman's Party, many of them of an extended duration, see Leila J. Rupp, "The Women's Community in the National Woman's Party, 1945 to the 1960s," *Signs* 10, no. 4 (summer 1985): 715–41.

109. Interview with Thomas R. Waring, Jr., Charleston, South Carolina, June 21, 1983.

110. Letter, Susan Frost to Nina Pringle, July 3, 1918, Pringle Papers.

CHAPTER 3: PATRON SAINT OF PRESERVATION

1. The origins of Charleston progressivism dovetail with the views of historian Samuel P. Hays, who argued that a national movement developed because the upper class took the lead, seeking to change municipal government to benefit its own ends. See Samuel P. Hays, "The Politics of Reform in Municipal Government in the Progressive Era," *Pacific Northwest Quarterly* 55 (October 1964): 159–68. For a summary and analysis

of factors limiting Charleston's economic growth for decades after the Civil War, see Don H. Doyle, "Leadership and Decline in Postwar Charleston, 1865–1910," in *From the Old South to the New: Essays on the Transitional South,* ed. Walter F. Fraser, Jr., and Winfred B. Moore, Jr. (Westport, Conn.: Greenwood Press, 1981), 93–106. A good overview of the Rhett years as mayor is contained in John J. Duffy, "Charleston Politics in the Progressive Era" (Ph.D. diss., Univ. of South Carolina, 1963). R. Goodwyn Rhett's ancestors came from Charleston. Rhett was president of the city's oldest and largest bank and was an Episcopalian who belonged to the prestigious St. Cecilia Society and the Charleston Yacht Club.

2. Duffy, "Charleston Politics," 49–51, 221–26.

3. Frances R. Grimball, "Old Charleston Lives Again," 299.

4. Register of Mesne Conveyance, Charleston County Courthouse, Charleston, South Carolina (hereafter cited as Register of Mesne Conveyance).

5. Letter, Thomas R. Waring to W. W. Ball, February 1910 (?), Ball Papers. Both Ball and Waring married two of the "six beautiful Witte girls" of Charleston, whose father was a well-to-do German banker and cotton merchant. The Ball Papers detail substantial real estate "fishing" on the part of both journalists in the waters of the Charleston peninsula. For the life and journalistic career of the influential Ball, see John D. Stark, *"Damned Upcountryman": William Watts Ball, a Study in American Conservatism* (Durham, N.C.: Duke Univ. Press, 1968).

6. Duffy, "Charleston Politics," 50.

7. *Yearbook,* City of Charleston, 1911 and 1912.

8. Charleston Real Estate Exchange, Charleston, South Carolina, Minutes 1929–1939. Letter, Thomas R. Waring to W. W. Ball, January 20, 1913, Ball Papers.

9. Register of Mesne Conveyance.

10. Myers, interview with Laura Bragg, March 27, 1974, Winthrop College Archives, Dacus Library, Rock Hill, South Carolina. A close friend of the three Frost sisters, Laura Bragg recalled weekend dances at the island pavilion before it burned, as well as group sleepovers in the crowded quarters of "The Ranch."

11. Register of Mesne Conveyance.

12. Ibid.

13. Letters, Thomas R. Waring to W. W. Ball, July 7, 1913; March 15, 1914, Ball Papers.

14. Register of Mesne Conveyance. Exact amounts are impossible to determine in that prior to the advent of the Internal Revenue Service, the "other considerations" noted in the Conveyance and Miscellaneous Deeds Books were not detailed.

15. Samuel G. Stoney, *This Is Charleston: A Survey of the Architectural Heritage of a Unique American City* (Charleston, S.C.: Carolina Art Association, 1944). For a thorough study of the earliest settlement and commerce in and around Tradd Street, see Robert Preston Stockton, "The Evolution of Rainbow Row" (M.A. thesis, Univ. of South Carolina, 1979).

16. Scrapbook, Society for the Preservation of Old Dwellings, SCHS, 27, contains a *News and Courier* article on 6 Tradd Street, site of the school. For a picture of the school, see Grimball, "Old Charleston Lives Again," 298. For key residential changes in the geography of lower Charleston in the years 1860–1880, see John P. Radford, "Culture, Economy and Urban Structure in Charleston, South Carolina, 1860–1880" (Ph.D. diss., Clark Univ., 1974).

17. Duffy, "Charleston Politics," 22.

18. Data on the health conditions of African Americans in Charleston in the Progressive period can be found in Duffy, "Charleston Politics," 28–29; see also Doyle W. Boggs, "John Patrick Grace and the Politics of Reform in South Carolina, 1900–1931" (Ph.D. diss., Univ. of South Carolina, 1977), 9, 48.

19. From a tribute to Susan Pringle Frost by Elizabeth O'Neill Verner in *Preservation Progress* 5, no. 4 (November 1960): 91.

20. Information from street house file furnished by Preservation Society of Charleston, Charleston, South Carolina. See also Stockton, "Evolution of Rainbow Row," 15–17.

21. Letter, Susan Pringle Frost to *NC*, February 24, 1941; republished in *Preservation Progress* 16, no. 1 (January 1971): 2, 6.

22. Interview with Laura Frost, Charleston, South Carolina, July 5, 1981; see also Alston Deas, "They Shall See Your Good Works," *Preservation Progress* 7, no. 3 (May 1962): 2–3.

23. Harriott Horry Rutledge Ravenel, *Charleston: The Place and the People* (New York: MacMillan Co., 1906).

24. W. D. Howells, "In Charleston," *Harper's Monthly Magazine* (October 1915): 756.

25. Norman Olsen, Jr., "Books as Gifts: An Overview," *Preservation Progress* 24, no. 1 (January 1980): 5.

26. Alice R. Huger Smith and D. E. Huger Smith, *The Dwelling House of Charleston, South Carolina* (Philadelphia: J. B. Lippincott Co., 1917). For a review of the career of Alice R. Huger Smith, see Helen McCormack, *Introduction to Portfolio of Eight Watercolors of Carolina Rice Plantations,* June 1972, in Alice R. Huger Smith Papers, SCHS. The manner in which the Smiths, father and daughter, reinforced and encouraged the work of the other can be seen in Martha R. Severens, "Reveries: The Work of Alice Ravenel Huger Smith," *Art Voices/South* (January-February, 1978): 74–76. Alston Deas, taped interview by Charles Hosmer, Jr., June 26, 1972, Hosmer Collection, Archives of American Art, Washington, D.C. (hereafter cited as Hosmer Collection), 1, identified the publication of *Dwelling Houses* as "the signal for the first awakening, general awakening . . . of interest in Charleston's early architecture per se." Charles B. Hosmer, Jr., *Preservation Comes of Age: From Williamsburg to the National Trust, 1926–1949,* 2 vols. (Charlottesville: Univ. Press of Virginia for the [National Trust for Historic] Preservation Press, 1981), 1:234.

27. D. E. Huger Smith and Alice R. Huger Smith, *Twenty Drawings of the Pringle House* (Charleston, S.C., 1913); see also Elise Pinckney, "Miss Alice Smith: Low Country Artist," *South Carolina Magazine* (June 1957): 6–7.

28. Deas, "They Shall See," 1.

29. Letter, Susan Frost to Irénée DuPont, August 2, 1918, Irénée DuPont Papers, Eleutherian Mills Historical Library, Greenville, Delaware; letter, Susan Frost to *NC*, February 24, 1941.

30. Letter, Susan Frost to W. W. Ball, June 8, 1916, Ball Papers.

31. Isabella Leland, "Susan P. Frost Put Sentiment First to Become Benefactor to Charleston," *NC*, September 21, 1958.

32. Interview with Alston Deas, Charleston, South Carolina, July 3, 1981; see also Deas, "They Shall See," 2; Grimball, "Old Charleston Lives Again," 300.

33. A cousin to Miss Frost and her successor as president of the Society for the Preservation of Old Dwellings, Alston Deas knew her activity better than most and

acknowledged that "circumstances" affected the quality of some house restoration. Deas, interviews with author, July 3, 1981; July 21, 1981; June 12, 1983.

34. John M. Vlach, "Philip Simmons: Afro-American Blacksmith," *Black People and Their Culture: Selected Writings from the African Diaspora* (Washington, D.C.: Smithsonian Institution, 1976), 37–40. Philip Simmons was one of only two practicing blacksmiths in Charleston in 1976. See also Vlach, *Charleston Blacksmith: The Work of Philip Simmons* (Athens: Univ. of Georgia Press, 1981); valuable insights on Charleston's African-American craftsmen and the tensions that developed between those "free brown elite" who sometimes formed alliances with socially elite whites and those darker skinned, illiterate and sometimes less-skilled former slaves who migrated to the peninsula can be found in Bernard Edward Powers, "Black Charleston: A Social History 1822–1885" (Ph.D. diss., Northwestern Univ., 1982).

35. Mamie Garvin Fields (with Karen Fields), *Lemon Swamp*, 29. Fields's husband was a bricklayer, and her father was a member of the carpenters' union; *Lemon Swamp* gives glimpses into the lives of craftsmen of several generations.

36. Telephone interview with Carl Boone (African-American contractor), Charleston, South Carolina, June 23, 1983; Deas interview, July 21, 1981; telephone interview with Philip Simmons, Charleston, South Carolina, June 12, 1983, highlighted Pinckney's reputation for "neat work"; obituary, *NC,* December 10, 1952.

37. Obituary, *NC,* December 10, 1952. The Ball Papers contain a neat, handwritten estimate, dated October 28, 1936, on Pinckney's letterhead stationery, for some general contracting work on a Ball property in lower Charleston.

38. *NC,* December 11, 1952.

39. Myers, interview with Bragg.

40. Interview with Alston Deas, July 21, 1981.

41. Eve Thompson, "A Stroll Down Stoll's Alley," *Preservation Progress* 7, no. 4 (November 1962): 2.

42. Telephone interview with Philip Simmons, June 12, 1983.

43. Letter, Susan Pringle Frost to *NC,* published December 13, 1952.

44. James M. Lindgren, "The Gospel of Preservation in Virginia and New England: Historic Preservation and the Regeneration of Traditionalism" (Ph.D. diss., College of William and Mary, 1984), 5. Lindgren's evocative study is a cultural history of two organizations—the Association for the Preservation of Virginia Antiquities and the Society for the Preservation of New England Antiquities—from their establishment through the Progressive era. A more recent examination of Virginia in the same period is contained in Lindgren, "'Virginia Needs Living Heroes': Historic Preservation in the Progressive Era," *Public Historian* 13, no. 1 (Winter 1991): 9–24. See also the pioneering preservation study of Charles B. Hosmer, Jr., *Presence of the Past: A History of the Preservation Movement in the United States before Williamsburg* (New York: G. P. Putnam's Sons, 1965), and the synthesis in Hosmer, "The Broadening View of the Historical Preservation Movement," in *Material Culture and the Study of American Life,* ed. Ian M. G. Quimby (New York: W. W. Norton, 1978), 121–40.

45. Letter, Susan Frost to Mrs. M. T. Coleman, July 15, 1915, NWP Papers, LC.

46. Letter, Susan Frost to W. W. Ball, June 8, 1916, Ball Papers; Frost to Ball, June 6, 1914, Ball Papers; letter, Susan Frost to editor, *NC,* January 20, 1947.

47. Letter, Susan Frost to Nina Pringle, April 8, 1914, Pringle Papers.

48. Letter, Susan Frost to Irénée DuPont, August 2, 1918, Irénée DuPont Papers.

49. Letter, W. W. Ball to Susan Frost, June 7, 1916, Ball Papers.

50. Duffy, "Charleston Politics," 29–30.

51. Ibid.

52. Letter, T. Allen Legaré and I'on Rhett to W. W. Ball, June 7, 1916, Ball Papers. Ball's real estate brokers pointed out that there was little likelihood he could gain more income simply because the streets around his property were hard-surfaced.

53. Duffy, "Charleston Politics," 214–16; Boggs, "John Patrick Grace," 69, 179–80.

54. Boggs, "John Patrick Grace," 180.

55. Letter, Susan Frost to W. W. Ball, June 8, 1916, Ball Papers.

56. Letter, Susan Frost to Irénée DuPont, November 14, 1919, Irénée DuPont Papers.

57. Ibid., August 2, 1918, Irénée DuPont Papers.

58. Register of Mesne Conveyance; letter, Susan Frost to Irénée DuPont, March 26, 1918, Irénée DuPont Papers.

59. Isabella Leland, "Picturesque Alley Makes Comeback," NC, March 2, 1957.

60. Register of Mesne Conveyance; letter, Susan Frost to W. W. Ball, December 13, 1913, Ball Papers; see also NC, March 3, 1957.

61. Letter, Susan Frost to NC, February 24, 1941.

62. See Simons genealogical chart, accession 229, Irénée DuPont Papers. Connections also established through interviews with Mrs. W. T. (Eleanor Pringle) Hart, Charleston, South Carolina, July 6, 1981, and Alston Deas, July 3, 1981, both cousins of Susan Frost, and telephone interview with Marianne Hanckel, Charleston, South Carolina, July 5, 1981.

63. Letter, Susan Frost to Irene DuPont, March 26, 1918, Irénée DuPont Papers; see also obituary notices on the death of Rebecca Motte Frost, July 7, 1971, in Susan Frost file, SCHS.

64. Register of Mesne Conveyance.

65. Ibid.

66. The long struggle of Susan Frost's management of the Miles Brewton House as a tourist home and her continuing indebtedness to Irene and Irénée DuPont and Mrs. W. K. DuPont is excruciatingly detailed in the Irénée DuPont Papers. See particularly Susan Frost letters to Irénée DuPont, April 23, 1920; April 28, 1920; March 30, 1921; and Irénée DuPont to Susan Frost, April 24, 1920, and October 13, 1922.

67. Duffy, "Charleston Politics," 279–80.

68. Marvin Cann, "Burnet Rhett Maybank and the New Deal in South Carolina, 1931–1941" (Ph.D. diss., Univ. of North Carolina, 1967), 114; Duffy, "Charleston Politics," 355.

69. Letter, Susan Frost to Irene DuPont, March 26, 1918; Frost to Irénée DuPont, August 2, 1918, both Irénée DuPont Papers. Frost's letter to Irene DuPont attaches a list of her present mortgages and proposed new mortgage figures (including repairs) for property at 6, 8, 10, 12, 19, and 23 Tradd Street.

70. Frances R. Grimball, "Miss Frost Restores Houses," NC, February 1, 1945; see also NC, January 16–17, 1939. Miss Frost rented her first office at 9 Broad Street in November 1918.

71. Letter, Susan Frost to Irénée DuPont, July 15, 1919, Irénée DuPont Papers.

72. Ibid.; letter, Susan Frost to Irénée DuPont, November 14, 1919, Irénée DuPont Papers, lists more than twenty properties for sale around the peninsula.

73. Letter, Susan Frost to Irénée DuPont, April 28, 1920, Irénée DuPont Papers; *NC,* May 4, 1920.

74. Interview with Mrs. Edward Manigault, July 14, 1981.

75. Interview with A. J. Tamsberg, Charleston, South Carolina, June 22, 1983.

76. Clare Jervey is sometimes cited as the first woman in business in Charleston. No city of Charleston *Directory* was published between 1900 and 1906, but the 1906 *Directory* identifies a business for the Misses Bailey and Jervey on Logan Street. Jervey's Stenographic Exchange was located on Tradd Street according to the 1911 *Directory.* The 1919 *Directory* was the first to identify an office for Clare Jervey's Stenographic Exchange on Broad Street, placing her in the professional district slightly later than Frost. Grimball, "Miss Frost Restores Houses," identifies Jervey as a pioneer businesswoman (Charleston Real Estate Exchange, Minutes 1929–1939).

77. Given a realtor's license for $25 as a joke in 1915, Eulalie Salley went on to become vice-president of the South Carolina Association of Real Estate Boards and was chosen the First Lady of South Carolina Realtors by the association in 1959. She led in the formation of the Aiken County Board of Realtors, and she eventually held almost every top office on it. For Salley's business career, as well as her unique contributions to the woman suffrage movement, see Emily L. Bull, *Eulalie* (Aiken, S.C.: Kalmia Press, 1973). President of the Aiken Suffrage League, Eulalie Salley once flew over the town scattering suffrage leaflets to the crowd below.

78. *NC,* October 8, 1960.

79. Letter, Elise Pinckney to author, February 8, 1980.

80. Marjorie Uzzell, "I Bought My House from Miss Sue," *Preservation Progress* 7, no. 2 (March 1962): 1–2; letter, Mrs. T. M. Uzzell to author, April 30, 1983; Carol Carre Perrin, "The Chisholme-Gilman Tenement: A Charleston, South Carolina, Preservation" (M.A. thesis, Wake Forest Univ., 1979), details the rich history of the property Marjorie Uzzell and her husband purchased from Susan Frost.

81. Ibid.

82. Interview with Laura Frost, July 5, 1981.

83. Interview with Alston Deas, July 21, 1981; Deas, "They Shall See Your Good Works," 2. Any substantive minutes of the Charleston Real Estate Exchange are nonexistent prior to 1929, by which time early perceptions of the merits of Susan Frost's real estate career had changed significantly.

84. Letter, Thomas R. Waring to W. W. Ball, October 10, 1919, Ball Papers.

85. Ibid., June 21, 1920, Ball Papers.

86. Letter, Susan Frost to Irénée DuPont, March 8, 1920, Irénée DuPont Papers; Frost to DuPont, March 12, 1920, and March 27, 1920.

87. The best authority on Rainbow Row is Robert P. Stockton. In addition to his expansive master's thesis on the East Bay landmark, Stockton authored a group of articles on Rainbow Row in late spring/early summer 1979 in his long-running "Do You Know Your Charleston?" series in the *News and Courier.* For other information on Rainbow Row, see street files, Charleston County Library, *NC* Collection, SCHS, the Preservation Society of Charleston, and the Historic Charleston Foundation. Photographs by George W. Johnson, c. 1920, showing the rundown condition of the lower East Bay neighborhood at the time Susan Frost invested in it can be found in the Gibbes Art Gallery, Charleston.

88. Stockton, "Rainbow Row," 93–100.

89. Letters, Susan Frost to Irénée DuPont, March 8, 1920; March 12, 1920; March 27, 1920, Irénée DuPont Papers. *NC,* February 24, 1941.

90. Susan Frost purchased buildings numbered 83, 87, 91, 93, 95, and 97 East Bay Street during April–May 1920. Irénée DuPont's financial assistance is documented in letters to Susan Frost, April 9, 1920, and April 24, 1920, Irénée DuPont Papers. See also register of Mesne Conveyance.

91. Boggs, "John P. Grace," 245.

92. Letters, Thomas Waring to W. W. Ball, March 20, 1922, Ball Papers.

93. Letter, Susan Frost to Irénée DuPont, October 12, 1922, Irénée DuPont Papers.

94. *NC,* February 24, 1941; letter, Susan Frost to Thomas Pinckney, December 23, 1939, Susan Frost file, CCA. The Frost file contains paving tax records that depict her struggle to keep interest payments current on East Bay Street properties.

95. Letter, Susan Frost to Irénée DuPont, March 24, 1925; see also Frost to DuPont, January 23, 1923, Irénée DuPont Papers.

96. Letter, Irénée DuPont to Winder Laird, August 7, 1923, Irénée DuPont Papers.

97. Albert Simons, "40 Years of Preservation," *Preservation Progress* 5, no. 3 (May 1960): 1. The keys to Charleston's cultural renaissance included the emergence of an active colony of artists on Atlantic Street near the Battery and the formation of the Poetry Society of South Carolina (composed mostly of Charlestonians) in late 1920. See also the chapter "Charleston Again a Center of Culture" in Robert Goodwyn Rhett, *Charleston: An Epic of Carolina* (Richmond, Va.: Garrett and Massie, 1940).

98. Interview with Elizabeth Verner Hamilton, Charleston, South Carolina, July 20, 1981. Etcher Alfred Hutty and writer Hervey Allen, one of the founders of the Poetry Society, also resided on Tradd Street at one time.

99. Letter, Susan Frost to Mrs. Ernest Pringle, May 12, 1931, Manigault House file, SCHS.

100. Letter, Susan Frost to Irénée DuPont, March 23, 1928, Irénée DuPont Papers.

101. Justice and Mrs. Lionel Legge moved into 101 East Bay Street in 1932, next to the rented Frost properties, and for several years they were the only whites in the neighborhood. Their experience and Dorothy Haskell Porcher Legge's contributions to Charleston's historic preservation are covered in an interview, Dorothy Legge with author, Charleston, South Carolina, July 13, 1981; "Preservation Profile: Dorothy Haskell Porcher Legge," *Preservation Progress* 26, no. 4 (November 1982): 3, 7. Mrs. Legge "sold" the first of Susan Frost's East Bay holdings for her in 1936 when she persuaded a New York couple to purchase 97 East Bay Street.

102. *NC,* February 24, 1941; Stockton, "Evolution of Rainbow Row."

103. *NC,* February 24, 1941.

104. Minutes, 1929–1939, Charleston Real Estate Exchange; see especially January 13, 1933. New rules adopted in mid-1931 called for 5 percent commissions on the first $5000 and 3 percent on the balance for city property, 5 percent on residences in suburban developments, and 10 percent on acreage and lots.

105. Ibid., September 11, 1929; see also Exchange Minutes, 1939–1947.

106. Ibid., May 1938; January 31, 1934; April 29, 1948; December 14, 1949; December 20, 1949.

107. Letter, Susan Frost to Mrs. Ernest Pringle, May 12, 1931, Manigault House file, SCHS.

108. Letter, Susan Frost to Irénée DuPont, March 2, 1931, Irénée DuPont Papers.

109. Letter, Susan Frost to William Sumner Appleton, July 30, 1920, Archives, Soci-

ety for the Preservation of New England Antiquities (SPNEA), Boston, Massachusetts. The driving force behind the SPNEA and a seminal figure in U.S. preservation history, Appleton apparently initiated the exchange with Frost. Theirs was a relatively small volume of correspondence but dealt with matters critical to Frost, including the Miles Brewton House, the Society for the Preservation of Old Dwellings, and efforts to save the Joseph Manigault House. The full impact of William Sumner Appleton's career is covered in Hosmer, *Preservation Comes of Age,* especially 1:133–82.

110. Letter, Susan Frost to "My Dear Nell" Pringle, March 7, 1934, Ravenel/Pringle/Childs Papers, SCHS.

111. Milby Burton, taped interview by Hosmer, June 27, 1972, Hosmer Collection.

112. *Preservation Progress* 5, no. 4 (November 1960): 91.

113. Letter, Susan Frost to *NC,* March 9, c. 1928, reprinted in *Preservation Progress* 7, no. 2 (March 1962): 2–3; Deas, "They Shall See," 1.

114. In May 1925, Susan Frost urged Mayor Stoney to support an ordinance prohibiting taking old iron and wood from the city. Stoney, in turn, urged his corporation counsel to work with Frost on the matter. See Hosmer, *Preservation Comes of Age,* 1:237.

115. Hosmer, *Preservation Comes of Age,* 1:236.

116. Interview with Frances R. Edmunds, Charleston, South Carolina, June 27, 1983.

117. Letter, Thomas Stoney to John T. Cosgrove, May 27, 1925, Thomas Stoney Papers, CCA.

118. Louis E. Storen, long known as Charleston's "dean of real estate," had great respect for the Frost's work. For a summation of Storen's fifty years on Broad Street, see David S. Farrow, "Louis Storen: The Dean of Real Estate," *News and Courier/ Evening Post,* July 7, 1981; telephone interview with Louis Storen, Charleston, South Carolina, July 10, 1981.

119. Nell Pringle, "Short Story on Susan Snow," n.d., Susan Frost file, SCHS.

120. On Hannahan's career, see Thomas R. Waring, Jr., "Real Estate: Business Fun for Fifty Years," *News and Courier/Evening Post,* January 9, 1983; telephone interview with Elizabeth Hannahan, Charleston, South Carolina, June 27, 1983.

121. Letter, Susan Frost to "My Dear Nell," May 12, 1931, Manigault House file; Frost to Nell Pringle, March 7, 1934, Ravenel/Pringle/Childs Papers, SCHS.

122. Letter, Burnet R. Maybank to L. Ostendorff (abutment clerk), November 23, 1936, CCA.

CHAPTER 4: A SMALL BAND OF US

1. Undocumented memorabilia of M. P. Fenhagen (daughter of Nell McColl Pringle and Ernest Pringle), penned to clarify the role of her parents in the preservation of the Manigault House, November 1953, Joseph Manigault House papers (hereafter cited as Manigault House file), SCHS.

2. Ibid. Discussions about saving the Manigault House, initiated by Susan Frost, prompted the issuance of a public notice calling for a meeting at the South Battery residence of the Ernest Pringles. Fenhagen recorded that "Sue Frost bemoaned that there was no society for the Preservation of Old Houses in Charleston and no treasury to draw on for such purposes," and in turn, "between the two, a spark was lit." In a short story about Susan Pringle Frost and the thirteen-year battle over the Joseph Manigault House, an autobiographical piece titled "Susan Snow," Nell McColl Pringle recorded much of

her own anguish over the fight. According to her version, she volunteered the initial loan and announced: "We will organize a 'Preservation Society,' and all of us together will save the Gault House and Gardens." Copy of "Susan Snow," unpublished ms., n.d., Susan Frost file, SCHS.

3. The first Preservation Society historian, Eola Willis, labeled Susan Frost "the moving spirit" of the group. See Eola Willis Papers, SCHS.

4. *NC*, May 5, 1920.

5. Eleanor Hart, "A Beginning in Preservation—As I Remember," *Preservation Progress* 7, no. 2 (March 1962): 11; letter, Ernest H. Pringle, Jr., to G. Corner Fenhagen, April 16, 1932, Manigault House file, SCHS.

6. Hart, "As I Remember," *Preservation Progress* 7, no. 1 (January 1963): 14; 7, no. 4 (November 1962): 12.

7. Kenneth Severens, *Southern Architecture: 350 Years of Distinctive American Buildings* (New York: E. P. Dutton, 1981), notes that the Adamesque style tended to be accepted in the United States in the late eighteenth century because it differed from Georgian, the style associated with the colonial phase of American history. The first U.S. handbook popularizing the Adam brothers' work appeared in 1797. The style was introduced in the South earlier than that, however, with the banquet hall that George Washington added at Mount Vernon.

8. "Do You Know Your Charleston? The Manigault House," *NC,* December 7, 1931.

9. Doyle W. Boggs, "John Patrick Grace and the Politics of Reform in South Carolina, 1900–1931" (Ph.D. diss., Univ. of South Carolina, 1977), 166.

10. "Architects Move to Preserve City," *NC,* April 10, 1931, 8–9a.

11. Eola Willis, a frequent writer and lecturer about Charleston's artists, art collections, and theater, was a factor in lowcountry cultural life for some sixty years. Eola Willis Papers, SCHS, contain some limited information on the early history of the Preservation Society as do the Harriet Simons Papers.

12. *NC,* April 22, 1920, lists all those attending the first meeting of what became the Society for the Preservation of Old Dwellings.

13. For a brief summary of the early career of Albert Simons, see Robert Stockton, "'Dean of Charleston Architects' . . . Remembers Early Restoration Work," *Preservation Progress* 20, no. 4 (November 1975): 6–7. Simons was involved in virtually every major phase of Charleston preservation work during the first three quarters of the twentieth century. He was personally part of numerous restoration projects and influenced countless others through almost thirty years on the Charleston Board of Architectural Review and as a leader of the local preservation community. See also Simons papers, SCHS. For his overall impact, see Hosmer, *Preservation Comes of Age,* 1:231–74.

14. *NC,* May 6, 1920; in a few short years, the Charleston Museum and the Preservation Society would be battling together to save both the Joseph Manigault House and the Heyward-Washington House.

15. Letter, Susan Pringle Frost to William Sumner Appleton, September 4, 1920, William Sumner Appleton Papers, Archives, SPNEA.

16. Susan Frost inevitably went back to the original title of the society and the overall purport of the word "dwelling" whenever she reviewed the history of the group. See *NC,* January 14, 1945; June 17, 1945. Alston Deas, "They Shall See Your Good Works," *Preservation Progress* 7, no. 3 (May 1962): 1–5, notes Frost's insistence on including "dwelling" as part of the title. James Lindgren, "The Gospel of Preservation in Virginia

and New England: Historic Preservation and the Regeneration of Traditionalism" (Ph.D. diss., College of William and Mary, 1984), stresses the importance of homes, particularly colonial-era buildings, as potent symbols used by historic preservationists to reaffirm old values and traditionalism.

17. D. E. Huger Smith and Alice R. Huger Smith, *The Dwelling Houses of Charleston, South Carolina* (Philadelphia: J. B. Lippincott Co., 1917), 375.

18. The Society for the Preservation of New England Antiquities was launched with a total of eighteen members and a treasury of $180. See Hosmer, *Presence of the Past,* 240.

19. Letter, Susan Frost to William Sumner Appleton, July 30, 1920, Appleton Papers, SPNEA.

20. Copy of notice of meeting to organize the Preservation Society, April 12, 1920, Manigault House file, SCHS. See also letter, Susan Frost to *NC,* April 25, 1933.

21. Letter, Susan Frost to *NC,* January 28, 1925.

22. Susan Frost spoke of the preservation of the original names of the streets of the city and all classes of buildings throughout the entire city at the May 6, 1920, mass meeting of the SPOD. See *NC,* May 6, 1920. At the June 1920 organizational meeting at the Joseph Manigault House, architecture, old homes, and "workmanship" (specifically mentioning wrought ironwork) were identified as within the purview of the group (*NC,* June 26, 1920).

23. One-page history of SPOD, including its standing committees, prepared by Eola Willis and contained in Harriet Simons Papers, SCHS.

24. Hosmer, *Presence of the Past,* 218.

25. Deas, Hosmer interview, June 26, 1972.

26. Albert Simons, taped interview by Hosmer, June 22, 1972, Hosmer Collection, 2.

27. Letter, Susan Frost to *NC,* March 9, c. 1928, as reprinted in *Preservation Progress* 7, no. 2 (March 1962): 2–3.

28. Michael C. Scardaville, "The Role of the Historical Profession in the Development of the Preservation Movement," paper delivered at the Teaching Historic Preservation Conference, Stagville Preservation Center, Raleigh, North Carolina, September 27, 1985, copy in possession of author.

29. Hart, "As I Remember," *Preservation Progress* 8, no. 1 (January 1963): 14–15. In her short story "Susan Snow," Pringle stated that her banker husband was "cold, unresponsive, if not irritable," when she approached him about saving the Joseph Manigault House, and he "fumed" at the "folly of meddling with progress."

30. Michael C. Scardaville, "The Selling of Historic Charleston," *Preservation Progress* 30, no. 2 (March 1986): 8. Throughout the 1930s, newspapers published letters and articles by SPOD members pointing to the necessity of preserving picturesque Charleston as a means of attracting the tourist trade.

31. Notice of meeting to organize, Manigault House file, SCHS.

32. Letter, Susan Frost to *NC,* January 28, 1925.

33. *NC,* January 14, 1945; June 17, 1945.

34. Hart, "As I Remember," *Preservation Progress* 8, no. 2 (March 1963): 18.

35. Manigault House file, SCHS.

36. Manigault House file, SCHS; Civic Club papers, SCHS, November 22 and December 27, 1922.

37. See Manigault House file and Civic Club minutes of late 1922, SCHS.

38. Civic Club papers, April 21, 1921, SCHS.

39. Charleston City Council Journal, November 28, 1922, Manigault House file, SCHS.

40. Interview with Thomas R. Waring, Jr., Charleston, South Carolina, July 6, 1981.

41. Register of Mesne Conveyance, CCA.

42. Undocumented memorabilia of M. P. Fenhagen, Manigault House file, SCHS.

43. Manigault House file, SCHS.

44. Few records exist to document the early years of the Preservation Society of Charleston. Sketchy details exist in the Preservation Society files and the papers of SPOD historian, Eola Willis, SCHS. Harriet Simons Papers, SCHS, contain a one-page list of original officers and committees. William Hanckel, "The Preservation Movement in Charleston 1920–1962" (M.A. thesis, Univ. of South Carolina, 1962), attests to having seen a "sparsely kept" Minutes Book for the period April 30, 1925, to January 4, 1934, which indicated minutes had never been read and seldom kept.

45. Albert Simons, Hosmer interview, 18–19. Simons thought highly of Deas and labeled his book *The Early Ironwork of Charleston* a "very excellent work . . . probably the best thing we have." Interview with Alston Deas, July 3, 1981.

46. Deas, Hosmer interview, 6, 9; interview with Alston Deas, July 3, 1981; one of the best assessments of Frost and her overall importance to Charleston historic preservation is Deas, "They Shall See Your Good Works."

47. Letter, Susan Frost to William Sumner Appleton, May 11, 1925; July 9, 1925, Appleton Papers, SPNEA.

48. Letter, Susan Frost to William Sumner Appleton, May 11, 1925; Appleton to Frost, May 14, 1925, Appleton Papers, SPNEA.

49. Letter, John Cosgrove to Thomas P. Stoney, May 29, 1925, Thomas P. Stoney Papers, CCA.

50. Thomas Stoney was mayor of Charleston from 1923 to 1931. It was Stoney who engaged the professional services of the Morris Knowles firm of Pittsburgh to do a survey and draft the historic zoning ordinance that the city council ratified in October 1931.

51. Letter, Thomas P. Stoney to John Cosgrove, June 1, 1925, Stoney Papers, CCA.

52. Minutes, SPOD, May 15, 1925, and June 3, 1925, as cited in Hosmer, *Preservation Comes of Age,* 1:237.

53. Marvin Cann, "Burnet Rhett Maybank and the New Deal in South Carolina, 1931–1941" (Ph.D. diss., Univ. of South Carolina, 1967), 97.

54. *NC,* December 1935. A musician, painter, and writer, and chairman of the Charleston Art Commission in the 1920s, as well as SPOD historian, Eola Willis spent many years researching the history of the American theater. Her book *The Stage in Charleston during the Eighteenth Century* was, in journalist Thomas R. Waring's view, "one of the distinguished contributions to the History of the Drama in America." See letter, Thomas R. Waring to Olivia Hobgood, April 18, 1932, Eola Willis Papers, SCHS.

55. Minutes, Ways and Means Committee, CCA, May 29, 1925.

56. J. Holton Fant, "Tea and Talk: A Preservation Memoir," *Preservation Progress* (Fall 1990): 1.

57. Memorabilia, M. P. Fenhagen, Manigault House file, SCHS.

58. Hart, "As I Remember," 19.

59. Fraser, *Charleston!* 381–82.

60. Thomas B. Stoney file, Charleston County Library, Charleston, South Carolina. In many ways the Cooper River Bridge was the legacy of Stoney's predecessor, John P.

Grace, who saw it providing access to area beaches, especially the Isle of Palms, which he projected would become a major tourist attraction.

61. Letter, Susan Frost to Irénée DuPont, March 23, 1928.

62. Simons, Hosmer interview, 35; Simons labeled the Mansion House crisis a "turning point in thinking about preservation in Charleston," Hosmer interview, 6.

63. Hosmer, *Preservation Comes of Age,* 1:243.

64. Stockton, "'Dean of Charleston Architects,'" 6.

65. Thomas Heyward House files, SCHS.

66. Ibid. Milby Burton inherited the commitments to save the Heyward-Washington House when he became director of the Charleston Museum in 1931. For his recollections of the project, see Milby Burton, Hosmer interview.

67. Deas, Hosmer interview, 13; Rowena Wilson Tobias, "Laura M. Bragg, Rejuvenator of Museums, Returns to Charleston after Retirement," *NC,* January 28, 1940.

68. Ibid.

69. Letter, Ernest Pringle to Corner Fenhagen, April 16, 1932, Manigault House file, SCHS.

70. Hanckel, "The Preservation Movement," 69.

71. Hart, "As I Remember," 19.

72. Ibid. Interview with Eleanor Hart, Charleston, South Carolina, July 6, 1981. Having viewed the Manigault House as a tremendous financial gamble from the beginning and having not been a party to the original commitment made in his home, Ernest Pringle understandably experienced resentment.

73. Letter, Susan Frost to Nell Pringle, December 2, 1931; May 12, 1931, Manigault House file, SCHS. Nell Pringle died in 1936 at age 58. The Pringle offspring believed her early death was hastened by the burdens of the Joseph Manigault House.

74. Letter, Susan Frost to Nell Pringle, March 7, 1934, Ravenel/Pringle/Childs Papers, SCHS.

75. Heyward House file, SCHS.

76. Interview with Alston Deas, July 3, 1981.

77. News clipping, October 23, 1928, SPOD Collection, SCHS.

78. Ibid., c. 1925, SPOD Collection, SCHS.

79. Deas, Hosmer interview, 4.

80. Frances R. Grimball, "Old Charleston Lives Again," 300.

81. *NC,* January 22, 1949.

82. Susan Pringle Frost, "Society Rescues Old Landmarks," *NC,* January 17, 1939.

83. Letter, Thomas P. Stoney to Susan Frost, April 17, 1929, Stoney Papers, CCA.

84. Letter, Susan Frost to *NC,* March 9, c. 1928, as reprinted in *Preservation Progress* 7, no. 2 (March 1962): 3.

85. Ibid.

86. *NC,* April 12, 1964.

87. Letter, Susan Frost to *NC,* 1937, SPOD Collection, SCHS.

88. Letter, Susan Frost to *NC,* April 25, 1933.

89. Hosmer, *Preservation Comes of Age,* 1:245–47. National figures included Fiske Kimball, Philadelphia museum director, and Leicester Holland, head of the Fine Arts Department of the Library of Congress.

90. "Do You Know Your Charleston?: The Manigault House," *NC,* December 7, 1931.

91. Letter, Alston Deas to Archer Huntington, January 21, 1932, Albert Simons Papers, SCHS.

92. Cited in Hosmer, *Preservation Comes of Age,* 1:248.

93. Ibid., 249. Milby Burton continued to serve as director of the Charleston Museum while heading the Preservation Society. Both men pressured Louise DuPont Crowninshield, who earlier had paid several months interest and taxes on the property.

94. Letter, Susan Frost to Ernest Pringle, April 18, 1932, Manigault House file, SCHS.

95. Letter, Ernest Pringle to Corner Fenhagen, April 16, 1932, Manigault House files, SCHS; letter, Alston Deas to Archer Huntington, January 21, 1931, Simons Papers, SCHS.

96. Letter, Warren Laird to Albert Simons, December 14, 1931, Simons Papers, SCHS.

97. Letter, Susan Frost to *NC,* April 7, 1932.

98. Letter, Susan Frost to Ernest Pringle, April 18, 1932, Manigault House file, SCHS.

99. Ibid., December 2, 1931, Manigault House file, SCHS.

100. Letters, Susan Frost to Nell Pringle, May 12, 1931; Frost to Nell Pringle, March 7, 1934, Manigault House file, SCHS.

101. Fuller details of Burton's role in saving the Manigault property can be found in Burton, Hosmer interview, 5–10.

102. SPOD Collection, SCHS.

103. Burton, Hosmer interview, 7.

104. Ibid., 4.

105. Ibid., 32.

106. Letter, Albert Simons to Warren Laird, December 17, 1931, Simons Papers, SCHS. Robert Whitelaw, dynamic director of the Carolina Art Association after 1931, reached the same conclusion as Simons, observing that Charleston had enough cultural institutions to "take care of" a city ten times its own size and that he likely expected more than the people could give. See Hosmer, *Preservation Comes of Age,* 1:255, and Whitelaw, taped interview by Hosmer, Hosmer Collection.

107. Insights into this problem can be seen in the series of letters and articles in the *News and Courier* in late 1933 promoting the necessity of preserving picturesque Charleston as a means of attracting tourist trade. See also letter, Nell Pringle to W. W. Ball, n.d., Manigault House file, SCHS, on the same subject.

108. Hanckel, "Preservation Movement," 15–16.

109. Letter, Susan Frost to *NC,* March 9, c. 1928, as cited in *Preservation Progress* 7, no. 2 (March 1962): 3.

110. Edward Twig, "Charleston: The Great Myth," *Forum* 103, no. 1 (January–June 1940): 1–7.

111. Ibid., 4.

112. Ibid.

113. Ibid., 72, 142, 207–8. Representative of some of the lowcountry responses to *Forum* was that of General C. P. Summerall, president of the Citadel, who labeled the Twig material "one of the most evil and dastardly libels that could be uttered."

114. In a letter to the *News and Courier,* April 25, 1933, Frost wrote: "Let us hope out of the present age of jazz music, impressionistic art and jig-saw architecture may rise a deeper sense of our own responsibility to the future generations in transmitting to them an architecture worthy to be preserved and a far reaching vision of beauty and truth."

115. Scardaville, "Selling of Historic Charleston," highlights the romanticist tradition and the role of artists such as Verner and Alice R. Huger Smith in educating both the local populace and the outside world to the architectural heritage of Charleston and the ambiance of an earlier era. See also Lyne R. Myers, *Mirrors of Time: Elizabeth O'Neill Verner's Charleston* (Columbia: McKissick Museums, University of South Carolina, 1983).

116. *NC,* April 4, 1935.

117. In a letter to the *News and Courier* in 1947, Susan Frost appeared upset on learning that many blacks had been forced to move "across the bridge and in the country" and now depended on bus service to get them to their jobs in the city.

118. SPOD Collection, SCHS.

119. *NC,* April 4, 1935.

CHAPTER 5: PRESERVATION WATCHDOG

1. Letters, Susan Frost to Irénée DuPont, March 2, 1931; May 4, 1929; March 17, 1931, Irénée DuPont Papers.

2. Letter, Susan Frost to Irénée DuPont, April 11, 1932, Irénée DuPont Papers.

3. Minutes of City Council, October 22, 1929, CCA, Charleston, South Carolina.

4. Ibid., September 10, 1929. While on a visit to Memphis, Tennessee, in late 1929, Mayor Stoney discussed zoning with its mayor, Watkins Overton.

5. Roy S. MacElwee, "The Preservation and Restoration of Charleston's Fine Old Architecture," *American City* 42 (February 1930), 134–35. See also MacElwee, "Charleston's Waterfront Driveways," *American City* 37 (December 1927): 741–44.

6. Alston Deas, "Charleston's First Zoning Ordinance," *Preservation Progress* 27 (January 1983): 3.

7. Deas, "First Zoning Ordinance"; minutes, Charleston City Council, April 8, 1930.

8. H. I. Brock, "The City That Lives As a Monument," *New York Times Magazine,* November 1, 1931. While the comprehensive ordinance covered every phase of the city's physical being and promoted health, safety, and the general welfare, it would be remembered most as the vehicle to preserve Charleston's old and historic buildings, chiefly from the Colonial period.

9. Samuel Gaillard Stoney, *This Is Charleston: A Survey of the Architectural Heritage of a Unique American City,* 2d ed. (Charleston: The Carolina Art Association, Historic Charleston Foundation, and the Preservation Society of Charleston, 1960), 134.

10. Carol Carre Perrin, "The Chisholme-Gilman Tenement: A Charleston, S.C. Preservation" (M.A. thesis, Wake Forest Univ., 1979), 122.

11. Ibid.; *This Is Charleston,* 134.

12. Albert Simons to Delos Smith, August 10, 1933, Albert Simons Papers, SCHS.

13. Ibid.

14. Robert Stockton, "'Dean of Charleston Architects . . . Remembers Early Restoration Work,'" 6–7; Hosmer, *Preservation Comes of Age,* 1:240.

15. Letter, Susan Frost to Albert Simons, December 21, 1933, Simons Papers, SCHS; Simons to Frost, December 23, 1933. Interview with Mrs. Edward Manigault, Charleston, South Carolina, July 14, 1981.

16. Ibid.

17. Visiting writers Clement and Gloria (Goddard) Wood expressed regret that the "frantic pursuit of the dollar" resulted in the reclamation of Cabbage Row and the dis-

placing of its longtime residents. See *NC,* December 25, 1933, and letter, Loutrell Briggs to *NC,* December 26, 1933.

18. Ibid., Susan Frost to Albert Simons, December 21, 1933, Simons Papers.

19. Letter, Susan Frost to James O'Hear, September 26, 1934, Susan Frost file, CCA.

20. Letter, Albert Simons to William Emerson, November 5, 1932, Simons Papers, SCHS.

21. Letter, Albert Simons to James J. Morrison, May 29, 1939, Simons Papers, SCHS.

22. Letter, Susan Frost to *NC,* March 8, 1935.

23. Letter, Aloysius Flynn to *NC,* March 6, 1935.

24. Letter, Susan Frost to *NC,* March 8, 1935.

25. *NC,* January 3, 1934; Michael C. Scardaville, "The Selling of Historic Charleston," *Preservation Progress* 30, no. 2 (March 1986): 7.

26. In 1934 a Department of Commerce housing survey cited Charleston as having the worst housing facilities of any city studied, with both African Americans and lower class whites living in substandard facilities. For more on the problem, see Marvin Cann, "Burnet Maybank and the New Deal in South Carolina, 1931–41" (Ph.D. dissertation, Univ. of North Carolina, 1967), 102–3.

27. *NC,* November 29, 1933; see also November 30, 1933, and December 13, 1933. Numerous letters to the editor also address this same subject.

28. *NC,* December 13, 1933.

29. Fraser, *Charleston!* 374.

30. Scardaville, "Selling of Historic Charleston," 8.

31. Letter, Albert Simons to James Morrison, May 29, 1939, Simons Papers, SCHS.

32. *NC,* December 8, 1933, clipping in PSOC scrapbooks, SCHS.

33. *NC,* 1937, PSOC scrapbooks, SCHS.

34. Michael Scardaville, "Elizabeth O'Neill Verner: The Artist as Preservationist," in Lynn R. Myers, *Mirror of Time: Elizabeth O'Neill Verner's Charleston* (Columbia: McKissick Museums, University of South Carolina, 1983), 19.

35. *NC,* October 23, 1933.

36. PSOC scrapbooks, SCHS.

37. *NC,* July 7, 1935.

38. Letter, Susan Frost to *NC,* PSOC scrapbooks, SCHS.

39. *NC,* April 4, 1935.

40. *NC,* August 20, 1938.

41. Letter, Burnet Maybank to L. F. Ostendorff (abutment clerk), November 23, 1936, Susan Frost file, CCA.

42. Maybank was a member of the state advisory board of bank control, the advisory board for public works, and the chairman of the South Carolina Public Service Authority. For detailed coverage of Maybank and the New Deal in Charleston, see Cann, "Maybank and the New Deal in South Carolina," 83–136.

43. Ibid.; between 1933 and 1938, when Burnet Maybank was Mayor of Charleston, the city added two municipal swimming pools (one white, one black), a fire station, a modern incinerator, a city prison farm, a new orphanage for African Americans, a yacht basin to further attract northern tourists, the Dock Street Theater, as well as several public housing projects.

44. For the life and career of this influential southern journalist see Stark, *Damned*

Upcountryman. After nearly two decades as editor of the (Columbia) *State,* Ball returned to Charleston in 1927 to become editor of the *News and Courier.*

45. Ibid., 44.

46. Letter, Susan Frost to W. W. Ball, August 17, 1943, Ball Papers; see also Frost to Ball, November 28, 1943, Ball Papers.

47. Letter, Susan Frost to E. Willoughby Middleton, December 12, 1940, Ball Papers; letter, Susan Frost to William G. Morrison, October 25, 1945, *NC* Collection, SCHS. Stark, *Damned Upcountryman,* convincingly argues that despite his love of what was left of old Charleston, W. W. Ball remained attached to the upcountry where he was born and reared and that his individualism and independence were the result of "the upcountry code."

48. Stark, *Damned Upcountryman,* 160.

49. Cann, "Maybank and the New Deal," 137, argued that the project insured Maybank's gubernatorial success in 1938. The Charleston mayor was chairman of the South Carolina Public Service Authority.

50. Letter, Susan Frost to William G. Morrison, October 25, 1945, *NC* Collection, SCHS.

51. In September, 1937, a decision favorable to the Santee-Cooper River project came from the federal district court and was upheld in February 1938 by the circuit court of appeals. The way was cleared for construction to begin when the Supreme Court refused to review the case in May 1938.

52. Cann, "Maybank and the New Deal," 162. See also letter, Susan Frost to *NC,* January 17, 1939.

53. Ball rationalized support of Maybank's pet project by arguing that since the government was already into the public power business with the TVA, South Carolina should get her share of federal dollars too. Once the Santee-Cooper project was safely underway, Ball resumed his vocal criticism. W. W. Ball's conduct is more fully explained in Stark, *Damned Upcountryman,* 160–61, 188–92.

54. Letter, Susan Frost to *NC,* January 17, 1939; letter, Susan Frost to W. W. Ball, January 25, 1939, *NC* Collection, SCHS.

55. Letter, Susan Frost to W. W. Ball, April 11, 1939, *NC* Collection, SCHS.

56. Herbert Sass, "The Cities of America: Charleston," *Saturday Evening Post* (February 8, 1947): 21, 70, 72, 75, 78, 80, 83; *Charleston Grows: An Economic, Social and Cultural Portrait of an Old Community in the New South* (Charleston: Carolina Art Association, 1949); and *Outspoken: 150 Years of the News and Courier* (Columbia: Univ. of South Carolina Press, 1953). Sass was one of the founders of the Society for the Preservation of Spirituals, created in the 1920s by whites to help preserve the words and melodies of songs sung by plantation blacks.

57. Susan Frost, *Highlights.* In the foreword Sass lauded the house restorations of Miss Frost, "carried out with limited means but enormous courage and enthusiasm," as the turning point in opening the eyes of Charlestonians to the aesthetically and practically valuable architecture around them (3).

58. Herbert Sass to Susan Frost, September 18, 1939, Herbert Sass Papers, SCHS.

59. Cann, "Maybank and the New Deal," 104–5.

60. *NC,* July 2, 1938.

61. Ibid.; letter, Susan Frost to W. W. Ball, July 1, 1938, *NC* Collection, SCHS. Frost called a special meeting of the PSOC at the Miles Brewton House and petitions were

circulated in several drug stores and hotels. Alston Deas, then on military assignment in Alexandria, Virginia, encouraged "Miss Sue" to continue the good work, expressing approval of her recent newspaper article on the old Medical College building.

62. William Means, "Fiddling as Rome Burns Reenacted Here," *NC*, 1939, PSOC scrapbooks, SCHS.

63. Letter, J. Franklin Burkhart to *NC*, 1939, PSOC, SCHS.

64. Letter, Susan Frost to W. W. Ball, January 25, 1938, Ball Papers.

65. *NC*, 1939, PSOC scrapbooks, SCHS.

66. Edward Twig, "Charleston: The Great Myth," *Forum* 103, no. 1 (January-June, 1940): 4.

67. *NC*, 1939, PSOC scrapbooks, SCHS.

68. Cann, "Maybank and the New Deal," 108–9.

69. Letter, Alston Deas to *NC*, October 30, 1938.

70. Letter, Herbert Sass to *NC*, 1939, PSOC scrapbooks, SCHS.

71. See particularly letter, Elizabeth O'Neill Verner to *NC*, October 1, 1938; Sam Stoney to *NC*, October 6, 1938; Josephine Pinckney to *NC*, October 25, 1938; DuBose Heyward to *NC*, November 7, 1938.

72. *NC*, September 30, 1938.

73. Letter, Susan Frost to Burnet Maybank, May 1937; letter, Susan Frost to J. H. Dingle, December, 1937, Susan Frost file, SCHS. See also *NC*, January 18, 1938.

74. Letter, Susan Frost to B. M. Thompson, June 2, 1941, Zoning Board files, CCA.

75. Letter, Susan Frost to T. W. Perry, August 14, 1942, Zoning Board file, CCA.

76. Letter, Susan Frost to Nina Pringle, January 5, 1943, Pringle Papers.

77. Ibid., December 15, 1942.

78. Details regarding publication of both volumes of house and family history can be found in letters of Susan Frost to Nina Pringle on December 16, 1943; May 30, 1944; October 14, 1944; November 25, 1944; and February 16, 1945, Pringle Papers. Frost, *Highlights,* and Mary Pringle Frost, *The Miles Brewton House: Chronicles and Reminiscences* (Charleston: Walker and Evans, 1939).

79. For an assessment of Robert N. S. Whitelaw's major contributions to the Charleston historic preservation movement, see Hosmer, *Preservation Comes of Age,* 1:254–73. See also Whitelaw, Hosmer interview. See also Stoney, *This Is Charleston,* which, several editions later, remains a vital catalog of the city's architectural heritage.

80. *NC*, June 17, 1945.

81. Whitelaw, Hosmer interview, 9.

82. Albert Simons, Hosmer interview, June 22, 1972.

83. Frances Edmunds was the driving force in the Historic Charleston Foundation for over thirty years, beginning as tours director in 1949 and serving as executive director from 1955–1985. She fought vigorously for the ongoing expansion of the "Old and Historic District." Edmunds won the prestigious Crowninshield Award of the National Trust for Historic Preservation in 1971, cited for having set the example for other communities in recovery of inner city districts as a result of rehabilitation of the Ansonborough section of Charleston through "pioneering use of the revolving fund." For a succinct preservation profile, see Bernard Groseclose, Jr., "Frances Ravenel Smythe Edmunds," *Preservation Progress* 17, no. 1 (May 1985): 3

84. Helen McCormack, taped interview by Hosmer, Hosmer Collection. McCormack, a native of Charleston, did the bulk of the work for the Carolina Art Association architectural survey and succeeded Robert Whitelaw as director of the group.

85. Burton, Hosmer interview, 20–22.

86. Deas, Hosmer interview, 26–27.

87. *Preservation Progress* 9, no. 1 (January 1964): 3–4.

88. For the municipal problems facing Charleston during and immediately after World War II, see Fraser, *Charleston!* 387–93, 399.

89. Letter, Albert Simons to Hasell Rivers, December 28, 1948, Simons Papers, SCHS.

90. *NC,* January 12, 1949; letter, Susan Frost to *NC,* January 1949, PSOC scrapbooks, SCHS.

91. *Preservation Progress,* organ of the Preservation Society of Charleston, frequently informed its subscribers of the vision and the financial sacrifice of its founder. A January 1971 issue (16, no. 1) reprinted her 1941 letter to the *News and Courier* detailing her rehabilitation struggles in southeast Charleston because it "might well serve as an incentive to today's restorationists."

92. Letter, Frances Ravenel Smythe Edmunds to author, June 2, 1981. Edmunds knew Frost well as a small child because her grandparents lived two doors away from the Miles Brewton House on King Street.

93. Letter, Susan Frost to *NC,* February 1947, PSOC scrapbooks, SCHS.

94. Grimball, "Old Charleston Lives," 298–300; Marguerite Steedman, "Miss Susan's Fight Saved Historic Charleston," *Atlanta Journal and Constitution,* March 18, 1951; Charlotte Walker, "Crusade," *Charleston Evening Post,* March 14, 1952; Frances R. Grimball, "Miss Frost Restores Houses, Fights for Women's Rights," *NC,* February 1, 1946; "AP Article Describes Tours of Historic Houses Here," *NC,* May 20, 1951; letter, Susan Frost to Nina Pringle, September 17, 1951, Pringle Papers, indicated local writer Herbert Sass wanted a picture of her and her dog to appear in an article he was doing for the *National Geographic Magazine.* However, the article, "South Carolina Rediscovered" (March 1953, 281–321), though rich in Charleston history, contains no mention of Frost, nor does her photograph appear. Letter, Susan Frost to Nina Pringle, January 10, 1946, indicated the *Saturday Evening Post* had a representative arriving the next day to take pictures in the Miles Brewton House drawing room for an article to appear in 8–10 weeks. No article was published.

95. On May 7, 1950, the *NC* ran a copy of a letter to the editor of the *New York Herald Tribune* by Albert Simons, written to inspire New Yorkers to save old houses in Washington Square from destruction. In telling the Charleston preservation story, Simons wrote of Frost: "With but little capital and rather less technical equipment but with the sort of faith that moves mountains, she has reclaimed one old house after another from slum occupancy to decent habitation. This she did long before early Americana became fashionable and before tourists in any Charleston." Remiss in sending birthday greetings on the correct day in 1955, the *News and Courier* issued an apology to Miss Frost a week later, said "happy birthday," and added: "We would be neglecting our duty if we failed to call attention to her work at every suitable opportunity."

96. *NC,* June 24, 1953. The Historic Charleston Foundation charged Sears with "ruthless destruction" in razing the Orphan House Chapel and maintained the national chain had "consistently turned a deaf ear to pleas from local and national organizations."

97. *NC,* May 6, 1948.

98. Letters, Susan Frost to *NC,* May 6, 1948, and June 30, 1953.

99. Ibid., June 30, 1953.

100. Ibid.

101. Letter, Charles B. Hosmer, Jr., to author, December 8, 1987. See also Hosmer, *Preservation Comes of Age,* 1:274.

102. *NC,* July 18, 1953.

103. Scardaville, "Selling of Historic Charleston," 10.

104. Ibid.; in 1959 the city council granted the Board of Architectural Review authority to review demolitions and alterations of pre–Civil War buildings in all parts of Charleston.

105. Letter, T. R. Waring, Jr., to author, September 16, 1980.

106. *NC,* May 6, 1948.

107. Letter, Susan Frost to Nina Pringle, January 22, 1953, Pringle Papers.

CONCLUSION

1. Register of Mesne Conveyance. Susan Frost sold the last of her six East Bay Street properties in July 1955.

2. Letter, Susan Frost to Nina Pringle, March 1, 1949, Pringle Papers. See also Frost to Pringle, December 16, 1947.

3. *NC,* December 18, 1941; noting disparities in appropriation of the Good Cheer Christmas Funds, Frost urged that need, not color, be the guiding factor in dispensing the monies.

4. *NC,* June 11, 1945.

5. *NC,* March 23, 1945.

6. Letters, Susan Frost to William Watts Ball, August 17, 1943, and November 28, 1943, Ball Papers.

7. *NC,* June 17, 1945.

8. Letter, Susan Frost to Nina Pringle, March 17, 1945, Pringle Papers, described one such occasion: "I went last evg. to such an intg. service in one of our Negro churches, a lovely little church, built many years ago, when they knew how to build; the Rector gave me a special invitation to come; he is a coal black Negro, looks as if he must be almost seven ft. tall and proportionally large; and had a very musical voice, very resonant, and he intoned a good deal of the Service. I have often been to his services."

9. Letter, Susan Frost to Nina Pringle, December 27, 1951, Pringle Papers; interview with Mrs. Edward Manigault, Charleston, South Carolina, July 14, 1981.

10. Interview with Thomas R. Waring, Jr., June 2, 1983. For the storm of controversy generated by the racial decisions of federal district court judge and seventh generation Charlestonian J. Waties Waring, his divorce and remarriage to a liberal Northerner, and his personal associations with African Americans, see Tinley E. Yarbrough, *A Passion for Justice: J. Waties Waring and Civil Rights* (New York: Oxford Univ. Press, 1987).

11. Frost, *Highlights,* 68–74. The Charleston canine lover published some of her favorite dog poetry in addition to the life stories of Cherie, Winsome (Winsie), Waysie, Stray Dog (Straysie), Jip, and Ashley Soluble Guano. See also Maude Waddell, "Where Birds Find Warm Welcome," *NC,* July 7, 1938.

12. See *NC,* March 9, 1951; April 9, 1945; March 18, 1945; letter, Susan Frost to *NC,* January 4, 1951, Ball Papers; letter, Susan Frost to Nina Pringle, December 27, 1951, Pringle Papers.

13. Letters, Susan Frost to Nina Pringle, January 4, 1945, Pringle Papers; also Frost

to Pringle, August 1946. For Frost's admiration of Sass and his work, see her letter to the editor, *NC,* January 24, 1948.

14. Interview with Mrs. Edward Manigault, July 14, 1981.

15. Letter, Susan Frost to Editor, *NC,* May 7, 1947, Ball Papers.

16. Letter, Susan Frost to Nina Pringle, February 1952, Pringle Papers.

17. *NC,* July 14, 1952.

18. Interview with Elise Pinckney, Charleston, South Carolina, June 10, 1983.

19. Ibid. Elise Pinckney was co-editor (with Alberta L. Quattlebaum) of *A Guide to St. Michael's Church Charleston* (Charleston: Nelsons' Southern Printing Co., 1979).

20. Letter, Susan Frost to W. W. Ball, January 19, 1945, Ball Papers.

21. Interview with Mrs. Edward Manigault, July 14, 1981; *NC,* August 12, 1952.

22. *NC,* February 16, 1947; challenging Police Chief Ortmann's "insinuations" of women as careless behind the wheel, Susan Frost argued that statistics would likely prove the opposite.

23. Ibid.

24. Interview with Mrs. Edward Manigault.

25. Ibid.; interview with Elise Pinckney.

26. The Julia Peterkin Papers, SCHS, contain her short story. Former archivist Harlan Greene, of invaluable assistance on this project, believed that Julia Peterkin was in the habit of writing down verbatim stories she heard and stated that he himself had heard the episode.

27. Letter, Elise Pinckney to author, February 28, 1980.

28. Elizabeth O'Neill Verner, *Mellowed by Time* (Charleston, S.C.: Tradd Street Press, 1941), 68–71.

29. Pat Conroy, "Shadows of the Old South," *Geo: The Earth Diary* 3 (May 1981): 64–82.

30. *NC,* January 4, 1958. The issue of the preceding day carried a full story of the honor to the pioneer restorer. The Charleston Federation of Women's Clubs *Yearbook* lists its Hall of Fame honorees.

31. Isabella Leland, "Susan P. Frost Put Sentiment First to Become Benefactor to Charleston," *NC,* September 21, 1958.

32. For obituary and funeral notices and editorial commentary see *Charleston Evening Post* and *NC,* October 7 and 8, 1960.

33. For a recent look at reformers in general in the Victorian era, with temperance as a focal point, see Gail S. Lowe, "A Bio-Bibliography of American Reformers, 1865–1917, with a Case Study of Temperance-Prohibition" (Ph.D. diss., George Washington Univ., 1992). A good overview of the rise of the "new woman" which incorporates the latest historiography can be found in Nancy Woloch, *Women and the American Experience,* 2nd ed. (New York: McGraw-Hill, 1994), 269–306.

34. Pringle, "Susan Snow," 3.

35. The continuities and collective patterns of reform are effectively treated in Robert H. Walker, *Reform in America: The Continuing Frontier* (Lexington: Univ. Press of Kentucky, 1985). On the woman question, see 93–104.

36. Noralee Frankel and Nancy S. Dye, eds., *Gender, Class, Race and Reform in the Progressive Era* (Lexington: Univ. Press of Kentucky, 1991), 4.

37. Martha Swain, "Organized Women as Force in the Community," paper presented at the Symposium on Women in Southern Society, University of Richmond,

1984, paper in possession of author. For the range of women's "municipal housekeeping" projects in the South and elsewhere, see Anne Firor Scott, *Natural Allies: Women's Associations in American History* (Urbana: Univ. of Illinois Press, 1991), 141–59.

38. Mary Vardrine McBee, founder of Ashley Hall, a private girls' school, was recognized nationally in the field of education. She was Civic Club president and received commissions from the governor of South Carolina to serve on the Charleston School Board (the first female member) and the State Welfare Board. Mrs. Julius Visanka served as both president of the Civic Club (1904–1908) and the Federation of Women's Clubs (for three years). She was also state federation president, a charter member of the Charleston Section National Council of Jewish Women and organized the Women's Division of the Red Cross campaign in 1917. She worked in a campaign to enlarge and improve local schools, and Charleston's first municipal playground was opened during her tenure as Civic Club president.

39. Woloch, *Women and the American Experience,* 302.

40. Lowe, "Bio-Bibliography of American Reformers," 121.

41. Such conclusions embraced both the Richard Hofstadter (*The Age of Reform: From Bryan to F.D.R.,* 1955) and George Mowry (*The California Progressives,* 1951, and *The Era of Theodore Roosevelt and the Birth of Modern America, 1900–1912,* 1958) views of reformers as old middle class concerned about loss of status, economic security and community autonomy and morality and the conclusions of key historians who challenged those interpretations of Progressivism, especially Samuel Hays (*The Response to Industrialism, 1885–1914,* 1957) and Robert Wiebe (*Search for Order, 1877–1920,* 1967.) Hays and Wiebe saw reformers as rational, responsible, enthusiastic and confident of making a better new world in modern America.

42. Letter, Charles Hosmer to author, December 8, 1987. In acknowledging that Appleton and Frost did not concentrate on single buildings the way most of their preservationist friends did, the "dean of preservation historians" admitted: "Frost was outstanding nationally in her ability to embrace Charleston's 'townscape.' Even Appleton talked more about individual houses than she did."

43. Letters, Susan Frost to John D. Rockefeller, Jr., April 28, 1938; Helen G. Spencer (for Rockefeller) to Susan Frost, May 4, 1938; Susan Frost to John D. Rockefeller, Jr., May 18, 1940; Helen Spencer to Susan Frost, May 24, 1940, Rockefeller Archive Center, Rockefeller Family Archives, Cultural Interests, Record Group 2, File 156, Pocantico Hills, New York.

44. Sharon McKern, *Redneck Mothers, Good Ol' Girls and Other Southern Belles* (New York: Viking Press, 1979), 4–5.

$\mathscr{S}$ELECTED BIBLIOGRAPHY

PRIMARY SOURCES

Manuscripts

Archives of American Art, Washington, D.C.
Hosmer Collection: Taped interviews, Charles B. Hosmer, Jr., with Milby Burton, Alston
  Deas, Helen McCormack, Albert Simons, and Robert N. S. Whitelaw.

Bancroft Library, University of California, Berkeley
Pringle Family Papers.

Charleston County Courthouse, Charleston, S.C.
Register of Mesne Conveyance.

Charleston County Library, Charleston, S.C.
Susan P. Frost file.
McBee biographical file.
Thomas B. Stoney file.

Charleston News and Courier, Charleston, S.C.
Miles Brewton House clipping file.
Heyward-Washington House clipping file.
Joseph Manigault House clipping file.

Charleston Real Estate Exchange, Charleston, S.C.
Minutes, 1929–1939.

City of Charleston Department of Archives and History, Charleston, S.C.
Charleston City Council, minutes.
Charleston Zoning Board file.
Susan P. Frost file.
John P. Grace Papers.
Tristram T. Hyde Papers.
Burnet R. Maybank Papers.
Thomas P. Stoney Papers.
Ways and Means Committee, minutes.

Eleutherian Mills Historical Library, Wilmington, Del.
Irénée DuPont Papers.

Gibbes Museum of Art, Charleston, S.C.
George W. Johnson Collection.

Library of Congress, Washington, D.C.
National Woman's Party Papers.

Perkins Library, Duke University, Durham, N.C.
William Watts Ball Papers.
Hemphill Family Papers.
Louisa and Mary B. Poppenheim Papers.

Rockefeller Archive Center, Pocantico Hills, North Tarrytown, N.Y.
Rockefeller Family Archives, Cultural Interests.

Society for the Preservation of New England Antiquities, Boston, Mass.
William Sumner Appleton Papers.

South Carolina Historical Society, Charleston, S.C.
Alston/Pringle/Frost Papers.
Alston/Pringle/Hill Papers.
Miles Brewton House file.
Century Club, minutes.
Charleston Board of Architectural Review papers.
Charleston City Federation of Women's Clubs records.
Charleston News and Courier Collection.
City of Charleston Historic Building file.
Civic Club of Charleston records.
Frost Family Papers.
Susan P. Frost file.
Heyward–Washington House file.
Jenkins Orphanage file.
Ladies' Benevolent Society files.
Ladies Fuel Society files.
Joseph Manigault House papers.
Julia Peterkin Papers.
Mabel Pollitzer Papers.
Mary B. and Louisa B. Poppenheim clipping files.
Ravenel/Pringle/Childs Papers.
Herbert Ravenel Sass Papers.
Albert Simons Papers.
Harriet Simons Papers.
Society for the Preservation of Old Dwellings, scrapbooks and files.
Alice R. Huger Smith Papers.
Elizabeth O'Neill Verner Papers.
Thomas R. Waring, Sr., Papers.
Eola Willis Papers.

South Caroliniana Library, University of South Carolina, Columbia, S.C.
Equal Suffrage League of South Carolina, minutes.

Winthrop University Archives, Rock Hill, S.C.
Taped interviews, Constance B. Myers with Laura Bragg, Carrie Pollitzer, Mabel Pollitzer, Eulalie Salley.

Government Documents

Charleston City Directory. Charleston—various publishers, 1890–1955.
Yearbook, City of Charleston. Charleston—various publishers, 1890–1955.

Newspapers

Charleston Evening Post
Charleston News and Courier
The Suffragist

Interviews and Letters

Boone, Carl. Telephone interview, June 23, 1983, Charleston.
Childs, Margaretta. Interview, July 8, 1981, Charleston; letter, May 20, 1981.
Deas, Alston. Interview, July 3, 1981; July 21, 1981; June 12, 1983, Charleston.
Edmunds, Frances. Interview, July 17, 1981; March 8, 1982; June 27, 1983, Charleston; letter, June 2, 1981.
Frost, Laura. Telephone interview, July 5, 1981, Charleston.
Hamilton, Elizabeth Verner. Interview, October 13, 1980; July 20, 1981; April 13, 1985, Charleston.
Hanckel, Marianne. Telephone interview, July 5, 1981, Charleston.
Hannahan, Elizabeth. Telephone interview, June 27, 1983, Charleston.
Hart, Mrs. W. T. Interview, April 27 1980; July 6, 1981, Charleston; letter, May 27, 1981.
Hosmer, Charles B., Jr. Interview, April 12, 1985, Harrisonburg, Va.; numerous telephone conversations and letters.
Legge, Dorothy. Interview, July 13, 1984, Charleston.
Manigault, Mrs. Edward. Interview, July 14, 1981; March 10, 1982; June 22, 1983, Charleston.
Pinckney, Elise. Interview, June 10, 1983, Charleston; letter, February 28, 1980.
Simmons, Philip. Telephone interview, June 12, 1983, Charleston.
Tamsberg, A. J. Interview, June 22, 1983, Charleston.
Waring, Thomas R., Jr. Interview, July 6, 1981; June 21, 1983, Charleston; letter, September 16, 1980.

SECONDARY WORKS

Books

Abbott, Shirley. *Womenfolks: Growing Up Down South.* New Haven, Conn., and New York: Ticknor and Fields, 1983.
Blair, Karen J. *The Clubwoman as Feminist: True Womanhood Redefined, 1868–1914.* New York: Holmes and Meier, 1980.
Bodie, Idella. *South Carolina Women: They Dared to Lead.* Lexington, S.C.: Sandlapper Store, 1978.
Bowes, Frederick. *The Culture of Early Charleston.* Chapel Hill: Univ. of North Carolina Press, 1942.
Breaux, Daisy [Calhoun, Cornelia Donovan O'Donovan]. *The Autobiography of a Chameleon.* Washington, D.C.: Potomac Press, 1930.
Brewster, Lawrence Fay. *Summer Migrations of South Carolina Planters.* Durham, N.C.: Duke Univ. Press, 1947.

Brownell, Blaine. *The Urban Ethos in the South, 1920–1930.* Baton Rouge: Louisiana State Univ. Press, 1975.

Bull, Emily L. *Eulalie.* Aiken, S.C.: Kalmia Press, 1973.

Bussman, Marlo Pease. *Born Charlestonian.* Columbia: State Printing Co., 1969.

Cardozo, J. R. *Reminiscences of Charleston.* Charleston: Joseph Walker, 1866.

Cash, W. J. *The Mind of the South.* New York: Alfred A. Knopf, 1941.

Clark, E. Culpepper. *Francis Warrington Dawson and the Politics of Restoration South Carolina, 1874–1889.* University: Univ. of Alabama Press, 1980.

Clinton, Catherine. *The Plantation Mistress: Woman's World in the Old South.* New York: Pantheon Books, 1982.

Conroy, Pat. *The Lords of Discipline.* Boston: Houghton Mifflin Co., 1980.

Côté, Richard N. *Guide to the Alston-Pringle-Frost Manuscript Collection in the South Carolina Historical Society.* Charleston: South Carolina Historical Society, 1990.

Cott, Nancy. *The Grounding of Modern Feminism.* New Haven, Conn.: Yale Univ. Press, 1987.

Coulter, E. Merton. *George Walton Williams: The Life of a Southern Merchant and Banker, 1820–1903.* Athens, Ga: Hebriten Press, 1976.

Degler, Carl. *Place over Time: The Continuity of Southern Distinctiveness.* Baton Rouge: Louisiana State Univ. Press, 1977.

Dinnerstein, Leonard, and Mary Dale Palsson, eds. *Jews in the South.* Baton Rouge: Louisiana State Univ. Press, 1973.

Douglas, Ann. *The Feminization of American Culture.* New York: Alfred A. Knopf, 1977.

Duke, Marc. *The DuPonts: Portrait of a Dynasty.* New York: E. P. Dutton, 1976.

E. I. DuPont de Nemours and Company. *DuPont: The Autobiography of an American Enterprise.* Wilmington, Del.: E. I. DuPont de Nemours and Co. (distributed by Charles Scribner's Sons, New York), 1952.

Easterby, J. H. *A History of the College of Charleston.* New York: Scribner's, 1935.

Ferguson, David. *Cleopatra's Barge: The Crowninshield Story.* Boston: Little Brown and Co. 1976.

Ferris, William, and Charles Reagan Wilson, eds. *Encyclopedia of Southern Culture.* Chapel Hill: Univ. of North Carolina Press, 1989.

Fields, Mamie Garvin (with Karen Fields). *Lemon Swamp and Other Places: A Carolina Memoir.* New York: Free Press, 1983.

Flexner, Eleanor. *Century of Struggle: The Woman's Rights Movement in the United States.* Cambridge, Mass.: Belknap Press of Harvard Univ. Press, 1959.

Folsom, Merrill. *Great American Mansions and Their Stories.* New York: Hastings House, 1963.

Frankel, Noralee, and Nancy S. Dye. *Gender, Class, Race and Reform in the Progressive Era.* Lexington: Univ. Press of Kentucky, 1991.

Fraser, Walter F., Jr. *Charleston! Charleston!: The History of a Southern City.* Columbia: Univ. of South Carolina Press, 1989.

Friedman, Jean. *The Enclosed Garden: Women and Community in the Evangelical South, 1830–1900.* Chapel Hill: Univ. of North Carolina Press, 1985.

Frost, Mary Pringle. *The Meaning of a House.* Charleston: n.p., n.d. [ca. 1920].

———. *The Miles Brewton House: Chronicles and Reminiscences.* Charleston: Susan Pringle Frost and Rebecca Motte Frost, 1939.

Frost, Susan Pringle. *Highlights of the Miles Brewton House.* Charleston: Susan Pringle Frost, 1944.

Gaines, Francis Pendleton. *The Southern Plantation: A Study in the Development and the Accuracy of a Tradition.* New York: Columbia Univ. Press, 1925.

Hall, Jacqueline Dowd. *Revolt against Chivalry: Jessie Daniel Ames and the Women's Campaign against Lynching.* New York: Columbia Univ. Press, 1979.

Henry, Allan, Jr., ed. *Frances G. DuPont: A Memoir.* Philadelphia: William F. Fell Co., 1951.

Hosmer, Charles B., Jr. *Presence of the Past: A History of the Preservation Movement in the United States before Williamsburg.* New York: G. P. Putnam's Sons, 1965.

————. *Preservation Comes of Age: From Williamsburg to the National Trust, 1926–1949.* 2 vols. Charlottesville: Univ. Press of Virginia for the [National Trust for Historic] Preservation Press, 1981.

Hungerford, Edward. *The Personality of American Cities.* New York: McBride, Nast and Co., 1913.

Irwin, Inez Haynes. *Story of the Woman's Party.* New York: Harcourt, 1921.

Jervey, Theodore. *The Elder-Brother.* New York: Neale Publishing Co., 1905.

Jones, Anne. *Tomorrow Is Another Day: The Woman Writer in the South, 1859–1936.* Baton Rouge: Louisiana State Univ. Press, 1981.

Jones, Lewis P. *South Carolina: A Synoptic History for Laymen.* Columbia: Sandlapper Press, 1971.

Kennedy, Roger. *Architecture, Men, Women and Money in America 1600–1860.* New York: Random House, 1985.

Kraditor, Aileen S. *The Ideas of the Woman Suffrage Movement, 1890–1920.* New York: Columbia Univ. Press, 1965.

Lander, Ernest M. *A History of South Carolina, 1865–1890.* Chapel Hill: Univ. of North Carolina Press, 1960.

Lane, Mills. *Architecture of the Old South: South Carolina.* Savannah: Beehive Press, 1984.

Lapham, Samuel, Jr., and Albert Simons. *The Early Architecture of Charleston.* Columbia: Univ. of South Carolina Press, 1927.

Leiding, Harriette Kershaw. *Charleston: Historic and Romantic.* Philadelphia: J. B. Lippincott Company, 1931.

————. *Historic Houses of South Carolina.* Philadelphia: J. B. Lippincott Co., 1921.

Lord, Clifford, ed. *Keepers of the Past.* Chapel Hill: Univ. of North Carolina Press, 1965.

Lunardini, Christine A. *From Equal Suffrage to Equal Rights: Alice Paul and the National Woman's Party, 1910–1928.* New York: New York Univ. Press, 1986.

Marion, John Francis. *The Charleston Story.* Harrisburg, Pa.: Stackpole Books, 1978.

Martin, Theodora Penny. *The Sound of Our Voices.* Boston: Beacon Press, 1987.

McCrady, Edward. *The History of South Carolina under the Royal Government 1719–1776.* New York: MacMillan, 1899.

McDowell, John Patrick. *The Social Gospel in the South: The Woman's Home Mission Movement in the Methodist Episcopal Church, South, 1886–1939.* Baton Rouge: Louisiana State Univ. Press, 1982.

McKern, Sharon. *Redneck Mothers, Good Ol' Girls, and Other Southern Belles.* New York: Viking Press, 1979.

Molloy, Robert. *Charleston: A Gracious Heritage.* New York and London: D. Appleton-Century Co., 1947.

Moltke-Hansen, David, and Michael O'Brien, eds. *Intellectual Life in Antebellum Charleston.* Knoxville: Univ. of Tennessee Press, 1986.

Myers, Lynn Robertson. *Mirror of Time: Elizabeth O'Neill Verner's Charleston.* Columbia, S.C.: McKissick Museums, Univ. of South Carolina, 1983.

National Trust for Historic Preservation. *Preservation: Toward an Ethic in the 1980's.* Washington, D.C.: Preservation Press, 1980.

———. *With Heritage So Rich.* Washington, D.C.: Preservation Press, 1966.

O'Neill, William L. *Everyone Was Brave: A History of Feminism in America.* Chicago: Quadrangle Books, 1969.

Patton, Sadie Smathers. *A Condensed History of Flat Rock: The Little Charleston of the Mountains.* Asheville, N.C.: Church Printing Co., n.d.

Pease, William H., and Jane H. Pease. *The Web of Progress: Private Values and Public Styles in Boston and Charleston, 1828–1843.* New York: Oxford Univ. Press, 1985.

Pinckney, Elise, and Alberta L. Quattlebaum. *A Guide to St. Michael's Church Charleston.* Charleston: Nelson's Southern Printing Co., 1979.

Pringle, Elizabeth Waties Allston. *A Woman Rice Planter.* Cambridge, Mass.: Belknap Press of Harvard Univ. Press, 1961.

Ravenel, Beatrice St. Julien. *Architects of Charleston.* Charleston: Carolina Art Association, 1945.

———. *Charleston: The Place and the People.* New York: MacMillan, 1906.

Reznikoff, Charles. *The Jews of Charleston: A History of an American Jewish Community.* Philadelphia: Jewish Publication Society of America, 1950.

Rhett, Robert Goodwyn. *Charleston: An Epic of Carolina.* Richmond, Va.: Garrett and Massie Inc., 1940.

Rogers, George C., Jr. *The History of Georgetown County, South Carolina.* Columbia: Univ. of South Carolina Press, 1970.

Rosen, Robert. *A Short History of Charleston.* San Francisco: Lexikos, 1982.

Salley, Katherine Batts, ed. *Life at Saint Mary's.* Chapel Hill: Univ. of North Carolina Press, 1942.

Sass, Herbert. *Charleston Grows: An Economic, Social and Cultural Portrait of an Old South Community in the New South.* Charleston: Carolina Art Association, 1949.

———. *Outspoken: 150 Years of the News and Courier.* Columbia: Univ. of South Carolina Press, 1953.

Scott, Anne F. *Making the Invisible Woman Visible.* Urbana and Chicago: Univ. of Illinois Press, 1984.

———. *Natural Allies: Women's Associations in American History.* Urbana and Chicago: Univ. of Illinois Press, 1991.

———. *The Southern Lady: From Pedestal to Politics, 1830–1930.* Chicago: Univ. of Illinois Press, 1970.

Severens, Kenneth. *Southern Architecture: 350 Years of Distinctive American Buildings.* New York: E. P. Dutton, 1981.

Smith, Daniel Elliot Huger. *A Charlestonian's Recollections, 1846–1913.* Charleston: Carolina Art Association, 1949.

Smith, Daniel Elliot Huger, and Alice Ravenel Huger. *The Dwelling Houses of Charleston, South Carolina.* Philadelphia: J. B. Lippincott Co., 1917.

———. *Twenty Drawings of the Pringle House.* New York: William Murrow Co., 1917.

Stark, John D. *"Damned Upcountryman": William Watts Ball, a Study in American Conservatism.* Durham, N.C.: Duke Univ. Press, 1968.

Stephenson, William. *Sallie Southall Cotten: A Woman's Life in North Carolina.* Greenville, N.C.: Pamlico Press, 1987.

Stevens, Doris. *Jailed for Freedom.* New York: Boni and Liveright, 1920.

Stipe, Robert E., and Antoinette Lee, eds. *The American Mosaic: Preserving a Nation's Heritage.* Washington, D.C.: US/ICOMOS, 1987.

Stoney, Samuel Gaillard. *Charleston's Historic Houses.* Charleston: Historic Charleston Foundation, 1949.

———. *Plantations of the Carolina Low Country.* Charleston: Carolina Art Association, 1938.

———. *This Is Charleston: A Survey of the Architectural Heritage of a Unique American City.* 2d ed. Charleston: Carolina Art Association, Historic Charleston Foundation, and the Preservation Society of Charleston, 1960.

Taylor, William R. *Cavalier and Yankee: The Old South and the American National Character.* New York: George Braziller, 1961.

Tindall, George Brown. *The Emergence of the New South, 1913–1945.* Baton Rouge: Louisiana State Univ. Press, 1967.

———. *The Persistent Tradition in New South Politics.* Baton Rouge: Louisiana State Univ. Press, 1977.

Torre, Susana, ed. *Women in Architecture: A Historic and Contemporary Perspective.* New York: Whitney Library of Design, 1977.

Trachtenberg, Alan. *The Incorporation of America: Culture and Society in the Gilded Age.* New York: Hill and Wang, 1982.

Verner, Elizabeth O'Neill. *Mellowed by Time.* Charleston: Tradd Street Press, 1941.

Vlach, John Michael. *Charleston Blacksmith: The Work of Philip Simmons.* Athens: Univ. of Georgia Press, 1981.

Wade, Richard C. *Slavery in the Cities: The South, 1820–1860.* New York: Oxford Univ. Press, 1964.

Walker, Robert H. *Reform in America: The Continuing Frontier.* Lexington: Univ. Press of Kentucky, 1985.

———, ed. *The Reform Spirit in America: A Documentation of the Pattern of Reform in the American Republic.* New York: G. P. Putnam's Sons and Capricorn Books, 1976.

Wheeler, Marjorie Spruill, *New Women of the New South: The Leaders of the Woman Suffrage Movement in the Southern States.* New York: Oxford Univ. Press, 1993.

Whitehill, Walter Muir. *Louise duPont Crowninshield, 1877–1958.* Winterthur, Del.: Anthoensen Press, 1960.

Wiebe, Robert H. *The Search for Order, 1877–1920.* New York: Hill and Wang, 1967.

Williams, George W. *St. Michael's, Charleston, 1751–1951.* Columbia: Univ. of South Carolina Press, 1951.

Williams, Norman, Jr., Edmund Kellogg, and Frank B. Gilbert, *Readings in Historic Preservation: Why? What? How?* New Brunswick: Rutgers University, Center for Urban Policy Research, 1983.

Wilson, Charles Reagan. *Baptized in Blood: The Religion of the Lost Cause, 1865–1920.* Athens: Univ. of Georgia Press, 1980.

Wood, Mary. *The History of the General Federation of Women's Clubs.* New York: General Federation of Women's Clubs, 1912.

Woodward, C. Vann. *The Burden of Southern History.* Baton Rouge: Louisiana State Univ. Press, 1960.

Yarbrough, Tinsley E. *A Passion for Justice: J. Waties Waring and Civil Rights.* New York: Oxford Univ. Press, 1987.

Articles and Essays

Abbott, Shirley. "The Charleston Inheritance." *American Heritage* (April 1987): 62–69.

Abernathy, Mollie C. (Davis). "Southern Women, Social Reconstruction, and the Church in the 1920s." *Louisiana Studies* 13 (Winter 1974): 289–312.

Allen, George Marshall. "Charleston: A Typical City of the South." *Magazine of Travel* (February 1895): 98–128.

Allen, Hervey, and DuBose Heyward. "Poetry South." *Poetry* 20 (1922): 35–48.

Allen, James H. "The Zoning Ordinance of Charleston." *American City* 46 (February 1932): 111, 113.

"Another Red Light District Gone." *Survey* 39 (October 27, 1917): 97.

Baum, Dwight James. "Glimpses of Charleston." *House Beautiful* (April 1921): 304–5.

Bland, Sidney R. "'Miss Sue' of Charleston: Saving a Neighborhood, Influencing a Nation." In *Architecture: A Place for Women,* edited by Ellen Perry Berkeley, 63–73. Washington, D.C.: Smithsonian Institution Press, 1989.

———. "'Miss Sue' Frost: Women of Firsts." *Preservation Progress* 26, no. 3 (August 1982): 4–5.

———. "Transcending the Expectations of a Culture: Susan Pringle Frost, a New South Charleston Woman." In *Developing Dixie: Modernization in a Traditional Society,* edited by Winfred B. Moore, Jr., Joseph Tripp, and Lyon G. Tyler, Jr., 245–59. Westport, Conn.: Greenwood Press, 1988.

Brock, H. I. "A City That Lives As a Monument." *New York Times Magazine* (November 1, 1931).

Campbell, Barbara Kuhn. "The 'Liberated' Woman of 1914: Prominent Women in the Progressive Era." *Studies in American History and Culture* 6 (UMI Research Press, 1959).

"Charleston." *Los Angeles Times Home Magazine* (October 25, 1959): 13–24.

"Charleston, South Carolina." *Antiques Magazine* 61 (October 1966): 527–30.

Childs, Margaretta P. "Elizabeth Allston Pringle." In *Notable American Women,* vol. 3, edited by Edward T. James et al., 100-101. 3 vols. Cambridge, Mass., and London: Belknap Press of Harvard Univ. Press, 1971.

Cohen, Daniel. "Charleston's Restoration Challenge." *Historic Preservation* 39 (January-February 1987): 31–39.

Conroy, Pat. "Shadows of the Old South." *Geo: The Earth Diary* 3 (May 1981): 64–82.

Coolidge, Nancy, and Nancy Padnos. "William Sumner Appleton and the Society for the Preservation of New England Antiquities." *Antiques Magazine* 129 (January-March 1986): 590–95.

Cotterell, Robert S. "The Old South to the New." *Journal of Southern History* 15 (February-November 1949): 3–8.

Deas, Alston. "Charleston's First Zoning Ordinance." *Preservation Progress* 27 (January 1983): 3.

———. "They Shall See Your Good Works." *Preservation Progress* 7 (May 1962): 1–5.

Derks, Scott. "The New Battle for Charleston." *Sandlapper* (March 1981): 28–31.

Dingle, J. H. "Charleston Is Looking Forward." *American City* 44 (January 1931): 19.

Doyle, Don. "Leadership and Decline in Postwar Charleston, 1865–1910." In *From the Old South to the New: Essays on the Traditional South,* edited by Walter J. Fraser, Jr., and Winfred B. Moore, Jr., 93–106. Westport, Conn.: Greenwood Press, 1981.

———. "Urbanization and Southern Culture: Economic Elites in Four New South Cities (Atlanta, Nashville, Charleston, Mobile) c. 1865–1910." In *Toward a New South: Studies in Post-Civil War Communities,* edited by Orville V. Burton and Robert C. McMath, Jr., 11–36. Westport, Conn: Greenwood Press, 1982.

Engelman, Uriah. "The Jewish Population of Charleston." *Jewish Social Studies* 13, no. 3 (July 1951): 195–210.

"Esthetic Zoning Established in Charleston, South Carolina." *American City* 44 (December 1931): 115.

Fenhagen, Mary Pringle. "A Long Shadow." *Preservation Progress* 8, no. 3 (May 1963): 1–2.

———. "Descendants of Judge Robert Pringle." *South Carolina Historical Magazine* 62 (July 1961): 151–64; 62 (October 1961): 221–36.

Freedman, Estelle. "Separation as Strategy: Female Institution Building and American Feminism, 1870–1930." *Feminist Studies* 5 (Fall 1979): 512–29.

Friedman, Jean. "Piety and Kin: The Limits of Antebellum Southern Women's Reform." In *Women and the Structure of Society*, edited by Barbara Harris and Jo Ann McNamara, 12–19. Durham, N.C.: Duke Univ. Press, 1984.

Garner, George. "An American City Which Should Be Preserved." *Manufacturers Record* (May 20, 1926): 79–80.

Garofalo, Charles P. "The Sons of Henry Grady: Atlanta Boosters in the 1920s." *Journal of Southern History* 42 (May 1976): 187–204.

Granger, Mrs. A. O. "The Effect of Club Work in the South." *Annals of the American Academy of Political and Social Science* 28, no. 2 (1906): 248–56.

Greene, Harlan. "The Preservation Effort." *Charleston Magazine* (November 1976): 36–39.

Grimball, Frances R. "Miss Frost Restores Houses, Fights for Women's Rights." *Charleston News and Courier*, February 1, 1946.

———. "Old Charleston Lives Again in Houses Rescued by Miss Sue." *Independent Woman* 25 (October 1946): 298–300.

Groseclose, Bernard. "Col. Alston Deas." *Preservation Progress* 29, no. 3 (March 1985), 5.

Harrigan, Anthony. "The Charleston Tradition." *American Heritage* (February 1958): 48–61, 88–93.

Hart, Eleanor. "A Beginning in Preservation—As I Remember." *Preservation Progress* 7, no. 2 (March 1962): 11.

———. "As I Remember: The Creation of the Preservation Society and the Disappearance of the Mocha Cakes." *Preservation Progress* 7, no. 3 (May 1962): 9–10; 7, no. 4 (November 1962): 12–14; 7, no. 1 (January 1963): 14–15; 7, no. 2 (March 1963): 18–19.

———. "Weighing Her Merits." *Preservation Progress* 10, no. 1 (January 1965): 1–6.

Hays, Samuel P. "The Politics of Reform in Municipal Government in the Progressive Era." *Pacific Northwest Quarterly* 55 (October 1964): 159–68.

Heyward, DuBose. "Charleston: Where Mellow Past and Present Meet." *National Geographic* (March 1939): 273–312.

Hollis, Daniel. "Yates Snowden." In *Outspoken: 150 Years of the News and Courier*, edited by Herbert Sass, ed., 87–91. Columbia: Univ. of South Carolina Press, 1953.

Hosmer, Charles B., Jr. "The Broadening View of the Historical Preservation Movement." In *Material Culture and the Study of American Life*, edited by Ian M. G. Quimby, 121–40. New York: W. W. Norton, 1978.

Howells, W. D. "In Charleston." *Harper's Monthly Magazine* (October 1915): 747–57.

Hudson, Berkley. "First Lady of Preseverance." *Historic Preservation* (November-December 1986): 59, 87.

Huth, Tom. "Should Charleston Go New South?" *Historic Preservation* 31, no. 3 (July-August 1979): 32–38.

Lander, Ernest M., Jr. "Charleston: Manufacturing Center of the Old South." *Journal of Southern History* 26, no. 3 (August 1960): 330–51.

Leland, Isabella. "Susan P. Frost Put Sentiment First to Become Benefactor to Charleston." *Charleston News and Courier,* September 21, 1958.

Lindgren, James M. "'Virginia Needs Living Heroes': Historic Preservation in the Progressive Era." *Public Historian* 13, no. 1 (Winter 1991): 9–24.

MacElwee, Roy. "Charleston's Waterfront Driveways." *American City* 37 (December 1927): 741–44.

———. "The Preservation and Restoration of Charleston's Fine Old Architecture." *American City* 42 (February 1930): 134–35.

Meder, Marilyn. "The Role of Women and Minorities in Historic Preservation." Washington, D.C.: The Preservation Press, 1977.

Mendenhall, Marjorie. "Southern Women of a 'Lost Generation.'" *South Atlantic Quarterly* 33 (October 1934): 334–53.

Moltke-Hansen, David. "Why History Mattered: The Background of Ann Pamela Cunningham's Interest in the Preservation of Mount Vernon." *Furman Studies* 26 (December 1980): 34–42.

Moore, Jamie. "The Great South Carolina Inter-State and West Indian Exposition of 1901." *Sandlapper* (July 1978): 11–15.

Moore, John H. "Charleston in World War I: Seeds of Change." *South Carolina Historical Magazine* 86 (January-October 1985): 39–49.

"More Than a Shade of Difference." *Preservation Progress* 9, no. 1 (January 1964): 3–4.

Olmert, Michael. "How Annapolis Keeps Its Charm." *Historic Preservation* 38 (May-June 1986): 49–54.

Paine, Judith. "The Woman's Pavilion of 1876." *Feminist Art Journal* 4, no. 4 (Winter 1975–1976): 12.

Peterson, Anne E. "Frances B. Johnston: The Crusader with a Camera." *Historic Preservation* 32, no. 1 (January-February 1980): 17–20.

Pinckney, Elise. "Miss Alice Smith: Low Country Artist." *South Carolina Historical Magazine* (June 1957): 6–7.

Pinckney, Josephine. "Charleston's Poetry Society." *Sewanee Review* 38 (1930): 50–56.

Pringle, Nell McColl. "Susan Snow." Unpublished ms. n.d.

Radford, John P. "Social Structure and Urban Form: Charleston 1860–1880." In *From the Old South to the New,* edited by Walter J. Fraser, Jr., and Winfred B. Moore, Jr., 81–91. Westport, Conn.: Greenwood Press, 1981.

Ralph, Julian. "Charleston and the Carolinas." *Harper's New Monthly Magazine* (January 1895): 204–26.

Ravenel, Beatrice St. Julian. "The Restoration of the Manigault House." *Journal of the American Society of Architectural Historians* 2, no. 4 (October 1942): 30–32.

Rittenburg, Sidney. "The Business Men and the Clean-Up Campaign." *American City* 16 (March 1917): 285–87.

Rowland, Lawrence S. "Alone on the River: The Rise and Fall of the Savannah River Rice Plantations of St. Peter's Parish, South Carolina," *South Carolina Historical Magazine* 88, no. 3 (July 1987): 121–50.

Rupp, Leila. "The Women's Community in the National Woman's Party, 1945 to the 1960s." *Signs* 10, no. 4 (Summer 1985): 715–41.

Salley, A. S., Jr. "Col. Miles Brewton and Some of His Descendants." *South Carolina Historical and Genealogical Magazine* 2 (April 1901): 128–43.

"Samuel Gaillard Stoney, 1891–1968." *Preservation Progress* 13, no. 3 (November 1968): 1, 6.

Sass, Herbert Ravenel. "The Cities of America: Charleston." *Saturday Evening Post,* February 8, 1947, 21, 70, 72, 75, 78, 80, 83.

———. "South Carolina Rediscovered." *National Geographic* (March 1953): 281–321.

Scardaville, Michael. "Elizabeth O'Neill Verner: The Artist as Preservationist." In *Mirror of Time: Elizabeth O'Neill Verner's Charleston,* edited by Lynn Robertson Myers, 17–25. Columbia: McKissick Museums, Univ. of South Carolina, 1953.

———. "The Selling of Historic Charleston." *Preservation Progress* 30, no. 2 (March 1986): 1, 6–12.

Scott, Anne F. "After Suffrage: Southern Women in the 1920s." *Journal of Southern History* 30 (August 1964): 298–315.

———. "Historians Construct the Southern Woman." In *Sex, Race and Role of Women in the South,* edited by Joanne V. Hawks and Sheila Skemp, 95–110. Jackson: Univ. Press of Mississippi, 1983.

———. "The 'New Woman' in the New South." *South Atlantic Quarterly* 61 (Autumn 1962): 473–83.

———. "Women in a Plantation Culture: Or What I Wish I Knew about Southern Women." *South Atlantic Urban Studies* 12 (1978): 24–33.

———. "Women, Religion and Social Change in the South, 1830–1930." In *Religion and the Solid South,* edited by Samuel S. Hill, Jr., et al., 92–121. Nashville, Tenn.: Abingdon Press, 1972.

Scott, Anne F., and Jacqueline Dowd Hall. "Women in the South." In *Interpreting Southern History: Historiographical Essays in Honor of Sanford Higginbotham,* edited by John B. Boles and Evelyn Thomas Nolen, 454–509. Baton Rouge: Louisiana State Univ. Press, 1987.

Severens, Martha R. "Reveries: The Work of Alice Ravenel Huger Smith." *Art Voices/South* (January-February 1978): 74.

Shick, Tom, and Don H. Doyle. "The South Carolina Phosphate Boom and the Stillbirth of the New South, 1867–1920." *South Carolina Historical Magazine* 86 (January-October 1985): 1–31.

Simms, William Gilmore. "Charleston: The Palmetto City." *Harper's New Monthly Magazine* (June 1857): 1–22.

———. "St. Michael's Church, Charleston." In *Historic Buildings of America,* edited by Esther Singleton. New York: Dodd, Mead and Co., 1906, 78–83.

Simons, Albert. "Architectural Trends in Charleston." *Antiques Magazine* 97 (April 1970): 545–55.

———. "Charleston's Story." *Charleston News and Courier,* May 7, 1950.

———. "40 Years of Preservation." *Preservation Progress* 5, no. 3 (May 1960): 1.

———. "Public Opinion Key to Preserving Local Values." *Charleston News and Courier,* April 14, 1942.

Simons, Albert, and Harriett P. Simons. "The William Burrows House of Charleston." *South Carolina Historical Magazine* 70, no. 3 (July 1969): 155–76.

Sklar, Kathryn Kish. "Hull House in the 1890s: A Community of Women Reformers." *Signs* 10, no. 4 (summer 1985): 658–78.

Snowden, Yates. "Charleston." In *Historic Towns of the Southern States,* edited by Lyman P. Powell. New York and London: G. P. Putnam's Sons, 1900, 249–92.

Steedman, Marguerite. "Miss Susan's Fight Saved Historic Charleston." *Atlanta Journal and Constitution,* March 18, 1951.

Stockton, Robert. "'Dean of Charleston Architects' . . . Remembers Early Restoration Work." *Preservation Progress* 20, no. 4 (November 1975): 6–7.

Stowe, Steven M. "The Not-So-Cloistered Academy: Elite Women's Education and Family Feeling in the Old South." In *The Web of Southern Social Relations,* edited by Walter F. Fraser, Jr., Frank Saunders, Jr., and Jon L. Wakelyn. Athens: Univ. of Georgia Press, 1985, 90–106.

Taylor, Elizabeth. "South Carolina and the Enfranchisement of Women: The Later Years." *South Carolina Historical Magazine* 80, no. 4 (October 1979): 298–310.

Taylor, Lloyd C., Jr. "Lila Meade Valentine: The FFV as Reformer." *Virginia Magazine of History and Biography* (October 1962): 471–87.

Temple, Wendy. "Low Country Women: Susan Pringle Frost: Charleston's First Lady of Preservation, 1873–1960." *East Cooper Magazine* 2, no. 2 (1988): 46.

Thomas, W. H. J. "Elizabeth O'Neill Verner: First Lady of Charleston." *Sandlapper* 8 (December 1975): 11–16.

Townsend, R. J. "Charleston Revisited." *Country Life* (January 1927): 34–42.

Twig, Edward. "Charleston: The Great Myth." *Forum* 103 (January 1940): 1–7.

Uzzell, Marjorie. "I Bought My House from Miss Sue." *Preservation Progress* 7, no. 2 (March 1962): 1–2.

Verner, E. P. "Artist Restores an Old Dwelling." *Country Life* (January 1931): 49–50.

Vlach, John M. "Philip Simmons: Afro-American Blacksmith." In *Black People and their Culture: Selected Writings from the African Diaspora,* edited by Linn Shapiro, 35–53. Washington, D.C.: Smithsonian Institution, 1976.

———. "Philip Simmons: Charleston Blacksmith." *Family Heritage* 2 (February 1979): 14–19.

Waring, Thomas R., Jr. "The Grand Old City of the South." *New York Herald Tribune,* April 6, 1930.

White, Charles Henry. "Charleston." *Harper's Monthly Magazine* (November 1907) 852–61.

Willis, Eola. "Catfish Row Comes Back." *Country Life* (April 1930): 49–51.

Wolfe, Margaret Ripley. "Feminizing Dixie: Toward a Public Role for Women in the American South." In John H. Stanfield II, ed., *Research in Public Policy: Historical and Contemporary Perspectives* 1. Greenwich, Conn.: Jai Press, 1987, 179–211.

Theses, Dissertations, and Unpublished Papers

Bland, Sidney R. "Techniques of Persuasion: The National Woman's Party and Woman Suffrage." Ph.D. diss., George Washington Univ., 1972.

Boggs, Doyle W. "John Patrick Grace and the Politics of Reform in South Carolina, 1900–1931." Ph.D. diss., Univ. of South Carolina, 1977.

Cann, Marvin L. "Burnet Rhett Maybank and the New Deal in South Carolina, 1931–1941." Ph.D. diss., Univ. of North Carolina, 1967.

Darney, Virginia Grant. "Women and World's Fairs: American International Expositions, 1876–1904." Ph.D. diss., Emory Univ., 1982.

Duffy, John J. "Charleston Politics in the Progressive Era." Ph.D. diss., Univ. of South Carolina, 1963.

Hanckel, William Henry. "The Preservation Movement in Charleston, 1920–1962." M.A. thesis, Univ. of South Carolina, 1962.

Lindgren, James M. "The Gospel of Preservation in Virginia and New England: Historic

Preservation and the Regeneration of Traditionalism." Ph.D. diss., College of William and Mary, 1984.

Lowe, Gail Sylvia. "A Bio-Bibliography of American Reformers, 1865–1917, with a Case Study of Temperance-Prohibition." Ph.D. diss., George Washington Univ., 1992.

Perrin, Carol Carre. "The Chisholme-Gilman Tenement: A Charleston, South Carolina, Preservation." M.A. thesis, Wake Forest Univ., 1979.

Powers, Bernard Edward. "Black Charleston: A Social History, 1822–1855." Ph.D. diss., Northwestern Univ., 1982.

Radford, John P. "Culture, Economy and Urban Structure in Charleston, South Carolina, 1860–1880." Ph.D. diss., Clark Univ., 1974.

Stockton, Robert P. "The Evolution of Rainbow Row." M.A. thesis, Univ. of South Carolina, 1979.

Swain, Martha H. "Organized Southern Women As a Force in the Community." Paper in possession of Sidney R. Bland.

Ulmer, Barbara B. "Virginia Durant Young: New South Suffragist." M.A. thesis, Univ. of South Carolina, 1979.

Wheeler, Marjorie Spruill. "New Women of the New South: The Leaders of the Woman Suffrage Movement in the Southern States." Ph.D. diss., Univ. of Virginia, 1990.

ℐNDEX